TWO BOYS

AT BREAKWATER

ALSO BY BOSTON TERAN

God Is a Bullet

Never Count Out the Dead

The Prince of Deadly Weapons

Trois Femmes

Giv — *The Story of a Dog and America*

The Creed of Violence

Gardens of Grief

The World Eve Left Us

The Country I Lived In

The Cloud and the Fire

By Your Deeds

A Child Went Forth

How Beautiful They Were

TWO BOYS
AT BREAKWATER

BOSTON TERAN

ISBN: 978-1-56703-016-7
Library of Congress Control Number: To come

Published in the United States by High Top Publications LLC, Los Angeles, CA and simultaneously in Canada by High Top Publications LLC.

Special Thanks to: "STRANGER IN PARADISE"—Music and lyrics by Robert Wright and George Forrest—Copyright © 1954 (Renewed) by Scheffel Music Corp All Rights Reserved International Copyright Secured Used by Permission... "COME GO WITH ME"—by Clarence Quick—Round Hill Music... "WE SHALL OVERCOME"—People's Songs Bulletin

Interior Design by Alan Barnett

Printed in the United States of America

To the Teranovas
who time after time were torn asunder
only to resurrect again when called upon
in other works…with other names

ACKNOWLEDGMENTS

To Deirdre Stephanie and the late, great Brutarian…To G.G. and L.S…Mz. El and Roxomania…the kids…our wonderful and enduring agent, Natasha Kern…Charlene Crandall, for her brains and loyalty…The Drakes at Wildbound, for their deft decisions…Janice Hussein…Jay Kenoff, for years and years of sharp legalese…And finally, to my steadfast friend and ally, and master at navigating the madness, Donald V. Allen.

PROLOGUE

DEAN TERANOVA WOULD REMEMBER THAT DAY, ALWAYS. He was with his mother. They were outside the New York Institute for Special Education, or as the people in the Bronx neighborhood called it—The School for the Blind.

There was a small building on the property at the corner of Williamsbridge and Astor where the Institute sold brooms and mops that the blind made there. His mother always bought extras and gave them to friends and neighbors in the apartment building. She was that kind of person.

They were standing in the shade of the Institute trees waiting for the streetlight to change when out of the clear blue, the boy's mother said, "Dean…I want you to remember…God is always working in your life… No matter what you think or what you're feeling…No matter how troubled your world…God is always working in your life."

That's all. She took a drag on her cigarette and they crossed the street loaded down with brooms and mops. She did not press the subject. She did not elaborate. It was just a statement of fact like she was ordering off a luncheonette menu.

Statements like this usually die on the mind. A clarity experienced before the moment passes back into the obscurity of indifference. It was the same with him, except he would have reason to remember. Because within the week that ten year old boy would be arrested for murder.

SAINT LUCY'S GROTTO

CHAPTER 1

"The crime...is life itself."

Not exactly a saying for meek shoulders. But his life was not exactly the business of meek shoulders. In the spring of 1957, Peter Prince walked out of his attorney's house on a warm Bronx night and into uncertainty. Would he ever see his son Guy again? Was he to be murdered?

He dare not look back. He knew Guy would be at the window watching him.

"The crime...is life itself."

People ask God to forgive their transgressions, but to what end? It is the age old tale of the ultimate exit strategy. The 'How to Guide' to get away with everything that has finally caught up with you.

He, at least, was not that kind of man. He did not need to look in the mirror to know who he was.

His Continental was parked across the street in front of Saint Lucy's Grotto. If you know the Bronx at all, especially the Allerton section, you'd have heard of the Grotto. It was right off Boston Road and home to Lourdes of America. Yeah, that's right...it was an actual replica of the Lourdes shrine in France.

They had a huge mock cave and a statuary Madonna where water poured forth at her bare feet and was there for the taking. There were benches facing the cave where the desperate, the lost, the needy, or those who just wanted to be one in prayer with the revered woman came to shed themselves of the world.

Before he got into his car, Peter stood at the iron fencing and looked into the silent cave. There were rows of candles in their blood red holders where people would drop coins into a metal box and buy the right to light one. From his pocket he took out a coin and flicked it through the fencing.

He had come here with his wife often after they were married. She'd had a number of miscarriages and was told she would never have children. She would fill a coffee can with shrine water, and each night dip her finger into the water and make a cross upon her stomach while she prayed.

A boy had been born, and the woman had died. It was as simple as that.

Peter got into his Lincoln. He turned over the ignition and reached under the seat where he kept a 9mm pistol.

He swung onto Boston Road heading toward Williamsbridge. He remained intent on the steam of headlights behind him. He changed lanes a few times to see if he were being followed.

When he passed the Melba Theatre, a hard dose of reality cut through him, the neon logo burning against the night sky. This was the neighborhood of his youth. He had lived in that theatre. And these were the blocks he'd roamed. The old dime store, the corner luncheonette. They were still there, the same drab, tired storefronts. The same front stoops, the same alleys where he'd played stickball and feasted on cigarettes and beer. There for a few precious moments in passing, then gone. His youth, gone. He was suddenly unnerved by the vicious hand of mortality.

At 222nd Street he turned. He was making for the thruway. In his rearview he caught sight of a Fairlane taking the corner. The streetlights strobing off its candy blue roof. It moved with such power he knew this was a muscle car, and if it was them, they could eat his Lincoln alive. He could feel his adrenalin taking over. He had his gun at the ready in his lap.

He passed under a sign: NEW ENGLAND THRUWAY—GEORGE WASHINGTON BRIDGE. He held to the left lanes. The Fairlane was a few cars back. It wasn't opening up, it was just following.

Approaching the sign for the Orchard Beach exit, he waited until the last moment, then he cut that Lincoln across three lanes. In a blare of headlights and car horns, he remained intent on the rearview, but the Fairlane didn't follow. It sped past the exit and on into a gallery of taillights.

He was on Shore Road now, heading toward City Island and New Rochelle. He kept watch, but the traffic had thinned out and there was nothing that aroused his suspicion. Once he crossed the Pelham Bay Bridge, Shore Road was mostly two lanes flanking the Long Island Sound, both sides of the road were heavily wooded.

He had about a mile to go before he'd be out of that Lincoln and gone. He had to slow down when he came to Bartow Circle. It was very dark there. He cruised along, passing the turn for City Island, and kept on Shore Road toward New Rochelle.

There were few cars, nothing that threw out a warning. There were no lights this way, no homes really, just the dark structures of the Split Rock Golf Course.

Prince was cooling out, figuring he'd licked it, when he suddenly heard a car come roaring up alongside him.

It had no headlights on. It was a big, dark painted Packard. It was in the oncoming lane. He could just make out the shadow of a man leaning out the car window with a shotgun.

He saw the weapon and his instincts for survival kicked in. He hit the brakes and spun the wheel. There was a flash of light from the gun barrel, and the windows of the Lincoln exploded.

TWO BOYS
AT BREAKWATER

CHAPTER 2

Blood is the ultimate fix.

Saw that graffitied on the IRT platform at White Plains Road. Really speaks to the heart, doesn't it? Nothing like waiting for the train in the predawn light and getting an eyeful of that. Of course, you can read that sentence about any which way, and it all comes out right every time.

You ever hear of the Pirates of Pelham Parkway? They were a headline once. Front page stuff for about five minutes in the Bronx newspapers of the day. Murder and death, death and murder. The eternal Playland carousel in all its burning colors, rising up over the boardwalk of our lives. That glow of amusement is always with us. Death and murder, murder and death.

Mister Dean Teranova gonna tell you a tale from his own special estate of mind. A very private place where there is no dental, no medical, no room and board, and where one is always decked out in their very best moldering clothes.

Back in '57 there was a pack of four kids who called themselves the Pirates of Pelham Parkway. Very creative, in a tragic, pathetic way. They were all about ten years old, and real shitasses who thought the world revolved around their own special brand of stupidity. You know that type of crowd. Every era has them. Every decade, every country, city, every corporate boardroom and school, every street corner, for Christ's sake. That kind of ratpack is and will always be with us…like Christmas and cancer.

• • •

Pelham Parkway literally cuts across the heart of the Bronx, if you believe the Bronx has a heart. It runs about two miles from Pelham Bay out past White Plains Road. It's a divided Parkway, the lanes of traffic separated by wide swaths of lawn and trees that had been planted back in the thirties.

No trains were allowed to cross it. Everything there went underground or swung out along the Esplanade. In an attempt to approximate class, no hotel or bar was allowed to front the parkway. By the late fifties, this was the last bastion of the white man before he fled to Westchester with his family from a plague of "spics" and "niggers," as he called them, who were spidering their way up from the Bronx River.

On the northwest corner of Pelham Parkway and Eastchester Road was the huge white edifice of the Bronx Municipal Hospital. On the southwest corner, there were vast open lots and a lone six story apartment building—1540. That's where the Pirates lived and plotted out their petty acts of manhood.

In one of the lots behind the apartment there was an excavation pit for a planned building where the dirt had been bulldozed up onto the sides framing it in like a bull ring. The pit was about three feet deep in water, filthy and stinking water, as a matter of fact. When they dug down, they'd hit a natural spring, but what gave the water its special odor was runoff from the machinery across the street at Bronx Municipal.

The Pirates had constructed themselves a raft from scrap wood and hammered up a flagpole of sorts where they hung a strip of white sheet with a not exactly stylish skull and crossbones. It was from there they ruled their filthy pond, kicking the ass of any transgressors who defied their domination.

Except, of course, teenagers who happened along and rained rocks down on them. For them, all they had in response were the venomous promises of revenge.

CHAPTER 3

THE FOUR WERE LAZING ON THE RAFT, listening to their transistor radios all cued up to WABC and blasting away as they smoked. Think "telling portrait of American youth on a perfect summer day." One of them suddenly said, "Who's that punk up there watching us?" The one who'd spoken was Wayne DiGiacomo, but everyone called him Jockstrap. The others looked to where Jockstrap was aiming a finger gun.

There was a scruffy haired, skinny sort of kid with hands wedged down in his pant pockets standing on one of those hills of bulldozed earth. Calling him a lonely looking silhouette was an understatement.

"That's the kid what just moved into the building," said Bill Mercurio. "His name is Duane…or Dean…Something with a D, anyway."

"How about Dipshit?" said Donny Gerundo.

"His family just moved up here from Florida," said Mercurio.

"Where did you pick up all that?" said Gerundo.

"The mouth," said Jockstrap.

Which meant Mercurio's mother.

"His name ain't Duane or Dean or Dopey or fuckin' Dipstick," said John Lombardi. He was lying on his back staring up at the sky. He started blowing funky smoke rings into the dead Bronx air. Lombardi was pretty big for his age, with a formidable head, so that everyone called him Pluto. When he was pretty much played out putting on his half-assed show, he went on, "I saw the kid this morning in the lobby with his mother. He's black."

"He's not," said Mercurio. "He's from Florida."

Gerundo, the centerpiece of this genius squad, kicked Mercurio in the back. "They got spades in Florida."

"You think I don't know that," Mercurio cried out, grabbing at where he'd been kicked. "He's just real tan," said Mercurio. "He's Italian. I heard the mother say so."

"They got spades in Italy. Jews, too," said Jockstrap. "They came here on the Mayflower."

Gerundo gave out with a grunt. "The Mayflower musta took a wrong turn somewhere unless the Pilgrims were all dagos."

"You're a fuckin' imbecile," said Mercurio.

"I was just making a joke," said Jockstrap.

"The only joke about you," said Gerundo, "is your fuckin' birth certificate."

"I think we call him Rochester," said Lombardi. He cocked his head to look at the others. "What do you think?"

That pack just lit up at the idea, Rochester being the name of the black character with the gravelly voice on the Jack Benny comedy show who played Benny's valet and chauffeur.

"Rochester," said Jockstrap, bobbing his head like a mule. "Does he have a shoeshine personality or what?"

"Second only to you, fool," said Gerundo.

Gerundo told Jockstrap to get the kid out of there.

Jockstrap stood up on the raft and it listed a bit as he began to shout out, while thrusting an arm in the boy's direction. "Hey, you…Rochester… Take a fuckin' hike. Disappear."

• • •

The kid with the scruffy hair and his hands in his pockets was, in fact, named Dean. He could hear that stocky kid shouting above the music. "Hey, Rochester…Take a hike. You hear me, Rochester?"

Dean looked around for a moment like there should be somebody named Rochester. But he didn't need a diploma to get the insults and barbs.

So much for stepping out to try and make friends. Nothing like being the unwelcome stranger. He wished they'd stayed in Florida instead of coming back to the Bronx.

He got the hint. Next time he was forced to go to church he'd light a candle for those kids. That they should drown in that rat sump.

Anger doesn't go away like bruises. It's a poisonous presence lurking there on the borders of one's existence that manages to touch the colors of everything that is the person. But kids don't know that. They live it, but they don't know it.

Dean walked the neighborhood alone trying to find a place for himself. At the end of the street there was, of all things, a stable where they kept horses. It was right where Stillwell Avenue butted into the Parkway. Believe it or not, and on weekends they even had horse rides around the corral for kids. He stood there watching a groom walk one of the horses. It all seemed so unreal, like his life at that very moment.

Dean was just entering the apartment lobby when the stainless steel elevator door with its porthole window opened, metal gears ratcheting, and here comes the four, loud and raucous, their radios blaring.

He wished he could just bleed into the bottle glass that framed the lobby because when they came upon Dean, he could see the crude and malicious joy on their faces.

They were calling him "Rochester" right off and swirling around him and he feared they might jump him, but after a rush of insults they were out the glass lobby doors.

He was hit with a sudden flash. One of those little epiphanies that if you don't do something about this situation right now, you could become their personal whipping boy who they invent new and inspiring ways to shit on.

When Jockstrap saw Dean swinging out of the lobby door he said, "We're in trouble boys…Rochester is on us."

When the others stopped and turned, Dean put up his hands. "I only just wanted to meet you guys. We moved here last week and—"

"You met us," said Merc. That's what his friends called him. "Now go meet someone else."

"Hey…I don't want trouble—"

"But we do," said Gerundo.

Dean saw Gerundo's eyes narrow as he smiled. The look was unmistakable. This guy carried an asskicking card around in his back pocket. They would have kept on, most probably, but another kid was passing by the front of the building who grabbed their attention.

CHAPTER 4

"Hey, Jew boy," shouted Lombardi. "How's life over at the Kennedy home?"

Then Merc got an insult in, "What you doin' out on the street? You 'scape out of your cage?"

The kid they were insulting was about their age. Maybe a year older. He kept pretty cool and collected to Dean's way of thinking. He was a handsome kid. A real Ricky Nelson type with Brylcreem black hair and he wore those Italian cockroach killers and black pants.

"The cops find your old man, yet?" Jockstrap shouted. He was following after the boy. He put a hand to his ear. "I can't hear you!"

The kid didn't respond. If it was a rise the ratpack wanted out of him, they better not hold their fuckin' breath.

"I can see you and your father celebrating Christmas up in Sing Sing," said Merc. "Hey...Jew boy. You deaf?"

How long this would have gone on, how bad it would have gotten, came to an abrupt finish when a woman stepped out onto her apartment terrace and began to rail at the boys for their filthy language. The four took off, sprinting up to Eastchester Road, shameless and laughing and already on the hunt for whatever next aroused their worst instincts.

The other kid never looked back. Dean watched him cross the street, then that expanse of lawn before sprinting across the Parkway. He was fast. He was making for the Kennedy Home which you could just see beyond the trees.

The Kennedy Home was an orphanage with a campus of maybe half a dozen well-built brick buildings that flanked the Central railroad tracks, which swung under the Parkway then along the Esplanade toward West Farms.

A few hundred orphans resided there. Everyone in Pelham Parkway knew of the place. It was named after Joseph Kennedy, the flier who had died during the war and was the older brother of John Kennedy, the senator from Massachusetts. The Kennedys had lived in a mansion over on Independence Avenue.

The orphans weren't allowed to go wandering off campus like that. And the remark about the kid's father and Sing Sing Prison. What was that about?

At least Dean was not alone in being hated.

• • •

When Dean entered the apartment, his mother leaned out the kitchen door. She saw her boy looked pretty despondent.

"I wish we'd stayed in Florida," he said.

"You'll make friends. You'll see. It'll just happen."

"Yeah. Like getting pneumonia…or run over by a truck."

"That is one creative way of looking at it."

He kicked at the wall with a sneaker. "We wouldn't have had to leave here if Daddy hadn't gambled away everyone's money and people were after him, and he had to sneak off to Florida like a stinkin' coward."

A moment later, who should lean out the kitchen door? The boy looked suddenly petrified.

"Yeah," said his father. "It's the stinkin' coward himself."

It took one swing with a hard, flat, open hand right across the boy's nose and mouth and the next he knew, Dean could hear the thud of his body slam against the wall.

Then there he was sitting on the floor, spread-eagled and dazed and bleeding all down his shirt, his mother kneeling over him, cursing out her husband.

"What's he supposed to learn from that?" she said. "Tell me, will you? I'd like to know."

"To see around corners," her husband said.

• • •

Dean sat in his room on the floor with his back to the bed, reading, as it was the purest form of escape that he knew from the hatred and unfairness he felt was aligned against him. He was facing the door with a lamp on the floor beside him to keep the darkness at bay, and while he hid in the pages he read, the world was nothing more than an incidental mistake, unreal and untrue. It could not really hurt him.

The door to his room opened and there in the half-light his father just stood.

"What are you reading?"

Dean held the book cover up to the light.

"*The Hunchback of*...I've heard of that," said his father.

He took a few steps toward his son who pulled back. His father leaned down and slipped a twenty dollar bill into the boy's shirt pocket.

"I'm sorry about tonight. Buy yourself a baseball glove...Or go up to Playland."

As he turned away, Dean held out the money. "I don't want it."

His father stopped, and then turned. The boy could not see if his father was infuriated or not. And as aghast as he was, Dean didn't care. Then Dean heard the old man laugh it off.

"Forgiveness is pretty pricey where you're concerned," his father said.

• • •

Calling me a Jew...Real creative geniuses, Guy thought.

He lay in bed in the dark on his back in the same attic room that had been set up for him originally at the Kennedy Home, in Weldon Hall.

He held a stiletto up to the moonlight, springing the blade then setting it back, over and over. He liked watching the moonlight flash on that reedy steel.

When the door opened suddenly, the light flooded in and he quickly slipped the knife between his hands then cupped them behind his head.

"No," Guy said to the ceiling, "I haven't jumped out the window... yet."

The priest approached. Saw the boy was lying on the covers and still in his street clothes.

"Would it be more comfortable sleeping in your pajamas?"

"You caught me, before I made my escape."

"We do have rules here."

"I know."

"You keep disobeying us. You keep walking off campus, there's no telling where this kind of attitude will end you up."

"You're stuck with me, padre. My lawyer says so. The court says so. As long as my old man stays missing—"

"You won't make us lose our compassion for you or your situation. If that is your aim."

"I don't aim that high."

"Eleven years old and already going on too smart for your own good."

The boy grinned.

The priest walked out, and the door closed, and the boy was in the dark again and he took out the knife and sprung the blade.

But now he kept thinking about one thing…the boy. The one who'd been out front of that apartment that was being ragged on. He couldn't shake the thought of him…or the feeling that came with it.

CHAPTER 5

THE NEXT DAY DEAN GRABBED A BUS TO ORCHARD BEACH. He brought swimming trunks, a bath towel, and a paperback he'd torn into parts.

Orchard Beach back then was called "The Riviera of the Bronx"—a slight overstatement, let me tell you. It was the creation of Robert Moses, an Oxford graduate and NYC public official known as "the Master Builder." No connection to Ibsen.

The halfmoon beach was part inlet, part breaker, part islands, and endless truckloads of garbage landfill. From time to time they'd even had to bring in more sand.

There was a hexagonal promenade building of stone and a central pavilion with locker rooms and showers and food stands and you could rent beach umbrellas. It was a madhouse during the summer and the first place where you could see the racial makeup of the Bronx changing. And if you dug down into the sand an inch or so, you'd find peach pits had been hid there to tear into your bare feet, and there were beer cans with sharpened edges and the occasional used "rubber."

After he'd swum and baked and stole glances at the passing girls in their bathing suits, the loneliness set in.

Dean walked up the beach to Twin Islands where the old stone breakwater struck out into Pelham Bay. He took up on some rocks where you could see the full expanse of the beach, and he got out his paperback and went to reading.

He was immersed in the book so long the sun's shadow cast a darkness over him.

"Hey, Rochester."

When he heard the name, his head shot up. It can't be—

"You," said Dean.

It was the kid who'd passed by the apartment building with the pop singer hair that the ratpack called "The Jew."

"The Kennedy home, right?" said Dean.

"Good memory, Rochester."

Guy read the look of absolute reproach on the boy's face. "I was just busting your ass. My name is Guy. What do you go by?"

"Dean," he said, standing.

"What's with that book, it's torn up."

"It was so thick I couldn't carry it in my back pocket. So I tore it all into parts so it would fit."

"That's one solution, Dante. Of course, you could have just left the fuckin' thing at home." He swiped it from Dean. Checked out the cover. "*The Hunchback*...we had to read that for English class last year. Quasimodo sure got fucked over, didn't he? But that's the way it is in this world. Hey...you hungry? I have money if you don't. I always have money."

Guy started back toward the shore. Dean followed. Guy was talking away. "I know why the idiots over at 1540 have it in for me. What's their beef with you?"

"I just moved into the building. I don't know anyone, and I was trying to—"

"The stranger comes to Dodge City episode, where all the townsfolk hate him. I faced that crap when they first stowed me away in the Kennedy Home. But I'm special circumstances."

Guy pulled a pack of Lucky Strikes from his shirt pocket. "You want a smoke?" He reached back with the pack.

Dean didn't smoke much but he took one.

"How old are you?" said Guy.

"I just turned ten in April."

"I'm eleven last September."

When they reached the shore, Dean stopped and lit up. He noticed something had caught Guy's eyes. Over by the benches where the old fogies could sit and bake their bloodless bodies in the sun, there was a man in a suit with a fedora. He was just standing there smoking, but Guy's whole demeanor had seemed to change.

"Hey," said Dean. "Something wrong?"

Guy was somewhere else.

"Hey." Dean nudged the kid.

"What'd you say?"

"Is something wrong?"

"Yeah, Dante. My whole fuckin' life."

Then his mood reversed. He was the Guy of a minute ago. He took a hellacious drag off the cigarette then pointed it. "You tore that book in parts so you could carry it in your back pocket. That's A-1 fuckin' priceless. Come on." He threw his arm over Dean's shoulder. "Let's get some food. I hear they specialize in ptomaine."

They started off toward the pavilion. Guy glanced back. The man in the dark suit by the benches was watching them, or was he just staring in their direction?

CHAPTER 6

THEY ATE AT ONE OF THE PAVILION TABLES. The sun was roasting the concrete and the salty air was gritty with hamburger grease and the smell of suntan lotion. It was so damn loud with teenagers and young mothers and their toddlers and everywhere endless transistor radios. Dean ate and watched, while Guy had a lit cigarette in one hand as he stuffed his face with a hamburger in the other. They had to talk loud to hear each other.

"You're all right," said Guy. "You know that?"

"Me? What do you mean?"

"You didn't ask about my father. Or that Sing Sing crack. Was he a racketeer? And how did I end up in that Little Orphan Annie asylum. I know you heard those dickless wonders. People don't usually know me one minute before they're choking me with questions."

Dean put his hamburger down. He wiped his mouth with the back of a hand. Guy was watching him intently. "I don't ask people things…that might hurt them. Besides…it's none of my fuckin' business."

"Yeah…I knew you'd be that kind of guy, Dante."

Dean grinned, then nodded.

And Guy said, "I got a plan for teaching those dickweeds a lesson, but I can't do it alone."

"I don't want any trouble with them."

"Well, you got it. I was coming up Eastchester Road yesterday. I heard them shouting at you from that stupid raft. Dante…at some point they'll go atomic and kick your ass. But I have a plan that will blow them out." He tapped the side of his head with the hand holding the hamburger. Bits of condiment flew every which way.

"What's with, Dante? My name is—"

"Dean, yeah. But Dante…you know who that dude was?"

"No."

"He was a wop back in the Middle Ages famous for writing this really gory story about hell."

Guy got up. Hamburger in one hand, cigarette and Coke in the other. He was on the move. Dean got up. It was follow or be left behind.

"You know what else?" said Guy. "When Dante wasn't writing about hell, he took time off to invent the machine gun."

• • •

On the bus back to Pelham Parkway, Guy opened up about his life. It was so hot that day the boys' sweaty shirts stuck to their seats. They sat where they could share an open window and take in something of a breeze. Of course, the stifling air came with an extra dose of bus exhaust.

Guy's father's real name wasn't Prince. It was Borlenghi. He was an Italian Jew who had graduated from Cornell University. He had been with Army Intelligence during the war and connected to the anti-fascist forces. That's where he met Guy's mother. She had died in 1950 in a hit and run accident outside their Riverdale mansion. Guy was only two, his mother was now just a few framed photos in their darkened mansion.

Guy's father had changed his name to Prince after his return to the States…Prince Electronics…Prince Restaurant and Bar Laundry…Prince Cigarette and Jukebox Distribution. Most of them were fronts financed through the New York protection rackets.

Guy spoke of his father with such intense adoration that whether Peter Prince was a racketeer as rumored mattered little. The boy was at one with the man, down to the soul of his very being. Dean didn't need the words— the boy's eyes spoke, his expression bled emotions, his hand movements harnessed his human energies. They were on a hot, full city bus but for Dean it could have been a scene straight out of a movie.

The father was, it turned out, the only living relative the boy had. And Dean learned why, after the father's disappearance, or murder, the boy had been sent to the Kennedy Home while Peter Prince's private attorney organized the estate and worked with the family court to determine Guy's future living situation.

The more Guy spoke of his father, the more Dean's own father became this unsympathetic stand-in. More a station of the cross in his son's life, where he must genuflect before moving on. Eddie Teranova would never have his own son's undying allegiance, and it was a painful revelation to the boy and one that filled him with resentment and jealousy.

What Dean didn't know was that he was being born out of these moments. He was being seeded with people and feelings and deeply real scenes that would one day become words.

CHAPTER 7

BUT ON THAT DAY, Dean was just a boy on a city bus listening to another boy tell him about the last night Guy saw his father alive.

Father and son had had dinner at Paul Daube's over on Courtlandt Avenue. It was a well-known steak joint a few blocks from Yankee Stadium where the ballplayers came all the time during the season. Hell…it was autograph central if you were a fan.

Guy and his father were regulars. The waiters knew the kid so well that they had a nickname for him…"The Young Prince."

Before they'd finished dinner, a man approached the table. He seemed to know Peter Prince.

"So," said the man. "Blood money paying for that meal?"

"Guy," said Peter Prince. "This is Sol Ross. He wants to have a talk, I bet. So…you finish your dinner while he and I go outside to talk."

"Why outside?" said Ross. "You too ashamed to talk in front of your kid?"

Peter Prince had stood by then. Guy saw that this Mister Ross had meant to rouse his father's ire. It did nothing of the sort. Prince set his napkin down.

Ross wanted to get in one last dig. "Guy…one of these days you'll learn the truth about your father. And he won't seem so dashing then, I bet."

The boy looked to his father to see what Mister Ross meant.

"It's my son who's dashing, not me."

Outside the restaurant Prince took out a pack of Lucky Strikes. Prince was closing in on forty and as far as Ross was concerned hateably good looking with his slicked back black hair and uptown suits and the always matching ties.

"No conscience," said Ross.

"I've been given enough conscience for it to be dangerous."

"But not enough for it to be effective?"

"I'm not in the presence of God here, or one of his archangels. So get on with it."

Prince saw Ross wasn't alone but partnered with another investigator who was leaning back against the hood of a DeSoto.

"You're a disgrace," said Ross in a loud voice. "To this country and to your religion. You fought for America and now you're a lacky for those wops at College Point."

This was a cramped everyday neighborhood and those passing could sure hear what was being said.

"You're why people call you money hungry kikes."

"Taking it right to the street," said Prince.

"Sure am, kike."

"Waste of time, boy…Waste of time."

Ross was only twenty-five and still in the early stages of manhood, so to be called "boy" racked up his ire. He was starting toward Prince to relate his feelings when the investigator with him called out, "Forget it, Ross. Don't dirty your hands on the mocky."

Ross was short, lean, and blond and stood there like some second rate James Cagney. "Eventually the dagos will see you're a liability and look to do you in. Then you'll come crawling to us for protection. You and that fag attorney of yours."

The man with Ross swung the driver's door open and got in.

Ross started for the DeSoto. "We know he's a faggot," said Ross. "You and him ever trade favors? Take turns getting each other off?"

As the DeSoto pulled away Ross spit out the open window, making sure he got Prince's suit pants and shoes.

Prince was half grinning when he noticed his son standing in the restaurant doorway. The boy seemed a little shaken.

"Who is he?" said Guy. "And why is he saying all those things about you?"

The father put his arm on his son's shoulder. "You might say he is doing me a favor."

"I don't understand," said the boy.

"You will…later. Let's take a ride."

• • •

Gardner Flynn lived in a well built, three story brick home on the corner of Bronxwood and Mace. The house faced Saint Lucy's Grotto. Gardner was a Fordham man, and Peter Prince's personal attorney and closest friend. He was not surprised father and son just appeared late that night. Gardner had gotten calls from well placed friends in the Bronx prosecutor's office that there was a rumor something dramatic was about to go down.

Gardner was quietly gay and had allies throughout the government who themselves were gay or had solicited him to represent relatives who were caught up in the raids of gay bars.

Peter told his son to go upstairs and watch television while he and Gardner talked. It was apparent there was trouble, and the boy refused, wanting to be at his father's side, but his pleas were steamrolled and up the stairs he went cursing under his breath.

The first floor of Gardner's house served as his law office, the den as his defacto library. Once the door closed, Guy snuck back downstairs to try and pick up what he could of the conversation.

"What's happened?" said Gardner.

"Ross made a dramatic entrance tonight at Paul Daube's."

"I've been getting calls…you know the kind. Plus…"

Suddenly a radio in the den went on, loud enough to wash out what was being said. The last of what the boy heard was "…I think from what I picked up today the house is being surveilled."

• • •

Guy was nervously killing time waiting, watching good old Ozzie and Harriet. It was a television world completely out of touch with his own, but one that intrigued him with its everyday white bread silliness. He dug Ricky Nelson though, especially when he got tuxed up and played the drums at some phony soiree, then hit the mic to rock up a storm.

In that black and white world one day you're just a goofus kid on a bland suburban street where there was no such thing as fear, or greed, no wrath, no violence, and part of an America at its most immediate and compelling. And next thing you know, you're carried off into the clouds of stardom between commercials. It was a hokey fraud that pissed Guy off, because it had a bite of him. He felt like kicking over the television until his father entered the room.

CHAPTER 8

PETER PRINCE HAD ON HIS GAME FACE, which the boy recognized in a heartbeat.

"Good news. You're gonna stay here with Gardner a few days."

"What?"

"Yeah."

"Where are you going?"

"Canada…on business."

"You're lying."

The father turned off the television.

"I'll bring you back plenty of fireworks. Remember how it's legal to sell them there."

"But not bring 'em back."

"We'll work that out. We did before."

The father started out of the room, but his son pressed in behind him.

"How 'bout the truth?" said Guy.

"How 'bout it?"

"You're leaving 'cause of what happened tonight."

"I'm leaving for a few days because it's necessary."

"Remember when you told me you'd never lie to me. Or did you forget?"

"I didn't forget. Though sometimes parents do intentionally misplace what they say. It's just the flaw of being a parent."

"It's not right."

The boy stopped. His father turned.

"Come on," said Peter. "Walk me out to the car."

The boy had begun to cry. "You're all I have in the world."

The statement hit the father dead center, his son's pathos not something he could easily bear.

"You have Gardner."

The father's voice was shaky.

"But he's not you," said Guy.

Peter looked down to the bottom of the stairs where Gardner stood waiting. "He's pretty damn good, though."

"What good is the truth," said Guy, "if you don't use it when it means something?"

Peter leaned against the stair rail. "Nothing near that smart should come out of the mouth of a ten year old."

"Eleven," said Guy.

"Was it pure luck...? Or are you that smart?"

"It was pure luck," Guy said, wiping at the tears.

Peter sat down on the stairs and pointed for where his son should squeeze in next to him. He put one arm around Guy's shoulders, and with the other, wrote an imaginary note in the air speaking out the words, "My dearest son...You are right...Your father is in trouble...but..."—he underlined the word—"...he has been in trouble before and gotten through it...And will again...Remember that...I will see you later...Your loving father."

He finished with a finger drawn exclamation point.

Standing, the father started down the stairs again, his son up and quick to follow.

"Take me with you," said the boy.

Peter looked back at his son. "No can do."

"Please?" The boy began crying out the words. "We can go anywhere... I don't care. Just don't leave me. Please...I can't bear the idea of not seeing you again."

The unbearable threat of impermanence, of being abandoned—even just a glimpse of it was too much.

At the bottom of the stairs Gardner could discern someone even as steeled as Peter Prince was stuck with the stark awfulness of it.

"What makes you even think such a thing?" said the boy's father.

"I just know. I do." Guy banged his hand again and again against the stair rail.

Peter took his son by the shoulders. "That isn't true. No matter what you think now. It isn't true."

"So you won't take me."

"I won't."

The boy pulled free. His hurt angling into anger.

"Walk me to the car?" said Prince.

"No."

"Kiss me good-bye?"

"No."

"Shake my hand?"

He put out a hand. The boy recoiled from it.

"Want to kick me once in the ass?"

The father turned just enough to make light of the moment. If looks could kill. A noisy breath came out of the kid's throat.

"Your father actually said that?" said Dean. He couldn't believe it.

Guy had been staring out the bus window, ashamed, because he knew he probably looked as vulnerable as he felt.

"That's what he said."

"You want to kick me in the ass?" Dean repeated, grinning.

Guy went back to telling Dean about that night. "My father was just starting out when Gardner reached into his pocket and said something like… 'I forgot to give you these.' They were keys and he tossed them, but they ended up on the hallway rug. I went and picked them up and handed them to my father. I put them in his hand. I can still see them. They were car keys, and I was thinking, maybe if I just hold his hand a minute longer, he'll take me with him."

But Guy shook his head. It hadn't happened, of course. It hurt Dean to see the kid suffering.

"You'll see him again," Dean said.

"Yeah," said Guy. "How the shit do you know?"

The boy sounded so bitter. Dean didn't know what to say. Guy looked to be radiating animosity, and ready to fight.

"How do you know?" said Guy.

"Because," said Dean.

"Because what, smartass?"

"Because…I'm a fuckin' genius."

Dean didn't even know what he'd said until he'd said it and then he couldn't even believe he'd said it. It was like there was another Dean inside his head who was the genuine article and brimming with self-assurance.

Guy blinked. Talk about the well-served answer. He threw his head back and cracked up. He swung an arm over the kid's shoulder. He then wrote an imaginary statement in the air with his finger… "I'm a fuckin' genius." Then he finished up with an imaginary exclamation point. "Totally rich," he said.

CHAPTER 9

THEY GOT OFF THE BUS AT GUN HILL ROAD. Guy had a hard on for that street sign and told Dean he was always conniving how he could steal one. Dean followed Guy along the train tracks that would pass the Kennedy Home. There were long stretches of trees framing the tracks and retaining walls made of corrugated steel or rotting brick.

Guy pointed out Hayden Hall, where he did his *Prisoner of Zenda* routine under the watchful eye of the fuckin' black robes. A section of retaining wall behind Lady Hall was rich with stock teenage graffiti. That's where Guy knelt down and shimmied loose a chinked up brick. He reached in and the next thing out into the daylight comes a crude, homemade pistol.

"Zip gun," said Guy. "It belonged to my old man. He made it as a kid."

Dean looked the weapon over. The barrel was a short section of sawed down piping strapped with metal flashing to a strip of varnished mahogany.

"No trigger," said Guy. "You pull the hammer. See. Single shot... Twenty-two caliber."

In Guy's other hand were a dozen shells. He loaded one into the pipe barrel. He stood. A passenger train came trundling down the Esplanade. It passed them in a rattling fury. Guy aimed. At the moment the passenger cars cleared, Guy fired into the trees across the tracks. There was a burst of leaves and dusty air.

"You're not gonna shoot them, are you?" said Dean.

"Better," said Guy, grinning. "We're gonna rat the fuckers."

• • •

Father Grace opened the wooden slat in the confessional. There in the shadows a man sat silently, keeping his face concealed. Out of shame, probably, the priest thought.

The confessant kept silent so long it was, in fact, the priest who spoke first.

"Are you here for absolution? Spiritual counsel?"

The man did not answer.

"Are you afraid to speak? Don't be. Nothing separates us from his love."

The man took a beat before responding. "That idea is as confounding as it is foolish," he said. "And when you consider it's fraught with inconsistencies, it really feels like a fraud, doesn't it?"

"If it is those things, why are you here?" said the priest.

The confessant moved slightly. "I was involved in the murder of that couple over on River Avenue...you might have read about it in the papers."

Father Grace was only twenty-four, and a Scarsdale boy to boot, but he had already heard his share of confessions. At Saint Lucy's, they kept you busy with the baring of private atrocities, so this was not new to him. But the calm in the tone of this man was what was so unsettling, his nihilism no less so.

"Are you here to seek forgiveness? To find peace?"

"No Father, I am not."

"Then why are you here?"

The man had a story to tell, and a reason to tell it, because he was like the knife that is sharp at both ends.

He had broken into the apartment in the two story house up on River Avenue and waited in blackness for the couple to come home. He had sat in a chair away from the door, a gun in his lap all decked out with a Sten. He was thirty and edgy, iron-eyed even to friends, the few that he had. Someone once told him that he was a monster in the shape of a man, which he took as a compliment before he stabbed her to death.

Leo Crab and his wife Tessie always walked home together from Pelham Park Station at the end of the day. He worked at Korvettes, and she was a domestic. Their life was as plain as the nose on your face—or was it?

He heard what had to be them climbing the stairs, lost in their small talk. A jumble of keys and the front door opened. One of them flipped on the light switch, but the room remained dark. They crossed to the kitchen in shadow, unaware of what awaited. She was carrying groceries and when she turned the kitchen light on, she saw a stranger in a sport coat and sneakers. He had a gun in his lap. The groceries fell from her hand as she gasped. He ordered her to be silent and as he stood, aimed the gun at her husband and said, "Drop the groceries and sit on the floor. You too," he said to the wife.

As they obeyed, the husband said, "If it's money you want—"

"If it's money I wanted, would I come to this dump?"

From the floor where she sat with the kitchen light on her, tiny and fragile, she asked, almost begging, "Then what do you want of us?"

The man set eyes upon the husband. "You served in Korea, right? A medic?"

"Yes."

"You were training to be a doctor. Then things went bad. You got yourself dishonorably discharged."

"Yes?"

"You work in shipping for Korvettes on Forty Fifth. But you make a little pocket money on the side performing abortions."

The husband glanced at his wife.

The man took a snapshot from his pocket and held it out for the husband to see. "You performed an abortion on a girl a few months ago. Her name is Vinci. But what would it matter? She probably didn't give you her real name."

"I can't see in this light," said the husband.

"Slide over next to your wife."

The husband crawled along with the gun barrel bearing down on him. He sidled up beside his wife.

The man held the snapshot out.

"I recognize her," said the husband. "A few months ago...Yeah."

"You performed the abortion here?"

"Downstairs...in the basement."

"What did you do with the fetus?"

"I put it in the furnace."

"Who brought her here?"

They didn't answer.

He put the snapshot in his coat pocket. He brought out another.

"Do you know this man? Did he bring her here?"

They both looked at the second photograph. It was of Peter Prince. There was an awkward silence. The woman looked to her husband. A moment passed between them that could have meant almost anything.

He pressed the gun against the woman's head, "What was that?"

The woman closed her eyes. She was on the verge of shivering tears.

"What do you want from us?"

"What do I want? The miracle of life means as little to me as it does to you…Does that explain it?"

The man leaned forward in the confessional and spoke through the partition to the young priest, repeating what he'd said in the apartment, "The miracle of life means as little to me as it does to you…You understand that? Don't you, faggot?"

What he'd suddenly heard, unnerved the priest.

"We know about your secret life, *Father Grace.* So when I'm done with you, go across the street and tell that fairy lawyer… He knows what we want."

CHAPTER 10

DEAN LAY IN BED, flushed with anticipation, like tomorrow was the second coming of the gunfight at the OK Corral. Next morning there he was behind the apartment building, shouting up to a third floor terrace, "Hey…Little Miss Jockstrap…Where are you, Little Miss Jockstrap…?"

Wayne DiGiacomo showed on the terrace, totally enraged at being insulted and what does he see but Dean pointing at the excavation pit. And there was Guy on the raft in the middle of all that scummed drainage. He was holding their pirate flag which he had doused with lighter fluid, and when he set the damn thing on fire you'd have thought Jockstrap had been nippled with battery cables.

Within fifteen minutes here they came. Puffed out chumps, four abreast, scooping up rocks as they slid down the hillside around the excavation site.

"What's with the rocks?" Guy shouted. "You got four. We're only two."

Dean was on the raft now kneeling on one knee over a piece of filthy burlap. It was covering something the four couldn't see but would jolt the shit out of them when the time came.

"Wade out here," Dean yelled, "or aren't you ready to mix up a little blood?"

Jockstrap flung a rock. It missed by a mile.

"That's a pussy throw," Guy shouted. "They got nuns over at the Kennedy Home with better arms."

Gerundo said nothing. He just slogged out into the water and the other three followed, dumping their rocks, the rust colored slop up almost to their knees, hurling curses, insults, coming out with war cries you could hear all the way to Eastchester Road.

As they charged the damn raft, Dean pulled aside the burlap and there on the raft boards lay four dead rats. Huge, filthy, toxic looking creatures with horrid teeth and cold eyes that had been shot dead by Guy's zip gun. Even Dean had plugged one. The rats hadn't stiffened yet but were painted with flies and they had these foot long tails. Perfect tails to hold in your hand then wrap around your wrist so you could use the dead vermin to whip your enemy with.

Dean had a rat in each hand. Guy, the same. The boys attacking didn't know that yet, but as they scaled up onto the raft, Gerundo was the first to have a rat whipped across his face. He could hear the fleshy thing thud against his nose and mouth leaving a trail of vermin blood and innards before he realized what Dean had hit him with.

Dean and Guy beat and struck the boys with impunity. The battle lasted a minute with the other boys jumping from the raft and scattering in defeat back to the edge of the pit.

The terrible simplicity of violence had played itself out and created a perfect map of all that was to come, but no one could foresee. Animosity knows no limits, and there were Guy and Dean on the raft holding the rats up in victory while Gerundo trudged up that earthen mound in defeat, the others behind him, he wiped vermin scum from his face and swore, "I will kill you."

CHAPTER 11

GUY WAS ALL REVVED UP. After they'd cleaned off the rat scurf, Guy was on Eastchester Road with his pocket transistor out and blaring away. He was cruising the curb and singing out loud to the Del-Vikings and waving to Dean, "*Love, love, love you darlin'...Come and go with me.*"

"What are you doin', man?" Dean shouted back.

"*Come, come, come into my heart...tell me, that we'll never part...*"

Dean saw now that Guy was trying to flag down a cab.

But no cab driver back in '57 was gonna stop and pick up some strange eleven year old rocking away to his radio right there in the street. But then the light changed, and cars got to backing up. Guy spotted a cab and grooved up alongside it. He was still singing as he pulled a wad of bills from his pocket no normal kid would be carrying. He flashed the money right in the cabbie's face. "Me and my buddy there got to get to Riverdale. What do ya' say?"

The cabbie looked like he was in discussion with his better judgment. But that lean green always carries the day. He jerked a thumb toward the back door.

Then there they were in the back of the cab like a couple of monied studs. With Guy still singing..."*Yes, I need you...Yes, I really, really need you...Please don't ever leave...*"

Then he pressed up behind the cabbie and said, "These are the Del-Vikings. Did you know they are one of the few integrated groups in America? I heard that on *American Bandstand.*"

"Fuck the Del-Vikings," said the cabbie. "And fuck *American Bandstand.* Now sit back and shut up."

Guy sat back and looked at Dean. They shared a secret moment as if they had been afforded some ancient wisdom. Guy whispered, "Fuck the Del-Vikings."

Dean whispered back, "Fuck *American Bandstand.*"

They were cruising out Gun Hill Road and living their own reality. A gritty breeze blowing through the open windows. It was like they owned the Bronx. Kings of the crowd, the traffic, the elevated.

Dean got suddenly curious. "Where are we goin', man?"

Guy slung an arm over the kid's shoulder. "Well, Dante…it's like Errol Flynn said in *They Died With Their Boots On*…'To Hell or to Glory.'"

• • •

They were going to Guy's house out in Riverdale. "Home of the rich and boss to the slaves," as Dean's father had jealously named it.

They got out of the cab at Independence Avenue and 252nd Street. Nothing but mansions. Big old stone or brick affairs set back from the street in the trees. Even the silence in this neighborhood cost big money.

Walking up the block Guy pointed out the mansion where the Kennedy's had lived. They were too young to appreciate all the ironies of Guy having lived across the street from *a* former Kennedy home to now living in *the* Kennedy Home.

They came to stone pillars that flanked a driveway and there Guy darted into the trees. Dean followed along a heavily wooded path to where a brick house with three story high chimneys stood. It looked to Dean like something out of Charles Dickens or Sherlock Holmes.

At the edge of the trees Guy looked about, then he sprinted to the back of the house with Dean right behind him. He got out his key ring and unlocked what was a servant's entrance to the kitchen. As they entered the house, they had no idea they had been seen.

CHAPTER 12

THE HOUSE WAS HUGE and still and dark as the blinds and drapes had been shuttered tight.

"The power's been turned off," said Guy.

Dean followed him through a stainless steel kitchen and then a dining room and a library. 'A library,' thought Dean. Everywhere cabinet doors were open, drawers pulled out. Their contents strewn about the floor. It looked like the proverbial cyclone had charted a course through the place.

"What happened?" said Dean.

"There's what they call a task force in the Bronx that searched the house to see if they could find anything to prove my father was a racketeer. Or…" his voice trailed off, "…that he was still alive."

Guy led Dean on into the enormous living room. It was two stories high. Dean looked up. The coved ceiling was hand painted, like you see in churches. There were angelic figures floating on clouds in the half dark ethos.

When he suddenly heard a piano somewhere, Dean looked around. Guy had disappeared. Dean followed the trail of music to a den. There was Guy sitting at a black, glossy baby grand, and he was playing with some serious proficiency.

"You play?" said Dean. "That's all right. You sound like Liberace."

"Fuck Liberace," said Guy. "And fuck Van Cliburn. Give me Jerry Lee Lewis."

He went slightly berserk while playing 'A Whole Lotta Shakin.'

Then he sprung up, "Come on, man."

Dean chased Guy up to the second floor, then the third. Nothing but hallways and doors, doors and hallways. Guy led Dean to his bedroom. It had been searched and was pretty well trashed like the other rooms.

"Help me move this bureau," said Guy.

They slid the heavy piece of furniture away from the wall. Guy knelt down. There was some kind of latch by the baseboard. It clicked and Guy lifted out a panel of flooring.

A space had been framed in between floors. Dean could see there were bottles of beer and packs of cigarettes stashed away. Beneath the beer were a couple of shoeboxes with what looked to be letters and paperwork. There was also a semi-automatic. Guy picked up Dean's worried stare.

"My father's gun from the war," said Guy, as he handed two bottles of beer to Dean.

He took out two for himself. Then Guy closed the floorboard and reset the latch. He and Dean slid the bureau back in place.

They sat in the living room like lords of the manor, drinking warm Rheingold from the can. They were kicked back on the couch with the transistor playing, treating themselves to a buzz.

"Hey, Dante…You ever been seriously drunk?"

"No…but my folks let me have an orange juice glass of red wine on Saturday nights. It's a dago thing with them. What about you?"

"No…But I am today. You ever chug a beer?"

"Never," said Dean, who began to sit forward to watch the spectacle that was about to go down. Guy put the can to his lips and arched back his head. Gulp after gulp after gulp. Dean could hear the kid swallowing over the music. Just imagine that. Then Guy shook the can to let Dean know it was empty. He crushed it in both hands and tossed it over his shoulder into the deepening dark.

"Fuckin' heroic," said Dean.

Guy sat back grinning pridefully, then let out a burp you could hear over in Jersey.

They talked and they laughed, and they smoked Lucky Strikes, and it was like they knew each other all of their lives.

One good fight will do it sometimes. Where you get to stand with someone against the bloodsuckers on your heels. Moments like that and the loneliness of your world can be suddenly cast from your being. And now you have this person, a friend, you don't need to explain yourself to, you don't have to fear how you'll be seen. Sitting in that big house under that coved ceiling with its angels, a Rheingold in hand, you become twice as smart, twice as fast, twice as tough, twice as cool as you were a couple of hours ago. Kick a little ass and you go from being a limp dick to a locomotive.

Of course, there are other things, unsaid things, secrets of the soul that don't come into focus until real time has passed. And the world comes closing in with all its manifest force, and you learn things like—who is irresistibly drawn to failure, and who is not.

Guy stood. He was flat out drunk and listing from side to side.

Dean privately smiled. "You're looking like you are about to tip over, man."

Guy wasn't listening. "Those four pricks. You get them alone and they're probably fuckin' snow cones."

"I wouldn't be so sure of that," said Dean. "Who cares anyway."

"You got a sympathetic streak in you, Dante. That's what makes you all right."

No one had ever expressed that to Dean, except maybe his mother.

Guy was staring up at the ceiling. He looked sad suddenly. Forlorn. "One night my father took my BB gun..."—Guy aimed the Rheingold can at the ceiling like it was a pistol, spilling beer as he went—"...and he shot at those angels. In the daylight you can see a couple of them have bullet holes in their asses."

Guy swigged the last of the beer, then tossed the can. It caromed off the wall. Guy was somewhere far away.

"Your father," said Dean. "You think he's alive?"

The boy fell into a terrorized silence. Dean watched the shadowy expression, it seemed so intimate and compelling.

"If he isn't," said Guy, "it's all my fault. I just know it."

Guy started to cry. He sat next to Dean.

"Why...is...it your fault?" said Dean.

Guy was sobbing now. He wiped at his eyes with a shirt sleeve. "I can't tell you," he said. "I just know."

Guy covered his face. Drunk as he was, he leaned over. His head came to rest in Dean's lap. Dean had no idea what to do or to say. He was a child emotionally frozen in place with the spreading dark upon the drapes, when a French door to the patio burst open and a figure rushed in and another came charging from the hallway. The boys were suddenly drowning in light and men's voices.

Guy's head came up. He saw a bulky outline bearing down on him. "Run," he shouted.

Dean sprinted from the couch without thinking, to escape into the shadows. Blind with fear, he had no idea who he was running from or why.

Guy was so drunk he stumbled as a man got a grip on his shirt. Dean was clotheslined by an arm around his throat and reeled from his feet choking. In the strafing arc of a flashlight Guy saw who it was that had hold of him. The man from the restaurant who had confronted his father, the one named Ross, with the task force.

"Let go of me, you fuck," the boy shouted. Guy started to violently kick and swing at his captor. Ross hit him across the face with a fist and the drunken boy dropped to the floor like a world of dead weight.

CHAPTER 13

THERE WAS A LESBIAN BAR IN THE EAST VILLAGE known as The Light Switch. It was a hangout for working girls and part of a chain of alternate bars and private clubs Gardner had put together for C.C. Carpetti. C.C. was the lesbian sister of Gino Carpetti, a hated Bronx racketeer.

The Carpettis ran a criminal organization out of Whitestone. And Gino, as cold blooded as he was, was not the force behind the family. The power to be reckoned with, the one Carpetti you better not cross, was the old lady herself, Maria Carpetti.

There was a hard animosity between brother and sister over what Gino Carpetti considered the depraved underpinnings of his sister's sexuality. By 1957 Carpetti was openly conspiring against his sister and even the threat of investigation by the Bronx Task Force did not frighten him off his path.

What did give Carpetti pause was all he'd learned about the River Avenue murders. And that is what led to Father Grace appearing at Gardner's front door unannounced and panicked.

The priest was a trembling wreck reliving those few minutes in the dark to Gardner and relaying events as he'd been ordered.

"What does it mean?" said the priest.

Gardner was sitting at his desk, hands folded, looking out the window toward Saint Lucy's. The messenger was out there watching. Gardner was sure of it. Watching to see how quickly the priest would rush to Gardner's house.

"It's just someone's creative way of passing me a message," said Gardner.

Father Grace stood before the desk like a man convicted of a crime he did not know or understand. "Why did they come to me?" said the priest.

"Because you are a priest in a confessional and sworn to secrecy…and because you are one of us."

Which the priest knew meant—homosexual.

Once Gardner was rid of Father Grace, he called C.C. at the bar. When she answered on her private line all he said was, "I'm thinking about moving to Florida."

"No kidding," she said. "Why don't you come on over and tell me all about it."

He hung up and got his car keys. He wasn't thinking about moving to Florida. He despised Florida. It was the land of varicose veins and urinary tract infections as far as he was concerned. But knowing their phone lines might be compromised he and C.C. came up with a simple code—I'm thinking about moving to Florida—which meant it was urgent they talk.

There was a bouncer at the front door checking ID's when Gardner arrived. He knew Gardner on sight and let him through the crowd and into the bar. He was mafia and had been hired by C.C., through Peter Prince. He wasn't there just to check ID's, but to keep out gawkers and men freaks.

It was wall to wall working girls, butch and femme alike. It was live music night in the back room that also served as a tiny dance floor. The lighting was moody and shadowed with cigarette smoke. At the entrance to the back room was a stairwell up to C.C.'s office.

C.C. stood smoking by a small one way mirror where she could look down through the colored lights to the tiny dance floor. She turned when she heard Gardner enter the cramped office.

C.C. wasn't even thirty, but she had the ambiance of someone who had burned through a lot of life, probably because she had. She wore her hair stylishly short and dressed Westchester—tailored slacks and vest. But when she opened her mouth, she was pure New York city cab driver.

"Florida," she said.

Gardner nodded.

She looked back out the one-way mirror, pointing the cigarette. "Half the time I'd like to just disappear down there in the dark. Become one of the friggin' invisible. Know what I mean? Punch a time clock. Be a bartender. Have a quiet little dolly over in Jersey."

"That's not your fate," said Gardner.

"Not yours, neither."

She pointed her cigarette toward the hallway. They entered a room where they kept the liquor. It reeked of cigarettes and stale beer. There was a single lightbulb they stood beneath.

In a half whisper Gardner laid out what had been told. C.C. listened, her lips pulled back against her teeth. Threatening a homosexual priest with some hardcore thug just to deliver a message was straight out of her brother's playbook.

"Gino is an insidious bastard," she said. "He would have made a great Pope…Don't you think?"

Gardner laughed at the cold horror of her comment.

"Well," she said. "How do you see all this?"

"He's tracked the girl all the way to River Avenue."

"But he doesn't have her…Otherwise I'd be in trash bins all over the city."

"He's also not sure you *do* have her…that's why the threat."

She rubbed at the spreading tension in her neck. "He's testing…I'm not sure I'm up to playing the tragic heroine."

"But here we are," said Gardner.

"Better sharpen up the kitchen knives…the family is coming to dinner. Do you think my brother can get to her?"

"He got to River Avenue, didn't he?"

"Prince got away though?" she said.

Gardner did not answer her.

"Is the baby alive? Or was it aborted?"

He did not answer that either.

"Silence is golden, but it's not very illuminating."

"I don't want you to be legally compromised."

"You mean you don't want yourself to be legally compromised."

"I don't want either of us to be legally forced to cut the other's throat."

She took a long drag on her cigarette then ground it out under the heel of her shoe.

"If I don't expose him, what will he think?" She paced a bit. She sat on a beer keg and rested her arms on her knees. She stared off into the shadows. After a while she smiled. "He won't know what to think. So, he'll stay enraged. Maybe it'll even give him cancer. One can only hope."

"He's going to believe you're holding the girl over him. She *is* our insurance policy."

"Sometimes I think…just have him quietly killed." She glanced up at Gardner. She knew he was nowhere on the same planet with that notion. "I can fantasize, can't I?"

She put on her best New York caustic smile and stood.

"Prince really threw himself into the fire doing what he did," she said.

"He did it for us…He did it for his son. Though the kid will never know. What choice did Peter have? He was marked either way."

• • •

The girl they had been talking about was a fifteen year old named Teresa Vinci. She was soft voiced, introverted and a looker. She had been shuttled from foundling to foster homes on Staten Island. She had been ill-treated. Then the Borea family hired her to work at their restaurant—THE OLD MILL out in Staten Island.

It was a well-known joint. People went there from all over the city. It even had a souvenir menu—Turnip Juice, Torpedo Juice…Octopus au gratin with apple in mouth (a mere $360) …African Leopard steak (order in advance 2 years) …Virgin Mermaid on Half Shell (reasonable).

Teresa was a good worker. She was polite. She kept to herself. She saved her tips. One day she gave notice. She said she was moving to Woodridge, New Jersey, and starting secretarial school. She told the landlady where she rented a room the same story. The landlady watched Teresa go down the walkway in the snow with her one beaten up piece of luggage and get into a black Lincoln.

Nothing more was seen or heard about her. She had quietly slipped into obscurity.

CHAPTER 14

THE BOYS WERE IN THE BACK OF ROSS' DEPARTMENTAL CAR. His partner, Nick O'Gorman, was driving. Guy was still pretty drunk and antagonistic. Fear had sobered Dean up considerably. The simple fact was, they were boys with a police investigator hovering over the seat and staring down at them as the car coursed its way through night traffic along Gun Hill Road.

"What were you boys doing there?" Ross said.

"It's my house," said Guy. "And I can be in there any time I want."

"I mean, what were you doing in the living room?"

Guy went silent.

"Drinking," said Dean.

"And what else?"

"Don't tell him anything," said Guy. "It's my house. We don't have to answer to him."

"Smoking," said Dean. "We were drinking some beer and smoking and hanging out."

"And what else?" said Ross.

"Drop dead," said Guy.

"You boys know what homosexuals are?"

O'Gorman glanced at his partner. Nick was a big clunky man, but he had a soft tone about him. And this line of pursuit—

"Sol—"

Ross waved him off.

"You know what they are," he said, looking from boy to boy. "Homosexuals...queers. Boys that have sex with other boys. Boys that take another boy's dick in their mouths...or jerk them off."

"Sol...cut it loose," said O'Gorman.

Ross was not having it. He was a tight young man, an exigent personality type with that big engine drive to succeed. Not the 'forgive your transgressions' kind.

Ross pressed his face toward them in the dark. The neon lights along the street flaring across the investigator's eyes. The boys were confined to that stare.

"You boys queer?"

Dean did not understand, but Guy did.

"You fuckin' shit," said Guy. He kicked at the seat.

"Sol," said O'Gorman, "let's have this conversation later."

"You're guilty, son," said Ross. "I can see it." He looked at Dean. "What was he doing with his head in your lap?"

Dean glanced at Guy for a moment.

"You don't need to look at him to know the answer," said Ross.

Dean couldn't breathe. He didn't know what to say. What to lie. He was not going to expose Guy talking about his father and crying.

"We were drinking beer..." said Dean, "...and smoking cigarettes."

"Wait till your parents hear what I tell them," said Ross. "You know how ashamed they're gonna be? How disgusted? You gonna ruin their lives."

• • •

Dean's parents had been contacted, as had Gardner Flynn. O'Gorman argued the boys should be brought to the Kennedy Home rather than the 49th Precinct, but Ross wanted to drop the hammer on them. Lock them up in some filthy, urine stained holding cell to see what he might be able to shake out of the little bastards about Peter Prince's disappearance. O'Gorman wouldn't have that and was a flat out no.

At the Kennedy Home, the two boys were separated and put in side-by-side offices. Ross knew Gardner Flynn was a fag and an attorney, so he'd deal with him last. When he told the Teranovas that he believed he had come upon the drunken boys at the beginning of a sexual act, they were a portrait of disbelief and dismay. O'Gorman didn't know if what Ross had told them was an exaggeration or a flat out lie, as Ross had been well ahead of him entering the room, but he kept still about it. From what O'Gorman could see, Eddie Teranova was bleeding anger and shame.

O'Gorman watched as Ross made it clear to the parents he did not want them to end up at juvenile court. What he did want was for the Teranovas to talk with their son, find out what he might have picked up or learned from Guy Prince about the boy's father. Had the youths shared secrets?

In a private moment, Ross took Eddie Teranova aside and warned him that Flynn was a homosexual and could not be trusted with their son's well-being. O'Gorman wondered if Ross came out of the womb a complete shit, but he kept it to himself, because the road to career advancement often goes through blind silence.

• • •

Dean was sweating out the moment when a world of terror would come through that door. This night was the first time that he realized the power of words. Words he could not understand yet he knew were designed to have a devastating effect on his life. He was bewildered in a way he did not know someone could be bewildered. He felt shame and regret, but for what, he did not know. He wanted to cry, but he would not give the world the satisfaction.

Then what does he hear...music coming through the wall right behind him. From the room Guy was in. It was his transistor radio blasting away... "*Dom-Dom-Dom-Do-Dom, Dom-Do-Dom...*"

Then someone—it had to be Guy—started tapping the wall with the flat of his hands. Like he was a fuckin' drummer or something.

As scared shitless as Dean was, he could not help but smile. He stood and what does he do. He started tapping back on the wall in time to the song, singing along.

"*Dom-Dom-Dom-Do-Dom, Dom-Do-Dom...*"

Then Guy started singing and drumming the wall even louder.

Dean heard someone yell, "What in God's name is going on here?" And that was the last of the music, all right.

When Dean was marched out into the hallway by O'Gorman, there was Gardner Flynn confronting Ross in the presence of the Teranovas and the Father Superior. "The boys had every legal right to be in that house," said Gardner. "You entered without a warrant and no reasonable claim to exigent circumstances. So you made up this crazy story about those children. Beware...You and Mister O'Gorman will have to legally answer for it."

O'Gorman could have predicted this, and he hoped to Christ that Ross could keep his mouth shut.

As Dean was led out by his parents, Guy shouted after him. "Hey, Dante...Fuck the Del-Vikings."

Dean got it and shouted back. "Fuck *American Bandstand*."

CHAPTER 15

THE RIDE HOME WAS ABOUT TWO MINUTES LONG. You could see the Teranova apartment from the Kennedy Home, and not a word spoken in the car. Only Eddie Teranova's narrowed eyes in the rearview on his son. As for Dean, he saw Ross there for a moment in his father's severe look of condemnation.

As they entered the apartment, Dean's mother, seeing how beaten and exhausted her son looked, tried to run interference. "Why don't we get a good night's sleep and talk about this in the morning."

"The hell with a good night's sleep," Eddie said. "We'll talk now." Then he came out with it. "Were you and that boy doing something disgusting in that house?"

"We were drinking beer and smoking," said Dean.

He saw his father did not believe him. That there was something akin to revulsion in his expression.

"And what else?"

"Nothing."

He shouted, "And—what—else...goddamn it."

The boy's mother saw her son was trembling.

"He answered you," she said.

"I don't believe him. I can smell a liar. You learn that in the war. He's hiding something."

Eddie Teranova walked out of the living room and into the kitchen. "He's a fuckin' liar," said Eddie.

Edith reached out and took her son's hand. There are all kinds of nightmares, she thought.

When Eddie returned with a glass of whiskey in hand, he said, "Those investigators need help to find the boy's father. Did you see anything? Did the boy say anything...Did you notice anything...? Anything unusual...? Strange or suspicious...? Anything that might be helpful to them?"

Dean sat on the edge of the couch staring down at his hands. He thought about the cupboard in the floor with the letters and papers and who knows what else. If I tell my father —he thought—will he not hate me?

The boy, you see, already believed his father hated him. He did not know why, only that it was so. That his father saw him as some sort of disappointing stranger who lived in the same apartment as he did.

"Remember what we talked about at the School for the Blind?" said his mother.

The boy looked up.

"What the hell does that mean?" said Eddie.

Dean understood his mother's quiet resistance. How she survived in a hostile world.

"We drank beer and smoked," said Dean. "And Guy told me how much he misses his father."

• • •

It was a bad week for both boys. Dean's father was either cruelly aloof or coldly grilling him about that night. Dean met with Ross and O'Gorman, who questioned him again.

Guy was confined to the Kennedy Home grounds where he was also questioned, denying always Ross' insinuations. He was also warned that one more actionable offense of the Home rules would find him shipped to a detention center in Elmira.

The boys finally hooked up where the train tracks passed behind Lady Hall. This was where they could talk and smoke and Guy would still be on the grounds.

"They still questioning you?"

"Yeah," said Dean.

"You didn't tell them anything about the space under the bureau?"

Dean flashed an angry look.

"Sorry, Dante…That was stupid of me."

Guy went and changed the subject, to get away from the shame of what he'd just asked.

"When you're an adult…What do you want to be?"

Dean flicked the ash from his cigarette like a pro. He kicked at the ground, thinking. "Taller," he said. "I want to be taller."

"Taller," said Guy. "That's fuckin' priceless."

"What about you?" said Dean.

"Me?" Guy was sitting on the ledge of the brick wall where his gun was stashed. He was staring at the burning tip of his cigarette which he held up to his face and blew on. "I want to be someone people fear. That when they see me…Wham! Know what I mean?"

Dean understood, the feeling anyway. The one that would keep the dogs off you. He could see being that person playing out his life on some terrible channel in his head. Getting even for some imaginary score.

A train approached. Its coupled cars violently shuttling along. The train horn blasted as a warning to keep back from the tracks.

Fuck it, thought Dean. As the cars came bearing down on him, he stepped close to the ties, then closer yet. So close the smell of iron burned his nostrils. A flood of windows went flashing by. Passengers staring at this crazy kid who was reaching out. The sweep of the air pulling at his hand.

Then it was gone. Leaving the air filled with dust and debris that had been strewn along the tracks.

"That probably gave a few of those donut holes a jolt," said Guy.

Dean tossed his cigarette away. He slumped his hands down in his pockets. Guy saw he looked visibly upset suddenly.

"My old man," said Dean. "He believes what those shit investigators told him about us. He rides me about us. Orders me to 'fess up." Dean got to biting at his lower lip.

Guy could imagine what had been said. More than imagine. He'd lived it…inside.

"I think my father hates me," said Dean. "Maybe he always hated me. I'm not crazy about him either."

"I'm sorry, Dante. I shouldn'ta took you up to the house."

"Fuck it," said Dean. "I got to get home before they send the cops out looking for me."

He started down the tracks. Guy stood. He watched Dean balance himself as he walked the rails. He'd noticed Dean from the first had this sway to his shoulders when he walked. Guy thought, very cool. He watched him and he watched him, and then who does he see—

CHAPTER 16

GERUNDO WAS MAKING HIS WAY UP THE TRACKS, ALONE. Guy saw him sometimes, as the kids' grandmother lived in a two family house about a block away on Ely Avenue and following the tracks past the Kennedy Home was a shortcut. They'd gotten nasty with each other a few times, but it never got violent.

Today it would be different. Gerundo saw Dean first. He'd been walking on the other side of the tracks, but he crossed over. That was when Dean saw him. And Guy knew.

It was a hot and humid day. The kind of day the sky was white and hurt the eyes.

"Well," said Gerundo, as he closed in on Dean.

Dean stopped but said nothing.

"Where's your fuckin' girlfriend?"

Dean felt a rising fear in his stomach.

"So…It's just you and me, cocksucker," said Gerundo.

Beyond the fear, something much more terrible was taking him over. The words had had no meaning before. They were just infantile insults. But now "girlfriend" and "cocksucker" were the calling cards of hatred that cut to the heart of a world closing in on him. A world where broken flesh and deformed manhood ruled the day.

Gerundo hit him so quickly, so squarely in the face, Dean was dropped. Stunned, he found himself sitting on the gravel alongside the tracks with blood pouring through his cupped fingers and onto the dried white stones.

Guy knew he'd do himself in if caught leaving the property, but he fuckin' did anyway. He was tearing it down the tracks when he saw Dean come firing up and going at Gerundo, driving him across the tracks and to the ground.

Dean was beating the kid across the face with a fist. All the rage that had accumulated—Ross's insinuations and threats, his father's prosecutorial questioning and animosity—he was not a boy in a fistfight on a brutally hot day in the Bronx, but another species of being altogether who had blown past all social norms.

A train was coming up the tracks and Guy couldn't get across in time, and there he was watching the fight through the strobing gap between passenger cars as the train went flashing past.

When Guy finally got across, he had to grab Dean under the shoulders and pull him off the boy. Dean was kicking and screaming, and Guy finally got him upright and they stood there staring down at a bloodied up and barely conscious Gerundo.

Gerundo was conscious enough to be whimpering. From all that adrenalin pumping through him, Dean shivered as if it were winter and not some sweltering day.

"Go home," said Guy. "Go on." Dean seemed too stunned at his own behavior to move. "Fuckin' go." Guy shoved him.

Dean pointed at Gerundo.

"It's just an ass kicking…He'll be all right," said Guy.

. . .

Gerundo had not come back home.

From the Teranova apartment terrace Dean could see across the Parkway, lights from a police car near the tracks left Dean trembling and sick to his stomach. His mother sensed something wrong and asked him about it and the boy lied. Guy called later from a pay phone in Linden Hall.

"He's dead," said Guy.

Dean felt as if he had fallen off the edge of the world.

"The police are out there now."

"But he was…What do we do now?" said Dean.

"I don't know. I'll call Gardner."

"We shouldn't have left him there."

"The little shit started the fight," said Guy. "Remember that."

Dean did not want to keep watching from the terrace, but he could not help himself. He saw the ambulance come. He was like something that no longer existed in his own body.

His mother questioned him, seeing how pale he was, how saddened and withdrawn. This is what he said to her, "…Sometimes when daddy calls you names and hits you, do you ever feel like hitting him back? I mean, hurt him."

This coming out of the mouth of her ten year old son frightened her to no end. She took him by the shoulders and gathering up all her motherly understanding and said to him tenderly, to somehow ease his fear, "You are my whole life…I'm the one person you never have to be afraid of."

He wanted to tell her he had done something terrible. To unburden his soul and make the world right again, but he could not.

• • •

Guy knew without fail Dean would eventually fess up. He was just too fuckin' decent to do otherwise, so he called Gardner Flynn from a payphone in the hall outside his room and told him what happened. Gardner asked for Dean's number, if Guy had it, and said he'd be right over.

Guy went out back of Lady Hall where kids from the Home had gathered to watch the police go about their business. Gerundo was lying alongside the tracks covered by a blanket. It was the first time Guy had ever seen the little shit with his mouth shut.

Guy took out a pack of Lucky Strikes and put one in his mouth and lit it. One of the kids got authoritarian with him.

"Hey, Prince…You better put that cigarette out."

"How 'bout I put it out on your forehead?" said Guy.

Guy walked away and crossed the grounds, smoking, making for the front gate because he knew his days as a resident of the Kennedy Home were coming to a fast close.

Late that afternoon, Gardner Flynn ushered Edith Teranova and the two boys into the 49th Precinct house where he'd already set up a meeting with investigators.

The air conditioning was out and the place was miserably hot. Fans had been set up everywhere. It was noisy, people came and went in handcuffs. In a private moment a fearful Edith took hold of Gardner's wrist, "The boys won't have to go to juvenile Hall… I heard the dead boy and his friends have been—"

Gardner tried to assuage her fear without lying, as she had no idea how bad things were in the summer of 1957 in New York, when it came to youth violence.

Youth violence meant teen violence. Teen violence meant juvenile delinquency. And teen violence was on a dramatic rise in the New York of 1957.

There were over one hundred gangs in the city. And not just Italian and Jewish gangs, but black and Puerto Rican gangs as well. And they were all fighting for the right to be lords of their own territory.

The week before, at a pool in Washington Heights, a lame white boy named Michael Farmer was brutally stabbed to death by black and Puerto Rican members of the Egyptian Kings and the Dragons.

People wanted justice. People wanted teen violence swept from their streets. They wanted juvenile delinquents incarcerated, and their wayward parents brought to task.

Amidst all the headlines of racism and hatred a musical was about to open called *West Side Story*, which would in time prove to fan the flames of personal outrage. Gardner Flynn knew there were convictions in the air, and children to be sacrificed.

● ● ●

The boys were placed in a small interrogation room to wait. They sat at a table side by side. There was no circulating air, not even a fan. It was like trying to breathe in sludge.

"You think they'd mind," said Guy, "if I light up?"

He was trying to be cool. Dean had other things on his mind.

"I don't know why you said anything to Gardner about being there. I hadn't told my mother. I wasn't gonna tell anyone. You'd a been outta this. What were you thinking?"

Guy looked at Dean. The scruffy haired kid, still a little dirty from the fight, his face banged up. Guy didn't know what to do when it came to the unimaginable truth of the feelings he sheltered.

He wanted to tell Dean that he loved him. He had loved him since he first secretly saw him at the edge of that pit, and then in front of the apartment building when he was being ragged on by those ratshits. And that everything Ross had said about him was true. He did not understand himself, yet he knew it to be true. But he was too afraid to say it, to admit it. Too afraid Dean would be lost to him. So what he said was, "I can tell them Gerundo jumped you, Dante. And all you did was fight back."

Dean just stared, then he shook his head. "They won't believe you, man. They won't believe us."

They just sat there after that, waiting. Each had tried to save the other, and in doing so, insured their own undoing.

CHAPTER 17

THE INVESTIGATORS DID NOT BELIEVE THE BOYS' STORY, especially after they learned of the incident with the rats. They thought it more likely the two had lain in wait for the late youth, as they knew Gerundo followed the tracks as a short cut to his grandmother's house. The fact that the boys came forward did play in their favor. But ultimately they were arrested and arraigned and sent to Spofford Juvenile Detention Center in Hunts Point to await trial for manslaughter. A charge that could keep them incarcerated until they were twenty-one.

That one of the boy's fathers was a known racketeer who had recently disappeared and was being investigated by a task force, only lent the whole episode an uncomfortable air of suspicion and violence. This, and the general atmosphere of the times, had Gardner deeply skeptical that the boys could get a favorable jury. Then he received a phone call from Judge Bishop of family court. The Judge wanted to meet privately. It was a stroke of luck…and here was why:

When Gardner Flynn graduated from Fordham Law back in 1952, he did what he could to conceal the fact that he was gay, so as not to derail a potential career. He'd had, at the time, very few relationships with men, and none of these was ever in the Bronx, where he might be seen by people he knew. His closest relationship was with a fellow student who lived in White Plains. The young man eventually went on to become an Irish Christian Brother preparing for his vows at Iona College in New Rochelle. He even taught for a time at Iona Preparatory School which was, in those years, on the college campus.

Gardner and he would meet at a small Italian restaurant called Trevi's on the corner of North Avenue and Shore Road. From there they would walk to Hudson Park, which was a quiet and shady strip with a small beach that looked out over the Long Island Sound.

It was through this Irish Christian Brother that Gardner one day received a call from a family court judge by the name of Bishop. He was a friend of the young man Gardner had the relationship with. It turned out the Judge's son had been arrested for solicitation in a gay bar by a vice officer. The year was 1954, and Gardner was one of the first attorneys to excel at the entrapment defense. He got the charges against the young man dismissed and the record expunged.

That same year, he received a second call. This was from the family attorney of a criminal regime out of the Bronx who had gotten Gardner's name from the same judge. It seemed that the daughter in this family had been arrested for the crime of solicitation by a vice officer outside Radio City Music Hall after the premiere of *White Christmas.*

The young woman's mother was desperate to have this 'issue' quietly disposed with. The girl's name was C.C. Carpetti.

• • •

Judge Bishop lived in Scarsdale on Fox Meadow Road. He was a tall and tailored fellow with prematurely white hair who could have easily stepped from the pages of *The Man in the Gray Flannel Suit.*

When he answered the door, Gardner thought the Judge seemed unexpectedly disconsolate.

"You all right, your honor?" said Gardner, walking into the house.

"I'm sorry about this," said the Judge.

"About what, your honor?"

The Judge led him to the dining room, and there at the table sat Ross and O'Gorman.

"I believe," said the Judge, "it is best I let you gentlemen talk privately."

Once the last of his steps could be heard climbing the carpeted stairs, Ross wasted no time.

"We want Prince. We know something went off between him and Gino Carpetti...or maybe it was that idiot son of Carpetti's... Christopher...If they didn't clip Prince out there on Shore Road, he's somewhere in hiding. And we believe you know where."

Ross stood now and came around the table where Gardner sat. O'Gorman hung back in the doorway.

"You know what's behind all this? And we want Prince to turn state's evidence," said Ross. "And we're gonna make your life fuckin' miserable until he does. And we know how. Like tonight for instance. Think about it...Mister Fag Attorney."

He walked out. O'Gorman took a moment. He was a good half foot taller than Gardner, but when he spoke he was neither aggressive or loud or crass. He seemed even conciliatory. "To prove what he's saying, Ross will ask the prosecutors to come down hard on those two boys. You don't want to see them incarcerated until they're twenty-one. And that will be just the beginning."

• • •

Gardner sat at the desk in his den, drunk and desolate, his eyes inflamed from crying. He had been rambling between rage and desperation. He was defenseless when it came to helping the boys and hated himself because of it.

C.C. came around the desk and pressed his head against her stomach to soothe him, as a sister might, or a mother or wife.

"I'd give it up to them, if I could," he said.

"Would you…Really? With all that entails?" she said.

It was the question he could not answer. And the one that marked absolute peril.

Suddenly there was knocking at the front door. Loud and relentless, then a voice calling out, "Flynn…I know you're in there."

Gardner got up and came around the desk. "It's the boy's father. Wait here."

He wiped his eyes and opened the front door and stepping out of the porch light was an enraged Eddie Teranova.

"Guess who just paid me an unwelcome visit," said Eddie.

"I was sure that would happen."

"They say that you have information that could benefit my son."

"If I did, don't you think I'd use it for both boys' sake?"

"I think your sake and my son's sake are very different."

"You'd be surprised."

"Ever since my son got involved with that—"

"This is not the time to cast judgments. We must stand together for—"

"I could beat the information out of you," said Eddie Teranova. "And no one would begrudge me for it. In some quarters, I might even be given a medal."

"I'd begrudge you for it."

Eddie turned to see a woman in the doorway to the den.

"Who are you?" said Eddie.

"I'm your basic issue Macy's dyke. And you ought to take a look at my left hand."

His eyes went to her hand. The light wasn't good down that end of the hallway, but it was enough to see she was holding a small but nasty looking semi-automatic.

• • •

The picture of Donny Gerundo they used in the newspaper was from his Confirmation. The article noted he was an honor student at Saint Clare's over on Hone Avenue and a member of the Legion of Mary Society. He was a good looking kid with a crew cut that was butch waxed. You'd have thought he was the Virgin Mother's own precious little package. But when an article came out about the Pirates of Pelham Parkway and that filthy sump, it dimmed the shine on his headstone some.

• • •

The trial lasted three days, the jury was out for less than an afternoon. In an atmosphere of societal retribution the boys were convicted and sentenced to incarceration until they were twenty-one. There was applause in the courtroom as the verdict was read.

Edith Teranova took a boy in each arm before they were herded away as if somehow now they were each her sons, and together as one. Her husband railed against the verdict he felt unfair, since much of it was based on salacious untruths about his son, who had been under the unhealthy influence of the older youth.

If you microfilm the local newspapers of the day or go to the Bronx Historical Society, you will find some telling black and white photos of the trial itself, and the times as well. One in particular was of the boys together in the court hallway surrounded by a bastion of prosecutors and police detectives, civil servants in middle age—all with a kind of uniform and impersonal drabness. And the boys, in their suits and ties and hair all neatly Brylcreemed as they stared into the grip of reporters and flashbulbs.

People have remarked on that photo. The expressions on the faces, the ambiance and atmosphere. And years later, after justice and divine vengeance had had their say, a writer used that photograph for the cover of a book about the boys. The writer, you see, felt it captured a moment in America when youth shed itself of an innocence that never existed.

CHAPTER 18

THAT WINTER THERE WAS A HORRIFIC KILLING. Some of the newspapers reported it as a murder, others took the more sensational approach and assigned the word—assassination.

The killing took place at Maria Carpetti's birthday party the week before Christmas. C.C. Carpetti's mother and brother lived in College Point on Powell Cove, which was just across the East River from Throggs Neck. Where Malba Drive intersected Summit Place, there were two rather stately brick homes that were almost identical and stood side-by-side.

They were both riverfront and had private docks. Maria Carpetti lived in one home, and her son Gino and his family lived in the other. Gino's oldest son, Christopher, inhabited the small guest house down by the dock.

To the outside world, the Carpettis seemed like any of the other Catholic families in College Point, except for the fact that their bloodline was violence.

It had snowed the day before, the streets and lawns were that beautifully smooth white. The Carpettis had a huge, lit tree on one lawn and a full-sized manger on the other.

Maria Carpetti's birthday was for family only—twenty, thirty guests. As crippling arthritis had confined Mother Carpetti to a wheelchair from an early age, she always set herself up in the sunroom so she could spend a little quality time with each family member as they first arrived. She was a merciless smoker with a voice like sandpaper. But her mind and senses were hard and clear as diamonds, and she was not to be underestimated.

C.C., as always, brought Gardner along, as he was like another son to Maria Carpetti. As they were coming up the shoveled walkway loaded down with presents, it was Gino, of all people, who opened the door. He wore a long flashy holiday scarf around his neck and a grin to match, but he was coldhearted through and through.

"Hello, brother," said C.C.

"I see you brought your wife along," Gino said, throwing Gardner a look.

"It must gall you to no end," said C.C., "that everyone knows your younger sister has a bigger cock than you...Oh, and Merry Christmas."

As they went into the house, Gino said, "Is that why Gardner always walks so funny? And Merry Christmas to you, too."

At family gatherings, C.C. had to run the gamut of quiet stares and uncomfortable silences. It usually settled down after the first hour or so, once the relatives were politely loaded. Occasionally one of the little ones would come right out and ask, "Are you queer?"

The time with her mother in the sun room and the door closed was always precious time. She knelt before the wheelchair with her head in her mother's lap, her hair being stroked by as case hardened a dago matron as ever there was one.

"I'm sorry, Mama," she whispered.

"For what?"

"For not being the girl you hoped for, with a couple of snotty, loud-mouthed kids and a selfish husband."

C.C. was ashamed she'd said it. Ashamed this feeling so overpowered her own natural feelings, but her desire for her mother's affection ruled all.

"Regret," said the older woman, "is not the worst form of grief. But it's damn close to it."

She had been looking out the sunroom window when she spoke, because she could see Gino and Christopher out there in the snow, alone, arguing. Christopher was twenty and taller than his father and already a terror.

"I've warned your brother not to cross the line with you, but it's getting so he can't even control his son. And it's affecting his judgment."

As C.C. stood and looked out the window, Missus Carpetti asked Gardner, "Those two boys...What's happened with them?"

"Guy Prince was sent upstate. The Teranova boy was incarcerated in the Bronx, so his mother would be able to see him regularly."

"Be careful," said Missus Carpetti to both her daughter and Gardner. "Because they kill the young ones, to get to the old."

There was a knock at the door. It was Leonard Ceraso. He was a youth who worked for Missus Carpetti as an errand boy. He explained that the bakery had called, and the cake was ready to be picked up, but C.C.'s car was blocking the driveway. She offered to move it, but her mother, who had been watching that endless familial conflict playing out on the snowy lawn, and finally fed up, said, "No…give Leonard your car keys. He can pick up the cake. You go out there and tell those two to get in here before the whole world knows our business."

Once outside, C.C. could pick up stretches of the argument. Christopher wanted the family to buy three hundred acres that flanked the Whitestone Expressway, to set up a commercial park that would include a fifty acre amusement center. Gino was against it. Believed it would be a breeding ground for "spics" and "niggers" from all over the five boroughs. That it would increase crime in College Point. Never mind the fuckin' nuisance lawsuits. But Christopher said, "We don't do it…Someone else will." And then he said something that stayed with C.C. "You owe me… Remember that," said Christopher. "You'd be doing time if—"

That's when they both saw C.C. was within earshot. They got very quiet.

"Mama wants you two inside," said C.C. "Like now."

The two men were trudging along behind C.C. all quiet like, when there was an explosion—

· · ·

One huge shock of flame scorched the cold winter sky beyond the rooftop. At first they thought it was a gas line that had failed, but upon reaching the front of the house they saw it was C.C.'s car. It was a crumpled mass with flames sheeting from the blown apart windows. The driver's door had been hurled a couple of hundred feet and now lay steaming on the neighbor's snow covered lawn.

People were massing in the street. Leonard Ceraso's mother had come running out of the house and was now trying to get as dangerously close as she could to see if her boy was alive.

Missus Ceraso had worked for Maria Carpetti for thirty years as housekeeper and aide. Missus Carpetti had helped raise Leonard herself. He'd been born with cerebral palsy and was physically challenged but was as decent a soul as the woman ever knew. Missus Ceraso had to be held back by Gino and his son because the truth was plain enough. The boy had been born into an uncertain world and he had died in an uncertain world.

The manger on the front lawn had been decorated with straw that got touched off by sparks from the explosion. So there it was, the wooden stable burning, the baby Jesus in swaddling, the Mary and Joseph, the three wise men and angels, their plastic bodies melting into the snow like steaming flesh then rising to heaven in black smoke.

C.C. stood before this fiery image, dumbstruck and staring at the inhuman reality in the driveway that had been meant for her.

SPOFFORD
Class of 66
—I fought the Law—

CHAPTER 19

DEAN TERANOVA WAS RELEASED FROM INCARCERATION at the end of April 1966. It was just short of his nineteenth birthday.

His whole life was a small box he carried with him.

It wasn't the old Bronx he stepped into. There were hardcore edges now—the mix of races, more traffic, endless graffiti in loud billboard colors. The buildings were all a little shoddier, there was more garbage. And the noise—everything seemed to be at loudspeaker pitch. But at least there weren't prison bars and walls between him and all that slightly polluted New York City sunshine. Take in a deep breath, Dante, and get a good toke of the Bronx right between your shoulder blades.

His father called to him. It was a shock Eddie Teranova showed up at all, even though he'd given Dean his word. He was leaning back against the hood of a yellow Mustang. He must have a scam going, thought Dean.

Dean didn't ask his old man where he was taking him. And Dean did not pursue the issue of his mother's death in that car accident. He did not believe his father's version of events. He never had, in the five years since Eddie Teranova had come to Spofford to give his son the tragic news. The boy silently chalked up what he'd heard as a lot of blow from a guilt ridden liar. Dean also believed the old man was only being nice to him now because he wanted something. And whatever that something was would eventually surface out of the pit that was his father's soul.

Eddie reached into the back seat and took a carton of Lucky Strikes from a stack and handed it to Dean. The youth saw right off there was no tax stamp.

"I got a thing going upstate with Indians on a reservation," said Eddie. "It's part of the connection I got working for me in Jersey."

Dean opened the carton and took out a pack.

"I help run a furniture store in Paramus," Eddie told him. "We import a lot of bedroom sets, living room sets, that kind of thing, from Canada."

As Dean slid out a cigarette he said, "Import...Is that what they call 'stealing' in the trade now?"

His old man took the comment in stride. But Dean could read the ill will behind the grainy smile. Dean lit up, then tossed the carton into that open box he'd brought with him from jail.

"What's with the box?" said Eddie. "And all those papers?"

They were crossing the George Washington Bridge at that very moment. It would always stick with Dean, that moment, whenever he even saw the bridge.

"I've been writing about everything that happened back in '57."

"What in God's name for?"

"Because I'm going to find out what happened to Peter Prince—and how it affected our lives."

"What...Are you serious?"

"I'm going to find out what this was all about. I've already written pages about the fight Guy and I had with Gerundo...and killing him... and how the task force used that and *other things* to threaten us with maximum sentences if we didn't 'fess up anything we might know. How they went to everyone...including you. And how you told me to put the blame on Guy, so they'd come down on him 'cause they wanted more pressure on him and Flynn. I'm going to find out...I'm going to get it all down on paper and blow it open."

"This sounds flat out infantile."

"Maybe...I don't know." He gave his father the caustic stare the old man had wrestled with in the past. "I'd like to know what mom would have thought about this."

His father's jaw clenched up and he got to rubbing his throat with the palm of his hand. That was a 'tell' Dean recognized. Eddie Teranova was choking on something he couldn't spit out.

"This is some kind of fantasy thing," said Eddie. "Some kid's fantasy. To burn the bad years out of your system. I get it. Write away."

"I'm past fantasy, Pop. I've been incarcerated half my life. I can't count the fights I've had. I've been stabbed and stitched up. Beaten with a metal bar. And raped...*twice*. Fantasy? Fantasy is rearview mirror stuff to me, Pop. I'm going to find out what happened because it's my life that got lost in there somewhere."

Eddie Teranova was suddenly looking into the tempered stare of a man disguised in the body of a teenager. He opened the window because he needed more air.

"Did they ever find out what happened with that kid blown up in front of the Carpetti house?" said Eddie. "No. All they found was one of his feet floating in the cove. You want to end up like that kid?"

"But, I'm not that kid."

CHAPTER 20

THE STEAK PIT WAS A TWO STORY, HIGHTONE RESTAURANT on Route 4, just across from the Bergen Mall. Eddie pulled into the lot and pointed out the furniture outlet beside it that he helped manage. As he parked in the back Dean saw some of the kitchen help was out there shooting craps. And it spoke to how the times had changed—half the workers now were either black or Puerto Rican. When they got out of the Mustang it was the first time Eddie Teranova spotted the tattoo on his kid's shoulder. He grabbed him by the arm.

SPOFFORD
Class of 66
—I fought the Law—

"You know what kind of creeps have tattoos?"

"Yeah," said Dean. "Marines and felons. And I'm no Marine."

Eddie took a sport coat from the back seat and tossed it to his son to cover up the tat. It was a classless shade of red and at least a size too small—but what the hell.

Eddie knew all the waiters and bartenders. He put on that phony charm facade his son knew all too well. The Steak Pit was subdued lighting and elegance, Louis XV and Persian décor, American cuisine with a few continental dishes to highlight the already extensive and upscale menu. The booth where they sat was soft leather and huge as a mothership.

Eddie Teranova ordered drinks and stuck to shallow small talk telling his kid about the ballroom upstairs and how Duke Ellington played there and Cab Calloway and Bob Crosby and his Bob-Cats and Killer Joe Piro and Xavier Cugat and his new babe, Charo.

Eddie had become a primetime name dropper, mentioning how a lot of the New York Yankees dined there. And Commander Whitehead of Schweppes Tonic Water fame. And that Bobby Darin had sung Mack the Knife to a ten year old girl who was having a birthday party. Through all the pointless chatter Eddie had no idea his son was emotionally breaking apart and finally had to excuse himself.

Trembling and pale, Dean Teranova stared into a bathroom mirror at some unpredictable stranger who had walked out of nine years incarcerated and into a quiet elegance he was not prepared for and had no connection with.

He hid in a locked stall and sobbed for a life forfeited, in part, by his own failures. A life undermined by fate and flawed choices.

He tried desperately to find his mother there inside him. To hear her voice. But it had been so long. He remembered the words, but not her throaty and floatish tone. *God is always working inside you. No matter how bad you think your life is.* He could at least envision her that day outside the School for the Blind. The heroine of some ghostly moment in his life, forever retreating with the years.

• • •

"You all right?" said Eddie, when his kid returned to the table.

"I'm not used to the world, yet," said Dean.

Eddie said he understood, but he didn't. He acted genuinely concerned, he wasn't. "When you're more grounded," said Eddie, "we'll talk out a few ideas for some action that might work for you on the side."

Something caught the father's eyes. "Look over there," he said.

At the entry to the Onyx Room a tall, and distinguished looking gentleman with wavy, grey hair and a dapper moustache had a crowd of restaurant employees around him.

"You know who that is?" said Eddie.

Dean had no idea.

"It's Cesar Romero."

"Never heard of him."

People at the tables around them had taken notice. A couple of women got up and all gushy asked him for an autograph.

"His movies are on *The Late Show…Million Dollar Movie*."

"What can I tell you?" said Dean.

"*Donovan's Reef?*"

"Nope."

"He's starring in a television series…*Batman*. He plays a character called The Joker."

"Never saw it."

"It's a hit show."

"Not at Spofford."

The maître d' walked Romero right past their table. He flashed a set of all time teeth. Romero just oozed old Hollywood.

"He's got an apartment in Teaneck...or maybe it's Tenafly," said Eddie. "I hear it's a real pleasure den...He's one of yours, by the way."

"Mine?" said Dean.

"Yeah."

"What do you mean?"

"He's one of yours."

"He went to prison?"

"Prison? Who said anything about prison?"

"You said he was one of mine."

"He never went to prison."

"No?"

"No?"

"Then how's he one of mine?"

"He's a fag...queer."

Eddie Teranova saw his son's eyes narrow, and he knew he'd made a poisonous misstep by what he'd said. The dark jawed face of the youth rose up from the table.

"What's wrong?" said Eddie, trying to cover for himself and seeming ridiculous in the attempt.

Dean took off his father's red sport coat and threw it at him.

"Why you—"

Dean walked out, leaving his father in the middle of an unfinished sentence.

In the parking lot, Dean went to the Mustang to get the box with his meagre belongings, but the doors were locked. Since the shortest distance between two points is the proverbial straight line, he made a fist and drove his hand right at the window. He had enough uncorralled rage to crack the glass with the first blow and he went through with the second, leaving streaks of his own blood in the wake.

Dean felt he had gone from one prison to another without hardly catching a breath or a break. He was carrying the box under one arm walking up to the highway when his father stormed out of the restaurant. He saw the open Mustang driver's door and the shattered window, and he lost it.

Dean was crossing the roadway, darting between a phalanx of traffic and when he got to the other side of Route 4 here came the Mustang skidding to a stop at the edge of The Steak Pit lot.

Eddie jumped out of the car. He went dago crazy, cursing his son out in Italian and English. The kid knew the language. His father kept shouting over the traffic, "There's something mentally wrong with you…in the fuckin' head. You'll be back in jail in no time. You hear me…you fuckin' prissy little fairy."

Dean put the damn box down, and what did he do, he started back across the highway at a dead run. Eddie saw the kid was coming after him. Not out of jail three hours and he actually looked like he was revved for a fight.

Now, Eddie Teranova wasn't the tough army officer of twenty years ago. He was a middle age slickster with polyester bellbottoms and white patent leather shoes and a floral shirt. And in a moment of measured desperation, jumped into the Mustang and took off.

There was Dean, left to eat his old man's dust kicking up from the parking lot gravel. Bent over, hands on his thighs, when he finally caught his breath and calmed a little, he started laughing. Laughing so hard he couldn't hardly contain himself.

The world it seemed, had gone stark raving mad while he'd been out of circulation.

CHAPTER 21

DEAN STARTED BACK FOR THE BRONX. He walked along the highway and didn't give a damn. He got hungry and tired of carrying that box and stopped at a diner on Route 4. It was one of those aluminum sided joints called Holly's, that looked to have been there since time immemorial.

He sat alone at a table in the back where it was quiet. He imagined himself like something out of Dickens, but with a Bronx accent. He was thinking about the life he'd plotted out for himself, but it sure hadn't started out as he expected. Suddenly someone slipped down into the seat facing him.

It was Ross himself. He didn't seem to have aged a bit, unfortunately. And he still had that same insufferably miserable stare.

He pointed at the hamburger weighted down with all the trimmings that Dean was eating. "Not like the crap you get when you're incarcerated."

Some nameless universal prankster must be fucking with my head, thought Dean.

"I see you and your daddy almost came to blows," said Ross.

He'd rehearsed confrontations like this in his head while he was locked away. Looking for the slick answers. Silence was better.

"Finish up," said Ross. "Then we'll get out of here."

Dean then noticed O'Gorman sitting at the empty table behind him. What did they think, he would try to sprint out of there with that box? O'Gorman didn't look so hot. And he shouldn't be wearing a suit anymore, but a friggin' toga.

While Dean ate, Ross reached for the box on the table to see what all those papers were about, but Dean was too quick with his arm and blocked the move.

While they led him to their car, Ross said, "How's your boyfriend doing?"

O'Gorman cut in. "They broke up years ago, didn't you know that?"

"No!" said Ross. "I did hear Guy Prince was offered a shortened sentence if he enlisted in the army."

"Yeah..." said O'Gorman. "So was Dean here. But he turned it down.

Did the full nine instead."

"Not a patriot, huh?"

They packed the kid and that box in the back seat of their sedan. Ross drove. They were heading for the bridge and Manhattan.

"You have one of two choices," said Ross. "You can work with us as an informant picking up what you can from Flynn and Carpetti. And what happened to old man Prince...or...You can get yourself convicted of some as yet undetermined crime."

O'Gorman reached over the seat and took the pack of Lucky Strikes from Dean's t-shirt pocket. He checked it out.

"No tax stamp." He showed Ross.

"You're gonna commit a crime," said Ross, "Even if you don't."

They crossed the George Washington Bridge. Light streamed through the girders, the river shimmered. It was turning out to be a beautiful day.

Then a thought hit Dean that shook him up. It was a deep, dark, dirty thought. The kind that comes from being indoctrinated by mankind while you're locked away...Had his father given him those cigarettes as a plant?

• • •

Dean had been to Gardner's home with his mother when they were preparing for trial. He had to get up his nerve before ringing the bell. When Gardner answered the door, Dean saw there was a party underway. Gardner was caught off guard by the ramshackle looking stranger with a cardboard box under his arm. Being a little lit on hash it took him a few beats to recognize the kid.

"Dean?" he said. "I thought you were getting out next week."

"They released me early. I didn't mean to...You're having a party."

He started to back off the porch, but Gardner wasn't having it. "What are you doing here?"

The kid cut a sorry figure as he said, "I had nowhere to go."

Gardner didn't bother to ask about Dean's father in all this, as he had a pretty sharp line on what Teranova was about.

Gardner led Dean through a hallway of partyers and up to the second floor, indulging in small talk along the way. There were some hipsters among the people there. But mostly it was the tie and jacket crowd, or those stylish Capezios and tops. There was music on a hi-fi and a bar had been set up in the dining room where they were knocking out cocktails. And that waft of pot in the air—Dean already recognized it real well.

The kid was collecting a lot of those invisible type stares. You know the kind, the ones that ask—what is that freak all about?

Two bedrooms on the second floor had been remodeled into a small apartment with a kitchenette and patio on top of the extended dining room. There was a private entry from an outdoor stairway up to the patio. It had been Gardner's first apartment from back when his mother was alive, and the family owned the building. Dean had been in there once with Guy, that was back before the trial.

"Stay as long as you want," said Gardner. "I'll get you a key."

"As soon as I rake in some money—"

"Forget it. We'll settle all that tomorrow."

Dean had set the box on a desk by the window. Gardner got curious and began fingering through what was a mound of handwritten or typed pages. "What is all this?" he said.

"I wrote about me and Guy and what happened that summer with killing Donny Gerundo."

Dean had been standing there in the middle of the room with his hands pressed down into his jeans back pockets like a true roadside tough, and not nearly the literate creature that Gardner knew him to be.

"You wrote about it?"

"Yeah."

"Why?"

Dean went over and rummaged through the box and out came this thirty or so page typed document. He handed it to Gardner who read the title:

The Pirates of Pelham Parkway
The True Story of How I Committed Murder

"They used that title in a newspaper story, so I stole it. Anyway, that's what Gerundo and the rest of them called themselves. I guess it means Guy and I now, too."

Dean pointed at the pages he had written. "I'd like you to read it, please. It's important."

"If that's what you want."

"Copies were sent off to a few magazines. You know, like *True Crime*… Good magazines. A guidance counselor at Spofford helped me compose the letter. Her brother is in that business… Getting stories in magazines."

Dean hesitated. He seemed a bit ashamed, maybe. "People like to read about murders. Especially if the person telling the story committed the crime. *And* was ten when he did the fuckin' deed."

"Why are you doing this?" said Gardner.

"To get in a magazine. Then to find out what really happened to Guy's father. And all the rest. You know what I mean."

Gardner took a long solitary breath. He knew, unfortunately.

"And then?" said Gardner.

"And then." The kid's whole body muscled up. "Then I would have done something. And my life wouldn't be a disgrace. I wouldn't get up every day feeling like a disgrace. Ashamed over my mother—dying while I'm incarcerated."

"I don't believe it's fair to put all that on yourself."

"Walk around inside my head for a while. Then come out with such high testimony."

There was much Gardner could say to alter the balance of the scales the boy was using to weigh out his life. But his instinct was to lean on silence. "Get some rest," he said. "There's food downstairs if you're hungry."

He started out of the room.

"There's one more thing," said Dean.

Gardner stopped. Thought—*All this so far isn't enough for one night.*

Dean took the pack of Lucky's from his t-shirt pocket. "I know you had a plan worked out that night to help Guy's father escape."

This took Gardner by surprise. Dean put a cigarette in his mouth and lit it.

"And how did you come by such knowledge?" said Gardner.

"Guy told me."

"And how did Guy come by such knowledge?"

Dean blew out the match. "He didn't. He said something sort of as an aside. It was just a detail."

"Is that so? And how did you come to know what this detail meant?"

"I had nine years to think about it."

CHAPTER 22

C.C. WAS KNOCKING DOWN VODKA IN THE KITCHEN with a cadre of women, listening to a political tirade in the living room when Gardner returned. She excused herself so the two could talk.

"It was him, wasn't it?" she said.

"None other."

"He looks—"

"Yeah. And then some."

He showed her the thirty pages Dean had given him. "He means to find out what happened to Peter. And all the rest that went with it."

She got a load of the title page. "Can he pull it off? He's only—"

"He was an honor student. And they didn't beat the brains out of him at Spofford. I can tell you that much. It's already gone to publishers."

"That means every fuckin' supervisor at Spofford had to know about it."

"I'm sure someone at Spofford has cued in the DA by now."

"Ross…Start listening for footsteps," said C.C. "The kid is putting a gun to his own head. He knows that, right?"

"I believe he's got a different worldview on the subject."

"Points of view don't mean crap when they come to foreclose on your ass. He's not doing us any good either. Is Guy—"

"He's not coming home to New York again," said Gardner. "He wrote me. He doesn't want to see the place."

"You put those two together—"

Gardner was fed up. He wanted to get wasted.

"We have another issue we have to deal with," said C.C.

She pointed to that political gathering going on in the living room.

"Next time I suggest having a party," said Gardner, "shoot me."

• • •

Charlie Merwin was a professor of philosophy at NYU. He was small and fair and always seemed to have too much energy for his boyish frame. He was a freak for the *Village Stompers* and the *Fugs* and anything political, and he was holding court in the living room with some of his diehard polemics.

Charlie was holding up a recent copy of *Time Magazine*—the one every homosexual in America was uncomfortably familiar with. That issue featured the two page essay entitled—THE HOMOSEXUAL IN AMERICA.

"*Time Magazine* says we're a pernicious sickness," said Charlie. "And if *Time* says it, its just got to be true."

Charlie was drunk, and he was waving the magazine around like it was a flag, quoting from memory… "In every walk of life…a pathetic second rate substitute for reality.

"But…but…our breakout is coming. And you know how I know?" He held up the magazine. "Articles like this.

"The writers can feel we're on the cusp. There's White Power…there's Black Power…there's women's rights…and there's us. The old order is coming apart. Ask Bobby Dylan…He'll tell you about where the losers are going.

"We need to take our identity to the streets. The world of business. Bars should be at the top of our list of attack. Ownership…liquor licenses. The right for us to have our kind of establishments. Free enterprise. And social freedom as one."

C.C. glanced at Gardner. He knew. If this was the rising tide of change, the mafia families that had been instrumental in the gay bar scene surviving were at risk. And they would not go gently into that good-night.

• • •

Dean sat alone in the dark at the desk in front of the window of that second floor apartment. Smoking and thinking and staring at a framed snapshot of Guy from somewhere back at the time of the killing that had been on the desk.

It was that look of his, the one of quiet loneliness and rebellion that brought back the letters that Guy had written.

After the trial, the boys were detained at separate locations for fear they might try and escape. There had been escapes from Spofford at the time, and the two youths together were considered troubled and cunning and primed to try and get out.

It was Gardner who'd brought Dean a letter from Guy. It was the unremarkable thoughts of an eleven year old youth until the last few sentences, where Guy admitted that he loved Dean, and he had from the first.

Alone in his cell, Dean could not read anymore. He never answered the letter—not the next, or the next or the one after that, not even the seventh, the last and shortest.

Hey Dante,

This is the seventh letter and will be my last. God rested on the seventh day… I think I'll take the hint. I wonder what he did for kicks after that. I'm sorry for writing how I felt if it fucked you up. Forgive me, if you can.

Guy

They never spoke again.

CHAPTER 23

THE HOUSE LOOKED LIKE THE TYPICAL SUNDAY MORNING after a Saturday night blowout. Dean came downstairs early with a cup of coffee and stepped over a pair of trousers. Nice touch, he thought.

He could hear Gardner talking away in legalese. Dean peered into the open door of Gardner's office. There was the attorney, neatly dressed, hair combed, shaved, talking into some kind of dictaphone. When he noticed Dean, he waved him in and shut off the recorder.

"You don't look like you were at an all night party," said Dean.

"It's a flaw of mine."

Gardner got right down to business. He reached for a file. Had Dean sit. From the file, he took a sheaf of papers and passed them to Dean. "The papers need to be signed," he said. "There's your mother's insurance policy for ninety thousand dollars, of which you are the benefactor." He then slid a bank passbook toward Dean. "That's a savings account with over thirty thousand dollars in your name that your father was forced to finance."

Dean set his coffee cup down and looked everything over. "I don't understand," he said.

Gardner cleaned up the confusion by explaining.

Edith Teranova had come to his house unexpectedly one day during the trial. She wanted to speak privately with Gardner. In his office, she told him with some trepidation, "I'm going to leave my husband when I think the time is safe. I want to get a job. The money will go to an insurance policy for Dean. And I would like you to be the executor of the estate."

"Missus Teranova," Gardner had said. "Are you in some kind of danger?"

"Have you ever felt as if you are? That there is a rising animosity against you?"

"Yes," said Gardner. "Quite often."

"I, too," she said. "But, of course, I always believe deeply God is working in my life. And that helps."

"I wish I could believe that," said Gardner. "But I don't. Even though I am Catholic."

"Well," said Edith, "I have a surprise for you."

"Yes?"

"That's when God's moral power is working its hardest. My son...will need friends after all this. I hope maybe you can consider that...if I am no longer here."

Listening to Gardner, Dean thought...*She's always here...encouraging you to get through all the ill treatments.* He wondered how in the fuck did she ever marry his father.

Dean held up the bankbook. "How'd you get this outta Eddie Teranova? Gunpoint?"

"After he failed trying to break your mother's written will, I got him work with a furniture outlet in Paramus."

"Importing suites from Canada...along with tax free cigarettes."

"You and he—"

"Unfortunately," said Dean. "We ate at a place called The Steak Pit. Food was great, the company a little hard to digest."

"The gig came with a caveat," said Gardner. "Your father had to cough up over ten percent, vig as they say, until you were released."

"He must fucking hate you," said Dean.

"It's not just the money, but to be handled by a 'gay' attorney."

Dean threw his head back and laughed out loud. He stood up. He started signing the paperwork.

"You could kick off a new life with that money. College...A business... Travel."

"I'm gonna get me a driver's license...A car...And a gun I can learn to shoot."

"You sure you don't want to lower the temperature a little on some of that?"

"I may run a little hot...Tell me about Guy."

"He earned himself a silver star and a purple heart, and an honorable discharge."

"Where is he now?"

"Let it be, Dean."

"Tell him I'm here...If you haven't already. And tell him...Well...Tell him we have unfinished business."

"Dean...I don't know if he can handle your unfinished business."

"It doesn't matter...because he'll know."

As Dean left the office, a man came striding along wearing the trousers that had been left by the stairwell. It was a disheveled and mussed up Charlie Meredith. He gave Dean a good looking over.

"Who are you?" said Charlie.

"Nobody," said Dean, starting up the stairs.

Charlie noted Gardner in the doorway. "They're growing a nice crop of nobodies this year, aren't they?"

You could detect the jealousy in Charlie's tone. Gardner made the introductions.

"You're him," said Charlie.

Dean didn't answer.

"A question...if I may?" said Charlie. "Do you think youth should set a higher standard than it used to?"

Dean knew the slant of the question. "Why bother to raise the standard, when you can just lower the ceiling?"

Entering the office, Charlie noted the look on Gardner's face. "You're not going to read me the riot act again?"

Gardner slammed the door. Dean waited. Eavesdropped a bit.

"Does C.C. run prostitution out of her places? No," said Gardner.

"She's still mafia," said Charlie.

"Does she deal in narcotics in her places? No."

"She owns it all. The liquor license...the liquor...jukebox concessions...cigarette concessions...laundry concessions...Prince fronted all that. But she got rid of him."

"That's...just bullshit talk," said Gardner.

"Gays should own and run businesses for gays. Not gangsters...even if they are gay. We'll run them out. Time and social pressure will—"

"You think C.C. Carpetti is just going to lay down and die at your feet?"

"No...she's gonna do what she did to Peter Prince."

"I don't want to hear that."

"Et tu, Brute? You're so fuckin' naïve," said Charlie. "One day she'll put a bomb under your car like they planted on hers out there at College Point. But don't listen to me. You don't have to raise your standard, just do like the Teranova kid says...Lower the ceiling."

CHAPTER 24

No one ever really knew the reason the Senior Editor at *True Crime Magazine* published THE PIRATES OF PELHAM PARKWAY. Even though the magazine stories were crude and sexual, *True Crime* had been, at the very least, a paean to law enforcement. But as the social order of the 1960s darkened before our silent eyes, the stories became more aberrant and amoral. Urban revolution and cultural dissonance were reshaping the human landscape of art and entertainment. Readers began to have more in common with the outsider, the rebel, the radical and misfit, even the murderers themselves. These became the heroes of the book rack world of magazines.

Maybe Dean had just innocently stepped through a historical moment of social change, and being outside the standard rules of storytelling he had included words like "queer" and "fag"—writing that this was how the police had mocked him and Guy Prince. And that the son of the missing gangster had admitted that he loved him. All this, coming from the youthful murderer himself, may have titillated or shocked some invisible audience and been its bestselling point.

Over time, rumors surfaced that Gino Carpetti and his son, had used their influence to see the story published, hoping it would resurrect the Peter Prince disappearance and smoke him out, if he were still alive. It was also suggested the District Attorney's office knew and let this happen, on the chance it would advance their case against the crime family. There was also this quiet grapevine about an underground of powerful gays in the arts that saw this story as an indictment on the institutional hatreds against them by the police and made a financial arrangement with the Senior Editor at the magazine.

• • •

The story was given a summer publication date. By then, Dean had gotten a driver's license, bought a souped up '62 convertible Impala with a 409, and through an intermediary of Gardner Flynn, secreted a pistol. He practiced on a makeshift target he had set up in the basement of the Flynn house on the corner of Mace and Bronxwood.

Gardner had kept faith with Dean's mother and convinced the youth to remain in the apartment on the second floor. In a private moment, after Gardner's paralegal had gone home, Dean stood in the office doorway and said, *"You never brought up the story...or the keys."*

Gardner sat back. He had been hoping to avoid this subject for as long as possible.

Dean stepped into the hallway and replayed that last night as Guy had described it to him on the bus back from Orchard Beach, with Peter Prince reluctantly heading out the front door. Guy brokenhearted for being left behind, believing his father would never return. Refusing to shake his father's hand, or to kiss him. His father joking, suggesting, that his son "kick him in the ass." The boy sitting at the bottom of the stairs, a defeated soul.

"And you," Dean said to Gardner, "took a pair of keys from your pocket and tossed them to Prince, saying, 'I forgot to give you these.'"

Dean pointed to where, he assumed, they'd landed on the floor and where Guy sat down and scooped them up. Guy saw they were *car keys* and wouldn't hand them over, hoping if he held onto them a little longer his father would relent and take him along.

Gardner remembered the night all too well, and to hear it played back—

"They were Peter's car keys," said Gardner.

"In your pocket? No way...No how. Those keys were to another car. One you had placed somewhere for Prince's escape. I think the car was in that wooded parking area along the Sound in New Rochelle. The place where the cars were found in the water along the shore and all shot up. I drove out there. There's plenty of places to stow a car away."

Gardner listened, then he lied with a perfect lawyer's pose. "You are not correct."

Dean wasn't buying it, not after all these years thinking it through. "What you are actually saying is...I'm not wrong."

"It's better if you are wrong."

"It's better if I'm correct."

CHAPTER 25

HE WANDERED THOSE FIRST WEEKS through a Bronx that *looked* like the old Bronx but was *not* the old Bronx. The Bronx he had been taken from in handcuffs was now a Bronx that had moved on without him. That reality struck with incredible force and robbed him of meaning and connection. He was like a character who had stumbled into a movie with a plot beyond his comprehension.

He went over to Pelham Parkway where he had lived with his mother and father. The sump with its filthy water was gone, replaced by an apartment and a school—no less. He was saddened to find it gone, though why he should he did not know. He had not yet come to realize that the past was like some beautiful horizon at dusk. Striking with memories, yet unattainable, because it was long past gone.

Somewhere in those troubled days and weeks, he began to see this other Bronx had something of him in it. It was a world trying to reinvent itself. Not just the buildings and the clothes, but the music and movies, the lingo, the different races and attitudes. Even the light that came down through the trees along the tracks where he had fought it out with Donny Gerundo, was reinventing itself.

And when that idea surfaced out of some perpetual reservoir of human surprise and took hold and challenged his will, so that when he lay in bed in the dark floating on the life raft of its very presence, and what it might mean, he began to feel hope.

He had not been to a movie in ten years, he had never seen a color television. He had not gone to a high school football game or dance. As a teenager he'd never gotten to run loose and wild. He had never had a date, had never been flesh to flesh with a girl.

The closest to that was being raped twice. Once by fellow inmates, an amped up version of the Pirates of Pelham Parkway. And once by a state guard.

• • •

89

On Sundays, Dean would take the subway down into Manhattan then to Washington Square. That was during the time when famous poets would come to the Square and recite their poetry, and cult writers would read from their works. Where singers and songwriters and bands on the cusp would strike out into the world with their songs and their music.

People were there to protest the war and the politics of the nation, to pass out leaflets about how the corporate rules of the road were defacing their lives, and that the elite and the powerful wanted to control their lives by silencing their passions. Everything to him was new and different and exciting, even a little dangerous. Dangerous because there were expectations with change, and expectations are known to have enemies.

"Hey... 'class of sixty-six...' Hey... 'I fought the law...'"

Dean didn't realize for a few moments that the girl standing there in the crowd just behind him and listening to Country Joe and the Fish was talking to him.

She was eighteen, probably. In funky jeans and a tight top with a Salvation Army coat. A real Salvation Army coat, with flashy brass buttons, even. She had black and wild short curly hair and dark skin to match and her eyes challenged you with a stare that dared you to stare back.

"What is that...?" she said, pointing to the tattoo on his shoulder. "Spofford...? A school?"

He was gonna tell her the truth, then thought better of it, "School... well, sorta."

She got closer and took hold of his arm without even asking and inspected the tat.

"I saw a guy with a tattoo recently. But he was totally zonked out in the front of a liquor store. His wasn't near as cool looking as yours."

All Dean could think of saying was, "No kidding."

"I go to NYU... My name is Elise...What's your name? You take classes here...Or do you go to Spofford?"

He didn't know what to answer, how to answer. The terror of actually speaking to someone in some interpersonal way about anything of himself took him over. His eyes got heavy lidded. He wished he'd worn sunglasses. He'd remember that for the future.

"No," he said. "I don't...I mean. My name is Dean. I don't go to NYU."

"You here to see the band?"

"Checking it out."

He noticed she slipped a neatly rolled joint from her pocket. She made sure he got a look. "What do you think?" she said. "Light up?"

He quietly freaked. Imagined Ross or the Feds swooping in and there'd he be, lunching at Rikers with the rape patrol.

Fate bailed him out.

Elise had come with a couple of girlfriends and they were hot to get on the move and slipped Elise one of those tell the guy good bye looks and let's get it out of here.

Elise scrambled among her friends for something to write with and to write on. She scribbled her name and phone number on a slip of paper then tore it in half. Half she slipped into his jeans pocket, the other half she gave him along with the pen.

"Let's see who calls first," she said.

He had never been in this situation and so was not in touch with himself or the moment. He added his last name and address instead of just leaving it with his first name and phone number. So you'd have thought he was filling out an unemployment form or a job application.

CHAPTER 26

DEAN WAS WAITING FOR THE IND. He stood alone at the far end of the subway platform smoking, really needing privacy from the world. A world he had not yet connected with. He looked at the scrap of paper with the girl's name and number and considered tossing it.

Dean was punished with edgy powers of observation. He could feel things before they happened, and this left him sensitive to the unknown around him.

Farther down the platform there was a young man, a shade older than himself. Good looking, too. Too much for his own good. The kind of youth they used to describe during his incarceration as "suicidally beautiful." He caught Dean's eye intentionally. The glance hung in the air like something unclothed for that extra moment.

Dean could hear the trains way down there in the dark, the iron screech of their wheels faintly as they made it through those diamond crossovers.

The youth kind of casually made his way down the platform. He was taking a pack of cigarettes from the pocket of his leather coat and then tapping a cigarette loose from the pack. He had a kind of centered grace, and not like he'd rehearsed the moves in front of the mirror, but more like God had gifted it to him.

Dean just waited silently as the young man positioned himself directly before Dean. He held up his cigarette and with his rather soft voice, said, "I noticed you were smoking."

"Was it that obvious?" said Dean.

The young man nodded.

"Got a match?" he said, holding out the cigarette.

"Nope," said Dean.

"How 'bout lighting my cigarette off yours, then?"

Dean took his cigarette and flung it down onto the tracks. The young man looked down to where it lay burning among the debris. "Well," he said, looking back at Dean. "That's a statement, isn't it?"

"I wonder," said Dean, "if I should have you tell Ross to go fuck himself. Or do I throw you down onto the tracks when the express comes by?"

All that suicidal beauty, Dean thought, and nowhere to take it.

• • •

THE FIFE AND DRUM was a neighborhood dive on Boston Post Road in West Farms. Police investigators congregated there. Homicide, vice, task force crews. No patrolmen, though. This was the exclusive domain of the white doo-wop crowd. What was left of it. A little jazz was all right, but none of that shit protest rock. None of that *'Eve of Destruction'* nonsense. Locals were okay to water there, strangers were hustled out with spartan efficiency.

Ross practically lived in the place. He carried a tab. He even parked a clean shirt and tie in a back office. That's how pathetic he was. Sitting at a table by the pinball machines airing out his professional miseries and wasn't Ross shocked when his informant was marched in by no less than a nineteen year old Dean Teranova.

"Ross," Dean shouted, scanning that packed dive. "Where the fuck are you?"

Brother, did this get the attention of a wall of unshaved and craggy faced hard cases.

Dean spotted O'Gorman first. After all, he was like a lighthouse squeezed in that nothing waterhole. And there was Ross beside him.

Dean pushed his way through the crowd, using the frightened informant as a shill.

"I think this belongs to you," said Dean, shoving the young man toward the table.

"You think you're gonna destroy my life," said Dean, "to get me to do your bidding. Not happening. And I want you to know. I can make your life pretty miserable."

"Is that so?" said Ross.

"I'm gonna write about this. I'm gonna write about you. I'm going to find out what I can about you and when I write about all this, I'm going to use what I find out about you. And there's plenty I already know."

"How many times have I heard that story," said Ross. "Your elevator is going down. So get used to it."

Dean was riding the rage of youth and wasn't leaving.

"Your wife tossed you out, and you stiffed your two kids on the alimony payments. Even when the court came down on you, you shit bagged your own."

Ross lunged at Dean. Got in one good shot and bloodied up the youth's nose pretty bad before he was restrained. But Dean kept right on.

"Your brother-in-law had to kick your ass to get the money, and word is, he left you on the front steps of your house weeping like a little girl."

They were pulling that bloodied kid out of there.

"They talk about you at Spofford," shouted Dean. "The guards...cops who came in. You're nothing in their eyes."

O'Gorman got Dean outside and flung him against a parked car. Dean had the breath knocked out of him. He was still game to have at it, but he'd have to get through a wall of full grown men behind O'Gorman, who had put out a stiff arm for Dean to keep back. "You made your point," O'Gorman said. "Let's leave it at that."

CHAPTER 27

DEAN WAS APPROACHING THE HOUSE the next morning after a rough and sleepless night walking the street, knowing one thing for sure—there was blood in the water and his presence was stirring it up.

And another thing—all this was the fuckin' sump behind the apartment with its shitass raft and lord Pirates, only on a grander scale. Something to remember to get down on paper.

"Hey."

Someone called out to him. "Hey…you…Dean Teranova?"

He turned to see a man stepping out of a parked Skylark. He wore a suit and a tasteless tie.

"Am I under arrest?"

"I don't know. Get in."

Dean saw there were two men in the back. All three looked pretty formidable, so he got in.

They drove in silence. When they started for the Whitestone Bridge and Queens, he knew this wasn't police.

"Let me ask you," said one of the men in the back, leaning forward and over the seat. "What do you think of the *FIFE AND DRUM.*"

They all cracked up laughing. Dean didn't know how to take it, so he just took it.

Out on Northern Boulevard, they pulled up to a beautiful Tudor mansion. Turned out it was a restaurant known as The Villa Bianca. Dean was wheeled through a busy lunch crowd and up to a private ballroom that was empty but for a young man at a back booth. One of the Beach Boy hits was playing on a loudspeaker.

Introductions were made. "This is Mister Chris Carpetti. Mister Carpetti…This is Spofford…Class of '66.

The man who'd spoken pointed at the tat on Dean's shoulder peeking out from under his shirt.

Chris Carpetti took a fork and used it to lift Dean's shirt enough to see the tat. Noted—I FOUGHT THE LAW—inked in red. "I fought the law," said Chris. "Bobby Fuller. I love that record." He sang a couple of bars, then had Dean sit.

Chris slid a carafe of coffee that had been on the table Dean's way. He motioned to his man to up the volume of the music.

"*Fife and Drum.* That place is some piece of work, ain't it?"

"I don't think I made their Christmas list."

"They wire us, we wire them. They have informants, we have informants. It's the double header that never ends."

Another Beach Boy record came on. Dean thought it must be their greatest hits or something. Carpetti sang along a little...

"You know how my aunt C.C. and Gardner got hooked up with Peter Prince?" said Chris Carpetti.

"No," said Dean. He poured himself coffee. "Mind if I smoke?"

"Smoke, man," said Chris. "I thought maybe you being one of them they told you. I mean, I got nothing against gays. I'm not like my father. He'd put a blow torch to the lot of you."

Carpetti bummed one of Dean's cigarettes. Listened to the music. *Surfer Girl...* The look on his face said 'too fuckin' much.'

"You familiar with Teatro Puerto Rico?" said Carpetti.

It took a minute for Dean to remember. After the war, Puerto Ricans had flooded into the Bronx. They'd called it the Great Migration. White and blacks alike wanted to know—great for who?

The 'Spics' had taken over Mott Haven. The Teatro Puerto Rico was the old Forum Theatre on 138th Street. It went strictly Spanish, live entertainment and music. It got hip. People from all over the city came there.

About two blocks from the theatre, C.C. bought a closed up bar. It was her first. It would be a private club for gays. Male and female. And called it THE U TURN. Reach a whole new crowd. She and Gardner were partners. He handled all legal work and contracts.

The place had to be rehabbed. They were alone there one night when they were confronted by a pimp thug named San Juan Dure. Drugs and prostitution to the gay crowd were his thing. And he had no intention of some white queers moving in on his territory. And he didn't give a shit if that dyke was a Carpetti.

He kicked the living crap out of both of them. He probably would have killed Gardner except for C.C. piercing his kidney with a letter opener.

When C.C.'s mother got word of what had happened, she brought the family together and ordered no one to touch this Dure. She would handle it herself.

"This," Chris Carpetti told Dean, "is where Peter Prince entered their lives. Did you know that Peter's older brother was a war hero...and gay?"

Dean had not.

"He had worked for my grandmother, and before he died he introduced her to Peter."

Chris Carpetti put a hand up to kill any talk while he listened to the music. It was still the fuckin' Beach Boys.

"I'm a California boy at heart," he said. "Surfing...the beach. A whole other worldview."

For a moment, Dean flashed on Guy and that first day at Orchard Beach—the Breakwater. Sitting here, now, was born out of that. It overwhelmed Dean suddenly. Because the unknown seemed to be expanding before his eyes. And owning him in ways he did not yet understand. Overwhelmed, he wished Guy were there.

"What I tell you now," said Carpetti, "I know by rumor. Dig?"

Dean blew out a long trail of smoke and leaned into the table as he nodded.

"Dure got sucked into a deal to go out to Jersey to meet some businessman who dealt in underage runaways from Canada for the sex traffic market. They were gonna bring a couple of young ponies...Samples, you know. White, young and pristine.

"Dure was a racist. The Spic hated whites, blacks. If he could turn them into junkies and whores he considered it a privilege. It got him off."

Carpetti repeated that everything he knew from there on he got second, or third hand. "The story," he said, "might have been through about as many hands as a roll of toilet paper."

Where Dure was finally taken, no one really knew. Jersey, Westchester. It didn't make a difference. What they did know was that someone or someones unknown had chopped his fuckin' hands off at the wrists. He was alive too when they did it. They could tell from the way the muscles were ripped from the bone that Spic must have fought like something crazed.

The hands were sent back to his people wrapped in wax paper. A not so subtle message—keep your hands to yourself.

Chris Carpetti had been intensely engaged in the telling of this story, that was no kidding. And the music. Those Beach Boy songs—

"In my room," said Carpetti. "I should have been born in California…
instead of wop New York."

There was a mournful innocence to the song that only made more
ghastly the story Dean had just been told. And would highlight with razor
sharp irony, what he was about to have laid on him.

"Well, Mister Spofford…Class of sixty-six. You may have thought you
had blood in the game before. But it's nothing compared to the blood you
have in the game now. You're in. Just like the Feds, and just like you, we
want to know what happened to Peter Prince. Some think the Ricans got
him. Some think they bombed my aunt's car. Yeah…run, rabbit, run, or
the dogs are gonna catch ya…Get my drift?"

Dean said nothing. He stubbed out his cigarette and just sat there.

"Twelve-twenty-one River Avenue in the Bronx…That address ever
come up?"

"No," said Dean.

"Not from Guy or his father?"

"Never met or talked to his father."

"No one talked of the murder?"

"No."

"Leo Crab…Tessie Crab. Their names ever come up?"

"Not that I know of."

"You know Gardner made a lot of money setting up phony birth cer-
tificates in Puerto Rico?"

"No," said Dean.

Twelve-twenty-one River Avenue. Check it out. Ask Guy…You can
split now."

CHAPTER 28

COUPLE FOUND MURDERED
IN THEIR RIVER AVENUE APARTMENT

Leo Crab and his wife Tessie were found shot to death in their second floor apartment at 1221 River Avenue. They had been murdered by an unknown assailant. There is as yet no known motive for the crime.

Neighbors had become suspicious when neither the husband nor his wife had shown up for work for over a week, nor had they been answering their phone.

Leo Crab, age 37, a former Marine, had been a shipping clerk the last seven years at E.J. Korvette's.

His wife, Tessie, age 35, worked as a domestic.

The couple met during the war, while Leo was stationed in San Diego. They have no children.

Leo is survived by his brother, Teddy Crab of Porchester, N.Y.

Funeral services will be held at Cook's Funeral Home on 190th Street, Bronx.

IT WAS A RATHER FACELESS ARTICLE FROM THE SPRING OF 1957. Not unlike the endless litany of similar articles that filled boxes and filing cabinets in thousands of dusty corners and locked up basement warehouses.

There were no follow-ups. Nothing other than that perishable xerox that Dean had gotten from the library and stood staring at in the Bronx sunlight.

• • •

Dean drove over to the River Avenue address. He found it under the Elevated and just up from Jerome. The neighborhood was pretty shoddy, and the address, one of those narrow turn of the century two-story brick apartments. The front unit had been turned into a barber shop with a bay window, but it was all boarded up now. The locks had been knocked out of the front doors, and the entry was showcased by a single naked bulb. The floor had those faded hexagonal black and white tiles, the white now as yellow as a set of dead man's teeth. There were cans in the hallway and a garbage in the air stink. There were the doors at the end of the hall and an iron stairway that led up to an open landing where there were two apartments.

He had bought an instamatic and was taking pictures with a flash when one of the apartment doors upstairs opened, and there came this flurry of people talking Spanish and then a man appeared. He was heading out and stopped when he saw this young white guy taking pictures. He came along the landing and in Spanish suspiciously said, "You with the Department of Health… About those goddamn rats."

He pointed toward the garbage cans. Dean could see a long tail skittering through the shadows behind the cans.

He'd picked up enough Spanish at Spofford to answer he was not from the City. The man grew more suspicious as he came down the stairs.

Dean had prepared a lie. "I'm doing a magazine article. I'm a writer…" He took a copy of *True Crime* from his back pocket. It was open to his story, which even featured his photograph. The man glanced at the magazine. From his look, he was not impressed.

"There was a murder back here in nineteen-fifty-seven." He held up a copy of the newspaper article. "I came to see if anyone was here now who lived here back in fifty-seven who could tell me about it."

The man had only been half listening. Dean could read the stare—Whitey was the outlier now and should be treated as such.

The man pointed down the hallway with pure disinterest. "Last door. A black lives there. He was a janitor for some of the buildings around here for a long time."

"Thanks."

Dean started down the hall. Could feel a cold set of eyes on his back, just to make sure he was not full of shit.

Dean knocked. He stood in the half dark alone while waiting before he heard shuffling feet. Then a door latch clicked, and then another. A chained door opened slightly. A small black man in his later years peeked out—"You with the Department of Health? 'Cause it's about time."

"No sir, I'm—"

"What you want then?"

Dean began the same lie. He held up the magazine. He thought to himself that he sounded like a door-to-door salesman. The man looked hard at the photograph, and hard at Dean.

The man reached through the narrow opening and took the xerox with two arthritic fingers and looked it over, all watery-eyed.

"After all these years," he said. "Finally...Finally...Someone come to write about the murders."

He handed Dean back the article and got this look on his face that gave the youth a sense of discomfort, as if something unhealthy was about to have at him.

"You here to write about the babies...? 'Cause someone should."

Dean did not know how to answer, so he tried just to be cool.

"I'm here to write about it all."

"And how they burned them up?"

Dean did not know if he had stumbled into something real or fake or just plain nuts.

"They burned up all those little ones."

The old man pointed past Dean's shoulder and Dean turned. There was a door that had a huge lock to keep it shut.

"I could show you the furnace where they did it."

CHAPTER 29

WHEN DEAN RETURNED TO THE HOUSE, C.C. was in the office with Gardner. They seemed on edge. He wasn't going to get right into it, except C.C. said, "What do you think of my nephew?"

Dean stopped in the doorway. He had the magazine rolled up in his hand. "He likes his music loud."

"That's just to drown out the screams."

"What did he want?" said Gardner.

Dean entered the office. Gardner was at his desk. C.C. was sitting back against the windowsill.

"Twelve-twenty-one River Avenue," said Dean.

This brought C.C. to her feet.

"And why did he give you that address?" said C.C.

"You both don't know?" said Dean.

"I think it's best you tell us," said Gardner.

Dean took the xerox of the newspaper story from the magazine. He handed it to Gardner. He looked it over and then he passed it to C.C.

"I have a strong familial compulsion to kill that son of a bitch." To Gardner, she then said, "You know where this is going. You can see the narrative."

Gardner put a hand up to suggest she calm down. "I can't see anything yet." To Dean, he said, "Did he give you this?"

"I got it from library files. Is Guy's father involved?"

"Involved how?"

"You're gonna make me chase you for that answer, aren't you?"

"Only for your own good."

"Why did Carpetti tell me all this?" said Dean.

"In case you didn't notice it," said C.C., "you just swallowed a question laced with strychnine."

"Your nephew also brought up a man named San Juan Dure," said Dean.

"I need a cigarette," said C.C. "You see what's going down here," C.C. said to Gardner.

Dean took a pack of Lucky's from his jeans pocket and slid it across the desk to C.C.

"I need to talk with Guy," said Dean. "Where is he?"

"Leave him be," said C.C. "Haven't you already done him enough harm?"

"What…what do you mean?"

"Let it go," said Gardner. Then, he said, "What did Chris tell you about this Dure?"

"What did she mean?"

"What she means and what she says are sometimes two very different things."

"I can do my own deflecting, Gardner, thank you. And I meant—"

Gardner cut her off. "What did Christopher tell you about Dure?"

Dean went through the story detail by detail.

C.C. had lit her cigarette and was flicking ash out the open office window. She was fed up. "That story," she said to Dean, "is bullshit. Dure roughed us up. My mother said she would take care of it—"

"I don't think we should get into this," warned Gardner.

"Fuck this kid," said C.C. "It's too late." To Dean she said, "My mother didn't hire Prince. It was Gino who did Dure in. I can't prove it, like I can't prove Hitler is dead. It was my brother who got word leaked out I'd ordered the murder. That's how I ended up with a bomb under my car. And you know why he's telling you all this?"

"You tell me," said Dean.

"Because you're blood in the water, boy."

Dean looked at Gardner. "I don't understand."

"They're feeding you," said Gardner, "misinformation. Half-assed facts. Knowing at some point you'll get entrapped and to keep from hard time at Rikers, you'll probably roll."

"Then you'll puke up what you know, or think you know," said C.C. "It's an old story. They know you're a target and are using you."

"It's C.C. and me they want," said Gardner. "They feel we're weak links. Being gay, we're vulnerable. You'll roll on us. And we'll roll on…You get the picture."

"And Peter Prince," said Dean. "Is that why you helped Guy's father to get out?"

"What else did you and Christopher talk about?" said C.C.

"Nothing."

"That's it? Anything else happen?" said Gardner.

Dean considered confiding in them about River Avenue and the tired out black man with that ring of passkeys undoing a fist sized lock on the door across from his apartment.

He'd flipped on a light switch, and there was a wood stairwell leading down to a grim, gray basement where dusty trunks were stacked against a wall. There was a coal chute up to the street that looked to be a hundred years old, and probably was. A cement trough went from it to a scarred boiler missing parts and pretty ruined looking itself.

The old man, whose name was Woodrow, had been a part time janitor for half a dozen buildings in the neighborhood.

"That's the boiler," he said. "Or was. That's where they burned up them babies."

"Did the police know about this back then?" said Dean.

"I didn't mention it after the murder. Being black back then was worse than it is now. Didn't want police trouble. A black man around when there's trouble, police automatically parachute him right into the middle of it. I'm old now…who'd give a shit."

Dean had taken out his instamatic, "Mind if I get some pictures?"

Dean confided to Gardner none of this.

Gardner picked up on the strange lapse of silence in the conversation. He looked across the desk. As he reached for a cigarette, he said, "I have a feeling there's more."

"I can't help how you feel," said Dean.

"Dean," said Gardner.

He looked across the desk. As he reached for his pack of cigarettes he said, "Nothing else."

Dean wasn't sure why he kept it from Gardner. Some sense of self-preservation, possibly. Some purpose that had not yet made itself known to him. Being raised by a lying slime like his own father might have heightened his instincts to keep a truth pocketed until the right time. Was he doing them right, or doing them dirt? He didn't know.

"I want to meet with Guy. Where is he?"

"Leave him alone," said C.C. "He can't afford you interfering with his life."

"I think his father is alive. I think," Dean looked now to Gardner, "you organized his *disappearance*. And Guy was never told. I think Guy needs to know. He has a right to know. Because I think we can find his father."

"Find him!" said C.C. She stared at the youth as if he were mad.

Dean shook his head, he thought he could.

"The task force tried for years," said Gardner.

"I know things they don't."

"You hear him," said C.C.

"Like what?" said Gardner.

"I…don't think I should…tell you…yet."

Gardner glanced at C.C. She was quietly enraged.

"I know what this is really about," she said.

Dean looked at her from across the desk.

"It's those unresolved emotions you've been carrying around—"

"I don't understand," Dean said.

"Trying to lure him back into your life because—"

"Don't go there," said Gardner.

"You can't come to terms with—"

"Don't."

"Who and what you—"

Gardner stood and shouted. "Goddamn, you."

C.C. tempered herself. "You destroyed him once when he was honest with you about—"

She stopped because Gardner had begun to make his way around the desk, and he looked prime for something nasty.

"All right," she said. "the long arm of mercy strikes again."

She went and sat on a couch at the far end of the office. She crossed her arms and refused to look at either man.

Gardner told Dean, "Go up to your place. I'll catch up with you in a few minutes."

As he left, Dean said to C.C., "I'm sorry for everything I'm not. But I'm not finished remaking myself."

Once it was just the two of them, Gardner said to C.C., "Guy should be told the truth after all this time."

"You mean the truth as it was ten years ago," said C.C. "'Cause there's a lot of truth between then and now we know nothing about. Unless you've been covering up."

"They need him dead…we need him alive."

"Christopher is making a move. Does he have my brother's blessing? If not, this will get ugly."

"Maybe we can help that along," said Gardner.

"You don't mean…" C.C. pointed upstairs.

Gardner made the trek upstairs and knocked on the hallway door to Dean's apartment. When Dean answered, Gardner handed him a buckslip. "I wouldn't call. I'd just show up and make my case. After all, it's been ten years."

Dean looked at the address and phone number. "I've never seen a desert."

"You know they want you to find him, so they can kill him."

"Yeah."

"And I want you to know we're using *you* in this."

"Blood in the water. I'm all right with that."

CHAPTER 30

WHILE DEAN WAS PACKING, HE GOT A CALL. He never got any calls. It was that girl. He recognized her voice right away.

"Looks like I called you first," she said. "Remember my name?"

He remembered. "Starts with an E…had five letters."

"Very good. You up for getting together? Going out into this big bad world?"

"I'm leaving for New Mexico in an hour."

Dean sat on the edge of the bed. He'd thought about her. He wanted to tell her about himself, but was afraid, unsure…even ashamed. He'd thought of a solution, a cowardly one he admitted to himself.

"I'd like you to get the recent copy of *True Crime Magazine*."

"That's a magazine with all these lurid covers."

"There's an article in it I wrote…" He lost his voice for a moment… nerves. "It's about, the Bronx back in fifty-seven…and a boy I killed in a fight."

There was a drawn out silence at the other end. He wished he hadn't answered the phone.

"Are you stoned?" she said.

• • •

Dean drove to Albuquerque in his souped-up Impala. He existed on amphetamines and truck stop coffee. He ate behind the wheel, and the country went by in a beautifully hallucinogenic tide of people and places and landscapes as alien to him as the moon itself. Every new stretch of road engaged and informed him of everything he did not know. That Chevy with its huge engine was like a rushing beast that was taking a bite out of time itself and made him free in a way he had not ever been before. Just being on the move can be its own form of profound.

He reached Albuquerque at dusk of the second day out. Not record time, but not bad either. He asked directions at a gas station and got a very strange reaction. He drove up into the Sandia Mountains just east of town and passed the tramway to the only road that led farther on up to where there was a funky trailer park and a bar known as THE MAVERICK.

Exhausted, he pulled off the road in the hills to rest until it was dark. After two hard days of anticipation and uncertainty he'd arrived at the here and now. He would write about all this later, and about confronting a reality you have no idea where it will take you, or how you'll end up.

• • •

While Dean had been driving across country, Gardner went with C.C. to meet with her mother at the house in College Point. The woman's health was compromised enough now she was entering a phase of being where the arc of time was moving against her. Her strength, she was not a woman of illusions. She had long since made friends with the inhuman shadows that pursue us all.

They sat in her office on a sunny day where she could look out the French doors and watch her two granddaughters playing with their nanny when the mood came over her.

C.C. had made the call to come over and talk, but her mother beat here to the punch. "You're here about the meeting between Christopher and Teranova."

"He told you?" said C.C.

"He came to me with the idea. He asked my permission. I gave it to him. Does this surprise you?"

"Yes, Mother."

"Good…Gardner…If you would be so kind as to leave my daughter and I alone for a few minutes."

He got up, and as always, kissed the woman, and she held his hand. There was a part of her, a selfish motherly part, that wished somehow in this life, C.C. and Gardner could be married and conceive children, even if they were gay. She did not believe being gay should get in the way of a sound marriage.

Once mother and daughter were alone, C.C. said, "You didn't authorize the Dure mur—"

"I know it. You know it. Christopher knows it."

"Then why let him—"

"I was making a move in conjunction with my attorneys…for after

I'm dead. Enough said on that. I don't know if Prince is alive. I don't know if Gardner does. Prince has kept your brother in check all these years with what he knows about his operation. Which has helped keep you alive. Besides me, of course.

"I don't know what will happen if Teranova and Prince's son find him. Guy Prince may know things that could blow our lives wide open and cause Gino to do something ill advised."

She glanced out the French doors. Watched her granddaughters consumed by all the earthly excitement of childhood.

"No one will be safe," said C.C.'s mother. "Not even Gino's own son. Listen, now. Those two boys are likely to be killed. That will bring everyone down on us. If I should be swept off this earth suddenly, you might have to have Gino killed yourself. I'd start thinking about that if I were you. And not a word to Gardner. He can serve you best that way."

Gardner was outside with the two girls. They were scrambling around him, and he—the tireless slave to their childhood excitements. Then C.C. joined him. She had lost that beautiful color to her skin, for the time being anyway.

As they walked to his car, who should they pass in the driveway but Missus Ceraso. She still worked for C.C.'s mother. And every day she came down the same driveway where her son had been killed by a car bomb. C.C. glanced at Gardner. They both had the same thought, one they'd discussed in the past.

C.C.'s mother had offered to pay the woman so she would never have to work again. But Missus Ceraso was old world Italian. A day's work for a day's wage. Besides, she had a secret prayer, hoping that someday, being there, she would learn the truth behind her son's murder and personally avenge her boy.

CHAPTER 31

THERE WERE STONE COLUMNS THAT FLANKED A DIRT ROAD to the entrance of the CLOUD AND SKY TRAILER PARK. It was set back among tall pines. Half a dozen roads with names like Apache Lane or Conquistador Way fed off into the wooded darkness. There was a sign outside the manager's office that read: PLEASE DON'T FEED THE BEARS. Dean noticed quite a few American flags hung from the trailers on stanchions.

Guy's address was down a long dirt road that said DEAD END. His was a beat up Airstream at the edge of the hills. There were lights on inside and the darkness made them burn all the more.

Dean took a breath and gathered himself. He knocked on the door but there was no answer. He called out, but there was no answer. He peered in through the screen door. It wasn't the big house in the Bronx the boy had grown up in, that was for sure.

"You looking for Guy?"

Dean turned. There was a young man in an army fatigue coat walking a dog.

"Yeah."

"He's over at The Maverick."

"Thanks."

"I see you got New York plates."

"Yeah."

"I hope the fuckin' place burns to the ground."

Dean waved cordially, "I'll let it know when I get back."

• • •

Dean was no bar expert. He'd only been loose on the street for a few months. The Maverick was a drinking bar. A mix of honkytonk and hipster, outlaws and arty types…and gays. That's where it had top spin from the bars down below in Albuquerque. Here the old rules of the road had been kind of run over.

On the juke, Johnny Cash was doing his rendition of Dylan's *It Ain't*

Me Babe.

Dean wandered through the crowd, wondering would he recognize Guy. A couple of times in that grainy bar light he thought—yeah, there he is—then no.

Finally, down that length of crammed bodies at the bar, Dean spotted him. He was side-by-side, sitting close, with a rough looking character, a little bigger and a little older than Guy.

Guy was smoking. He had a moustache now and longish hair and he wore a black t-shirt and his arms and back were muscled. Even sitting, Dean could see Guy was taller than he was.

Guy was drunk. He was shooting down a boilermaker, and he wore this freewheeling smile until something up that crammed length of bodies at the bar gave him a good old fashioned shock. For a moment he tried to suppress the reaction, kill it off. Get cool and distant as a piece of slab stone. Good luck.

As Dean made his way down the length of that bar, Guy may have been listening to the fellow he was drinking with, but he was already somewhere back in time, back all those years to Pelham Parkway before context was required for every little thing. When life was simply immediate and cool and full of promise.

"Hello, Guy."

Guy did not pretend he had not seen Dean coming. He did not give away whether he was shocked. He had drunk his way through a thousand personal torments, what's one more, more or less.

"What year is this?" Guy said to Dean.

"What?" said Dean.

"What year is this...nineteen what?"

The fellow at the bar with Guy gave this stranger from out of nowhere a good looking over as he tried to figure out what this conversation was all about.

"What year?" said Guy.

"Nineteen sixty-six," Dean said.

"It's not nineteen fifty-seven?" said Guy.

"No."

"You sure?"

"Even a fool knows the year he got released."

"Who is this?" said the fellow with Guy.

But Guy didn't answer. He was on his own flight path, and his drinking partner was not included.

"This isn't the Bronx," Guy said to Dean.

"Not unless I made a wrong turn somewhere."

"And you would never do that?"

"I did once."

"So Pelham Parkway isn't around here, either?"

"No."

The fellow sitting there wanted to know who this new player was, and what was happening.

"And that sump," said Guy. "That filthy, wonderful sump with its raft and rats?"

"Gone," said Dean.

"Gone?"

"There's a school there now."

"A school."

"Mother Butler Academy."

"Mother Butler...Mother fucker."

"You two know each other, I guess," said the fellow with Guy.

"And the Kennedy Home?"

"Still there."

"And the Pirates of Pelham Parkway. What happened to those boys?"

"All grown up, I guess...and gone their ways."

"Except for Donny Gerundo."

Guy had said that with a prize fighter's efficiency. "Except for Donny Gerundo," said Dean.

"Are either of you two gonna give me an answer as to what the fuck is going on?"

"He's still dead," said Guy.

"Still dead."

"And my old house...what about it?"

"Don't know."

Guy turned to the hulky character he was with. "You should have seen the house I lived in with my father. It was a palace. The fuckin' living room was larger than this whole bar. No kidding."

Guy reached for his shot of whiskey and bottle of beer. He downed the shot and chugged some beer right behind it. Dean could see the turbines were going full throttle inside Guy's head.

"There were beautiful angels painted on the coved ceiling," said Guy. "The living room had a coved ceiling. You know what a coved ceiling is?"

The fellow he was with got pissed off. "I know what a coved ceiling is."

"My father used to shoot at those angels with my BB gun. He was a trip."

"You guys know each other obviously. So…is somebody gonna introduce somebody to somebody?"

"No," said Guy. "There is no somebodies here. Only nobodies."

"If you don't mind my asking…What was your father shooting at those angels for?"

Guy answered his friend, but he was looking at Dean. "They were eavesdropping," he said.

"Eavesdropping." The fellow drank, and he laughed, and he shook his head. "Eavesdropping on what?"

"On mortal man," said Guy. He took a few slugs of beer. "You know something about mortal man, don't you?"

He had been talking to Dean.

Guy was pretty ripped.

"You see where this is going," said Guy.

"I see where it's been," said Dean.

"You're priceless."

"But not where it's going?"

"This isn't going anywhere, if you ask me," said the young man sitting alongside Guy. He had become that inconvenient third wheel, and he was none too pleased with that reality. There was a hint of animosity in his voice when he said, "My name is Lou. Guy and I run together…Sort of."

"This is Dante," said Guy. "Who shows up when it suits him or when he shouldn't. So," he said to Dean, "finish looking politely hopeful for whatever is on your mind… and go."

Guy's eyes had narrowed in the same way that they had as a kid. And there was that sharp tweaked up tone in his voice. The sentences always had movement in them. That first day at Orchard Beach, Dean had picked all that up about him.

"No matter where you go," said Dean, "or where I go, the Bronx is unfinished business in both our lives."

CHAPTER 32

DEAN WALKED OUT OF THE MAVERICK in quiet despair and was driving back down the mountain for home when a pair of headlights rolled right up on his ass. He could make out in the sideview mirror a red pickup. A big old Apache 10 with a horn blowing and front bumper shimmying from a loose bolt. And there was Guy leaning out the window demanding Dean pull the Impala over.

The two lane road was dark and deeply wooded and there were turns and little traffic, thank God, because Guy gunned it and was alongside the Chevy which had picked up speed.

Guy was enraged and kept demanding Dean pull off onto the shoulder, but Dean was keeping it coldblooded. They were approaching the trailer park when Guy put his boot to the floor. The road curved there, and Guy didn't give a damn. The pickup surged, the vehicles shadows climbing through the lights against the huge trees. He cut the wheel. He cut it so hard he left a trail of smoke from the skidding tires and the red pickup fishtailed and blocked both lanes fuckin' flat out.

Dean came to a desperate stop on the shoulder of the road with his headlights practically kissing the trees. Dean got out of the car fuming. "That was a brilliant move."

Guy was already standing in the middle of the road holding a bottle of beer like it was some kind of pistol. "Why didn't you just pull the fuck over then?"

Dean didn't answer. He leaned back against the Chevy, stuck his hands down in his pockets and stared.

"You just show up out of nowhere. The ghost of nightmares past… after ten years. No warning. No phone call. Not even a *letter*."

Dean took the dig. "Gardner thought it best," said Dean, "I just show up. I took his advice. I guess it was wrong advice."

"No…Gardner's got too much irony in him. He knew if you called, I'd blow you off. And he didn't want that to happen. Well…you're required to come up with some kind of answer. What is it? The grand entrance… Are you going to keep me in suspense?"

"Unfinished business," said Dean.

"What does that mean? You and me?"

"Your father."

"My…" Guy threw his arms out in some wildly dramatic gesture. "Are you some kind of incarceration casualty? Or are you looking for a way to untrivialize yourself?"

"I believe he's alive. I believe that night he left he had a plan of escape that Gardner had helped him prepare."

There in the throw of the headlights, Dean could see an uneasy tension coming over Guy.

"My father wouldn't just cast me off…"

"Maybe the situation demanded it. Maybe it was the only way to keep you safe. Maybe—"

"How many maybes are you carrying around in that head of yours? And how did you come to all these maybes?"

"Nine years incarcerated thinking about our lives," said Dean.

A car came down the road and had to brake dramatically and swerve to keep from blowing apart Guy's pickup. It was loaded with drunks who gave Guy hell, shouting obscenities, and a girl in the back yelled out, "You complete zero, loser. You want to get yourself killed?"

"I'm considering it," Guy yelled back. "So, why don't you drag your asses back here in about ten minutes, and if you see me lying in the road run me the fuck over."

They sped off into the light cursing Guy out with an almost preternatural pleasure.

In the throw of headlights, Guy caught a momentary grin on Dean's face.

"There's nothing like a genuine sense of purpose, is there?" said Guy.

"I'd be careful. I hear *the road* is littered with them."

"That's rich," Guy said. He headed for his pickup. "Follow me."

They pulled into THE CLOUD AND THE SKY. They parked in a clearing among the trees near Guy's Airstream. Both men got out. Dean went to the shotgun door where a box of files were on the seat.

"I want to show you something," said Dean. "I met with Chris Carpetti."

"I know."

"You know…Gardner, right?"

"Yeah. And he sent me a copy of your magazine story."

"I had one here for you."

"You weren't exactly honest, were you?" said Guy.

Dean took out a pack of Lucky's from his pocket. "About?"

"How much you got off beating the shit out of that punk."

Dean lit a cigarette. It was a full dose, that little comment. "Being that honest about myself is an emotional achievement I have not quite conquered. But I hope to, by the time I'm finished."

"You had no problem being brutally honest about the rest of us… *mortals*." Guy didn't wait for a response. "I also know about the whole car key story."

"Gardner told you everything."

"Except that you were coming. I realize now he was preparing me."

"What about the keys?"

"I don't know," said Guy. "You could have heard me wrong. I could have been wrong. I have a lot of miles between me and that night. I just don't know."

Dean smoked. There was a lot of stark space in the air between the two of them. Guy had intentionally lied to Dean about the keys. Dean was testing him with his stare. He put the cigarette between his lips. He bent down and began to rummage through that box of open files on the seat.

Guy watched him. Dean had grown tougher looking and become more beautiful because of it. It made Guy think of the Montgomery Clift character in the movie *Red River*. This blending of rugged masculinity and almost feminine detailing to the features.

Dean stood up. He was holding an envelope. "Twelve-twenty-one River Avenue."

"What is that?" said Guy.

"An address in the Bronx that Chris Carpetti gave me."

Dean took out a handful of snapshots of the building and handed them to Guy. He leaned down to see them better in the car light.

"You know that place?" Dean said.

"Should I?"

"Never seen it? Never been there?"

Guy had intentionally lied again. "No," he said. "Not that I remember. Why?"

Dean handed Guy a copy of the newspaper clipping of the murder.

"Look at the date. It's right around the time your father disappeared."

"What does it mean?"

"If you've never been there…I guess it doesn't mean anything."

CHAPTER 33

DEAN TOOK BACK THE SNAPSHOTS and put them in the envelope. He did the same with the newspaper clippings all the while trying to cover his disappointment. That was when Guy noticed what might be a tattoo on Dean's shoulder. He pulled up the sleeve, and that it was.

"You're the last person in the world," said Guy, "I would ever guess gets himself inked up."

"It was a graduation memento to myself...for the nine years."

Guy took the lit cigarette from Dean.

"Incarceration was nasty bad upstate," said Guy. "And don't let them bullshit you that upstate is soft time. There were real skull crackers among those hillbillies. So I applied to enlist and fight the Viet Cong rather than face my remaining sentence."

"I had a run-in with Ross after I got out. He tried to entrap me on a solicitation charge."

"Ross...that prick asked a judge to deny my request in the military until I ratted out my old man."

They passed the cigarette between them now. Each taking a puff or two, flicking away the ash, talking, sharing a private detail here and there. For a few minutes they were a single grain of being, borne from a moment in nineteen-fifty-seven.

"It's never gonna let us go," said Guy. "Is it? That's why I'm out here. In Lone fuckin' Ranger country."

"Do you miss it?" said Dean. "The Bronx...home. You know what I mean."

Guy was reluctant to answer, and he was not about to hide behind some well-meaning sentiment. Dean didn't press it.

"You want to—" Guy jerked a thumb toward his trailer. "I keep a virtual liquor store in there. Besides the obligatory drugs."

"Thanks for the offer, but—" Dean put a hand out for them to shake.

"What does that mean?"

"It means I'm going back..."

"Tonight?"

"Tonight."

"Why?"

"You told me to get out of here fifteen minutes ago."

"Fifteen minutes is a lifetime, sometimes."

"I think it's best. I see you're torn."

"Try it from my side."

"Yeah, I'm sorry for just showing up."

"No, you're not. You wanted to catch me napping, so to speak. Maybe so you'd have the edge."

"Maybe because I felt it was necessary."

"Necessary because…?"

"I knew you'd lie to me."

"Fuck you."

"I'm not going to argue over things that are unprovably true. You're too damn clever…and too damn decent."

Dean slammed the shotgun door and started around to the driver's side with Guy right behind him.

"That's right," said Guy. "Pump your chest and go to the head of the class. *While* you're working it."

"I believe your father is alive. And people are still fighting to this day over something he did, or knew, or did not do. And I intend—"

A pair of headlights came pouring down the road and straight at them.

"Shit," said Guy.

• • •

A white van came lumbering toward them with the radio pounding out a baseline, then the van made this jerky stop. The doors swung open. Lou stepped out into the night along with half a dozen of his work pals or former bedmates.

"What are you doing just walking off on me like that?" he said to Guy.

"You're trivializing yourself with this kind of drama," said Guy. "Go home."

"Get him out of here," said Lou, meaning Dean, of course. "So we can talk."

"Sorry…that just doesn't sound or feel like me," said Guy.

Dean knew this was the full dose of no good. It was like every nothing argument in Spofford where guys stumblefucked over their own dicks in the race to prove they were fools. Dean had walked around the front of the Impala and leaned down and reached in the shotgun door window.

Guy noticed Dean took something from the glove compartment but could not quite make out what it was.

"Get out or it could get ugly," said Lou. "I'll even toss in gas money."

"I can be asked," said Dean, "but I can't be ordered. It just doesn't fit in with my plans."

"Don't fuck with this kid, Lou," said Guy. "You got three inches and thirty pounds on him. But he did nine years incarcerated in the Bronx. And you know what that's like...it's combat training on amphetamines."

Enough of this, thought Lou. Fully pissed, he went at Dean and he hit him so hard the youth was thrown back against the Impala. He came in for the next blow when Dean hit him under the chin. But it was no ordinary punch. Dean had taken a duster from the glove compartment. Guy could see it now. It was a nasty piece of brass engineering. A primitive but effective pain delivery system.

You could hear Lou's gasp over in the next county. Lou dropped to the ground and sat there like some stunned, crosslegged Buddha.

This wasn't the penny loafer crowd that worked in downtown highrises or department stores and liked to dress up occasionally. These were the fight and fuck in the raw boys who took pride in their dirty fingernails. They were ragged and plastered and getting a little unnecessarily unhinged.

Guy got between them and their target. The fact that Guy carried a gun didn't hurt either and flashing it had the desired effect. "Why don't you take Lou into the trailer...someone light up a joint. What do you say? We don't want to make a documentary out of this," said Guy.

Then there they were, walking Indian file. A wasted conga line. The drunk in front rolling a joint, behind him was Lou being led along. Being helped along. Behind that, Guy and the rest of the bar boys. And by his Chevy standing alone, was Dean.

The drunk with the joint was the first one in and he turned on the hi-fi. Guy had huge speakers and you could hear The Byrds doing *Mr. Tambourine Man* all the way down the canyon. They were just hoisting Lou up the steps and into the trailer when the drunk lit his joint up.

Dean saw this momentary spark and the interior of the Airstream flashed with light and then there was an explosion.

THE PIRATES
OF PELHAM PARKWAY

CHAPTER 34

It wasn't until the next day that Guy regained consciousness. He woke to find himself a patient at Presbyterian Hospital. The light on the walls from the sun was so bright his eyes burned and left him barely able to see. He was floating on a tide of confusion and nausea before the figure of a man came into focus sitting in a chair in the corner of the room.

It was Gardner.

"You're awake," he said. "Thank God."

"Where am I?"

"Presbyterian Hospital."

"What happened?"

"You don't know?"

"Would I ask if I did?"

"The fire department said there was a leak in a propane tank in your trailer and a spark set off an explosion."

He lay there looking up at the ceiling. He seemed to remember a shrill, punishing sound. Like those you think you hear in your dreams.

"I got a terrible pain on the side of my head," said Guy.

Gardner explained how the screen door had been blown off its hinges and hit Guy square in the head. And his shirt sleeve, that had caught fire somehow. Dean had rushed to the trailer through the scattering drunks to throw himself on Guy and smother the flames that were scorching his arm. He had dragged Guy clear back to the cars.

Guy looked down at his arms. The one burned was bandaged from wrist to elbow. The other had an IV.

"The others…Lou…?"

"Dean went in after them. He got the three out. He was the only person there sober. Two are in a room down the hall. One is in intensive care."

Guy lay there looking up at the ceiling. Details began to draw together. Like thousands of small amoeba seen through a microscope.

"A propane leak?"

"That's what the preliminary investigation says." Gardner came over and leaned down. He glanced at the door to make sure he was not overheard.

Before Gardner said what he thought, Guy cut him off. "I'm already there."

Gardner stood up.

"Where is he?" said Guy.

"Dean?"

"Who the fuck do you think?"

"He's gone."

"Gone? When?"

"Last night?"

"Where?"

"Back to the Bronx. I believe he intends to confront the Carpettis."

Guy tried to gather himself and sit up. He went in one direction, but the room went in another.

"Help me get up and out of here," said Guy.

"I think they mean to keep you here for observation."

"Observe this," he said and yanked the IV from his arm.

• • •

A thunderstorm swept over the city the day that Dean returned.

"Would you like to get stoned tonight and listen to the rain?" she said to Dean over the phone.

Elise had called him on a chance. She lived in a stuffy little apartment in Brooklyn with three other girls who were all students at NYU, studying film. She'd take the train to the Bronx.

He picked her up at the elevated on White Plains Road and Pelham Parkway, where she ran to his car and shook off the rain.

The smell of the concrete on a warm rainy night and the sound of water slashing up from the wheels in that long steady drone. The lights of the shops reflected there in the drenched streets made their colors all fluid and alive and turned a simple ride into a thing of beauty.

A mist covered the streets and hung over the night and there she was curled up on the car seat. "I read your story," she said. "I read it in the dark with a single candle for light. And I put on albums of movie music I thought would fit the mood just right."

He was unsure and way too sensitive to ask what she thought, but as they drove, she leaned over and kissed him and then she sat back with a hand out the window catching raindrops in her palm. That bit of business alone was more alive and filled with meaning than anything she might have said.

They left the terrace door open and his apartment kept dark, except for one single candle she had brought just in case. They sat together on a cozy old couch and watched the rain anoint the windows with a moonless sheen like a scene from a movie you remember long before you've even ever seen it.

"Can I ask you a question?" she whispered.

"Yes…"

"You won't be upset…embarrassed…or ashamed?"

A confluence of emotions overcame him before she even asked, because somehow, he knew. His unsure movements, he believed, had given him away.

"Are you a virgin?"

He had lived the question in his mind so many times, he wondered, would the perfect answer of being raped twice in jail qualify. In the fullness of an identity he might have been able to address this. But he was trapped in the uncharted state of the life he had lived so far and so was incapable.

His silence made it easy for her. She stood in the terrace doorway with the lights from the apartments across the street a rainy dream lit backdrop as she slipped off her dress.

He was in the moment with her, and yet he was miles away. He was in her presence, yet he was alone. And that aloneness, he realized as he made love, opened doors in him he had never experienced nor even vaguely understood. Dean Teranova was a stranger with a history to someone named Dean Teranova.

As they lay together on the couch with the softness of her mouth against his neck, she whispered, "You and Guy must have loved each other very much. For him to admit he was there to try and save you, and for you to want to lie that he wasn't, says it all. I have never had anyone like that in my life. I have never been touched by such a moment. And it makes me hurt to know what I missed."

When she had fallen asleep, he slipped out of the room. He went silently down into that empty dark house and sat on the stairs, maybe the same stair where Guy had sat on that fateful night he last saw his father.

CHAPTER 35

DEAN LAY THERE ASLEEP IN THE DARK ON HIS BED. He lay on his stomach, loose from the sheets in the beauty and power of youth. A life for the imagination with all its complex forces and the need and desire to be at one with that was so intense it almost hurt.

The blinds were pulled open and sunlight poured in with brutal suddenness, all hot and white. Dean was driven awake. His eyes wandered. He looked up.

Guy stood over him.

"When did you get here?"

"Just did."

"What are you doing here?"

"The timeless question," he said, somewhat acidly. "And ill fuckin' timed, if you ask me."

Guy pulled the next set of blinds to make the room as unbearably bright as possible.

Dean cupped a hand over his eyes. "How's the arm?"

"Good enough to knock you out, if I care to. And no tricks either."

Dean rose slowly. Got his feet on the floor. His head listed from the weight of the headache he had earned. He pointed to a Formica table strewn with open beer bottles. "Find one that's not empty. Preferably one without a cigarette butt in it."

Guy went from bottle to bottle, holding each to the light. Most were pretty scroungy with old smokes.

"How is everyone back there?" said Dean.

"Coming along. You did well. They send their thanks…even Lou."

He passed Dean a bottle. Dean chugged the flat, warm brew. His mouth felt like half of New York had tramped through it.

"The investigators still think it was a faulty tank," said Guy.

"Did they ask your opinion?"

Guy grabbed Dean's jeans from the floor. "They couldn't handle my opinion."

"What is our opinion?"

Guy flung the jeans to Dean. "Get dressed. We're gonna go summon up the past."

Dean stood, pulled his jeans on. Guy quietly watched him. Dean partly turned away.

"What does that mean?" said Dean.

"Twelve-twenty-one River Avenue?" said Guy. "And don't look surprised. It's just a little too phony at this point on your part."

Guy started for the door. "Don't forget your car keys."

"What changed your mind?"

Guy turned. "The good Lord appeared to me in a dream…and bearing a faulty propane tank."

• • •

Dean was behind the wheel. Guy had brought along a couple of beers. He reached for a pack of Dean's cigarettes on the dash and lit one up. He turned off the radio. He didn't want to be talking over shitcan music. He drank and smoked and sat there like he was in some cocktail bar.

"You know a street called Shrady Place?" said Guy.

"No."

"It's a short block up a hill. A dead end. Couple of houses on each side. It looks more like a driveway than a street. It's just off Kingsbridge Terrace by the Jerome Reservoir. My father used to go up there all the time to hang out with a fella named Dicky Palazzo. He took me with him a lot of times. He knew Palazzo from the war. He was a conduit, I heard, between the crime syndicate and the Army. After the war he led a very dubious existence. A real law straddler. A favor man. Know what I mean? I saw Carpetti at his house. I saw Feds at his house."

Guy told Dean that Twelve-twenty-one River Avenue was really one night in his life. A night that started out at Palazzo's up on Shrady. Dicky had friends over for the usual play cards, get loaded and talk fifties trash. You know…Yankees versus Dodgers…women they knew and wanted to bang or had banged. That night the killing of Anastasia was a hot topic. A call came in and Palazzo shouted from the kitchen it was for Prince.

Guy would hang out with the men in an easy chair, half watching the tube, half listening to their talk. The call was from Leo Crab. He said his car had broken down and he needed a ride. It was, Guy would learn, a flat out lie.

Palazzo must have sensed it because he took Peter aside and they talked for a few minutes. Through two sets of doorways Guy could watch the men from where he was sitting. Palazzo was about the same age as Prince. He was a sharp faced dude, who could see a lie before you even thought of it. And he didn't take lies lightly. These men always had schemes going and they had learned to carry an extra set of eyes in their back pockets. Or maybe in the place where their hearts were supposed to be.

Once Peter got Guy back in the car, he'd said, "I don't have time to take you home. And there's something I have to take care of, so you'll have to wait in the car. Understand?"

"What are you taking care of?"

Peter Prince did not answer. He drove down Jerome looking touchy. He turned off the radio. He was preoccupied in some private matter and when Guy went to turn the radio back on his father slapped his hand away.

Where Jerome crossed River Avenue, Peter had turned. Twelve-twenty-one was just under the elevated. There had been a time, long past, as they were erecting that steel monster of a subway when twelve-twenty-one was being considered for the station. For about five minutes, the people that owned the property thought they were gonna be rich. Now they were just dead and forgotten. That's how easy your life can turn. Tonight was no different.

Peter had found a spot just past the building to park.

"You stay in the car. You keep it locked. Understand?"

"Sure," said Guy, as he leaned around and peered over the back of the seat. "What's in there?"

Peter went to get out.

"Give me the keys, at least, so I can play the radio and not be bored to tears."

He tossed his son the keys.

"Now," Peter had said. "What did I tell you?"

"Stay in the car under penalty of death."

Guy watched his father hurry off. He watched as he entered the building. Guy turned on the radio and waited. Trains came, and trains went, passing overhead. The world around him tremoring. Song after song, time stretched and then slowed and soon he could not stop looking back and watching. He grew anxious and was at war with his father's orders.

Maybe if I just peek in the front door window, he thought.

CHAPTER 36

IT WOULD HAVE BEEN A SIMPLE, attractive place back when the Yankees were known as the Highlanders and playing ball at Hilltop Park in Washington Heights, rather than half a dozen blocks south of there at the Stadium.

Now, it was just a filthy, gray looking place where you could spit at subway cars from the roof as they went slamming past. Guy looked up a few steps at a set of double doors with their glass panes that must lead to the apartments.

He cupped his hands and tried to peer in, but the glass was too marred and grimy. One door didn't even have a knob and Guy just fingertipped it open.

The entry was ill lit—no surprise there—and no different than endless other entries. A tiny alcove with black metal stair railings that led up to an open walkway where there were two apartment doors, white hexagonal tiles on the floor and partway up the walls, tiles missing, tiles cracked, the grouting stained and whittled. Two garbage cans side-by-side. And just above them a pair of mailboxes. A tricycle lay on its side against the wall, it was missing its front wheels and handlebars.

It had a smell, like the air in there went back decades. This was the kind of place where nothing is recorded, where lives come and go with the invisible pull of years.

Guy heard voices from one of the upper apartments quite suddenly. They grew louder and closer, and before he had time to gather himself and get out, an apartment door swung open and there stood a man in an undershirt and nice pants. He was hard looking, muscular. He was upset. He was talking Italian when a woman from inside the apartment called out. She sounded anxious. Then he heard his father's voice, "I'll take her. I'll take them both."

He thought if he could slip back down the hall where it was dark—but too late. There was his father in the doorway now, beside the man in the undershirt, and with a woman who was following after his father. She was saying, "Maybe we should take the girl to a hospital?"

That's when Peter Prince saw his son down on the first floor landing beside the garbage cans. Enraged he said, "What the hell are you doing there?"

Guy pointed toward the entry, "I got worried—"

"God damn you," said Peter, "go back to the car. Unlock the doors and wait."

Guy ran out. The last that he heard was his father saying, "I'll carry the girl. You bring—"

Guy was so shaken when he got to the car, he dropped the keys in the gutter. Starting to pick them up he cracked his forehead on the door handle. He was in the car wiping blood from his eyebrow when his father and the man in the undershirt slid a barely conscious woman across the back seat.

Doors were being slammed. His father was starting up the engine when the woman bent down and said to Guy, "Here…take this."

Guy was staring at a newborn baby wrapped in a blanket. He could not move. His arms paralyzed in his lap.

"Take the goddamn baby," ordered his father.

The woman tried to seem calm, but Guy could hear her voice was racing. "It's okay…take it…but hold it tight…Okay? …Okay?"

"Yes, ma'am."

A moment later he had a baby in his arms and the car was speeding toward the Concourse.

"This never happened," said Peter Prince.

"What?" said Guy.

"Tonight…this. It never happened. Do you understand? We will never talk about it…You will never ask about it…You will never speak to anyone about it…Not even Gardner…Especially Gardner…Do you understand?"

Guy just sat there holding this strange baby and looking into his father's unrelenting stare.

"Well, do you?"

"Yes!"

"Say you understand."

"I understand."

"Swear to me on your life."

"I swear."

Then Peter Prince noticed. "You're bleeding. You have blood on your forehead and eyebrows."

The boy wiped at his head with the back of a hand, cradling the baby in the other.

"What happened?" said Peter.

"I dropped the car keys and when I bent down to—"

Peter Prince cut the wheel in toward the sidewalk where he'd spotted a couple of payphones.

"I've got to make a call. I'll just be a minute." He pulled to a stop and parked. He bent over the seat and looked in the back. The girl's eyes were barely slits of an opening, but she was conscious. "You'll be all right here with my son," said Peter.

He jumped out of the car.

There was an unearthly silence inside that Lincoln, even with all the traffic streaming past on the Grand Concourse.

"Is the baby all right?"

Her voice was barely a whisper but it surprised Guy coming out of the silence like it did. He looked into the back.

"What?"

"The baby—"

"Yes…He's…Hey…is it a boy or a girl?"

"What?"

"Is it a boy or a girl?"

"A boy."

"He's all right. He's asleep."

He could just see over the rim of the seat and with the headlights of traffic flaring past he realized for the first time she was no woman, but a girl really.

"How old are you?" he said.

"I'm sixteen. How old are you?"

Her voice was so shaky.

"I'm eleven."

"You're Mister Prince's son?"

"Yes."

"What's your name?"

"Guy."

"My name is Teresa…Teresa Vinci."

They were quiet after that. Guy was nervous with the waiting. He just wanted to talk.

"How do you know my father?"

"He came to The Old Mill…It's a restaurant."

"I know that place…on Staten Island."

"I worked there as a waitress."

"They got that crazy menu."

"Your father saved my life."

"He did?"

Guy could see his father was in a phone booth talking. He slammed a fist against the booth glass.

"I won't die," she said, "will I?"

CHAPTER 37

"Where are we going?" said Dean.

As Guy had told the story of that night, he guided Dean out Pelham Bay Park and up Shore Road.

"I'm taking you to the house where we brought the girl and her baby… if I can find it."

They had to pass the same inlet by Grey Mare where Peter Prince's Lincoln had been discovered by the police in the rocky shoals.

"Do you want to stop here?" said Guy.

"Not now. You know…I've never been here…to this place. Passed it." Dean slowed a bit. "Gardner told me."

There were a few people parked there and fishing. It was a quiet, lovely place really, framed as it was by deeply shading trees.

Dean had been watching the rearview since they left the Bronx. "I'm gonna kick it for a bit in case we were being followed."

Guy looked back. "Sounds about right."

Guy gunned the Impala. That monster engine fired and he peeled off Shore Road and up Pelhamdale Avenue, turning onto Main Street and then back down Weyman until they were within spying distance of Shore Road again.

They watched and they waited, and Guy continued on how that night they had driven past the City Island turnoff. The Lincoln's headlights washing over a black cape of trees and undergrowth and the sign for the bridge which meant they were heading up into Westchester on Shore Road. There, a slight mist had begun drifting in from the Atlantic.

Peter Prince had followed Shore Road through Pelham Manor and into New Rochelle past Travers Island and the New York Athletic Club and blocks of post war apartments and once glorious homes and an old time strip mall.

It was slow going in the mist and he turned up a street and then onto another. Guy could see a house in the sweep of the Lincoln's headlights through unkempt trees that framed the driveway and a low stone wall. It was a large two story house with a tile roof, and the property stretched up most of what was a small street, or a short block. There was one light on the portico and another behind a drawn curtain in what must have been a sitting room or den.

And there was a school—yes, a school, a high school maybe, from its size—that Guy could see from the driveway. A great stone gray edifice. And with the moon that night obscured by a runner of clouds it looked like some gothic manor whose stock and trade was grim proceedings.

They pulled off the street, father and son reflected in the windshield staring and silent. The driveway was gravel and the sound the stones made under the tires was like dry bones giving way to the earth. Branches wrinkled slowly with the breeze. Beyond the house was a trellis for the garden and a gazebo that shined under a spot of moon like a white crown.

Peter Prince had pulled up to the house. "Stay here," he told Guy. He got out and hammered at the front door with a fist.

"Where are we?" said that weak voiced girl in the back.

"I don't know," said Guy.

The front door swung open, and there stood a woman in a long throw of light. She bent down to look in the car where Peter was pointing.

Things happened quickly after that. The woman passed across the headlights, a smoky figure, a little older and lean, who opened Guy's door.

"I'll take the baby," she said.

Peter Prince was already carrying Teresa into the house. The woman with the baby a few steps behind him.

Nothing had been said to Guy. He was just left there like some unwanted stranger, is what he thought. Though he knew it was not really true. He could not help what he felt.

He finally got out and walked up the front stairs. The door still being open, he saw there in the atrium a stone fountain and on the back wall a hand-carved crucifix nearly as tall as a man.

The woman carrying the baby crossed back through the atrium and called out to Guy's father in a strained voice. She saw the boy now standing there at the entry and she ordered him to "come in and close the damn door."

Then something about the boy caught her eye, and she stopped. Her mood seemed to soften a bit, "You're bleeding," she said.

CHAPTER 38

THE SCHOOL GUY HAD SEEN THAT NIGHT came upon them so fast they'd almost passed it. Seeing it was like a mere afterthought. At the corner of Shore Road and Centre Avenue, Dean pulled over. There was a high black wrought iron fence that spanned a block. Beyond it was a huge playing field with browning summer grass, and beyond that the stone gray edifice larger than even Guy remembered.

"Is this it?" said Dean. They'd parked in front of a small playground with swings alongside an apartment building while Guy looked across the street at what was Isaac E. Young Middle School.

"That's it," he said. His voice filled with anticipation. "Those towers… man."

Guy remembered being able to see the school from the driveway of the house, so the plan was to start up Centre Avenue going block by block until they found the place. The first street they came to was Hanford. At the corner is where Guy had seen this low stone wall and he knew. He ordered Dean to turn there and as they did, goosebumps rose across Guy's back and arms. He grew pale with the blood leaving his head.

The Chevy slowed past a driveway that curved toward the house. The driveway was mostly dirt now and a bare remains of gravel. The trees had grown dangerously high and dipped and were knotted together, a number of which had withered from lack of sun and were nothing but rot and kindling that created this wall of the living and the dead.

"Ten years," said Guy.

The house was still as he remembered, with a tile roof, though some of the tiles were missing or lay about loose. The stucco was a Mediterranean shade of taupe with long rust stains from where the gutters had given way.

As he passed the farther driveway entrance, Dean slowed to a stop. From there, he could look straight toward the garden, or what was left of one. There were trellis walkways and that gazebo—there was also a woman standing there.

She was watering the bushes with a hose. The spray came out in a dying arc. She might have been about forty, her hair hung loosely. She was wearing sneakers and a poncho. Her free hand held what had to be a joint. The *Rubber Soul* album was playing on a stereo in the house. The music drifting out a set of open French doors.

"Miss Havisham, I presume," said Dean. "Is it her?"

"At this distance…after all these years."

"How do we make the approach?"

"We? I go over there. I introduce myself. I ask her… she freaks out…"

"She's smoking a joint right out there in the open. The timing couldn't be better."

"For who?"

Dean noticed Guy hesitate.

"I need a minute. I'm feeling…very unsettled."

Guy had been suddenly confronted with the vast emptiness of lost years and unanswered questions. His human misery draped in mystery about to be faced. The fallout from the past was a racing heartbeat and shallow breathing.

"It feels like when I was getting ready to go into combat. Get what I mean?"

"Yeah…that's me every day," said Dean.

"No kidding. Is there anything you can do about it?"

"Sure…I don't kill Donny Gerundo."

• • •

Rose Berghich was the daughter of Nat Berghich, former mayor of New Rochelle and part owner of the Davenport Sand and Swim Club on New Rochelle Creek. A graduate of the Ursuline Academy for Girls and Vassar College, dear Rose Berghich was a restless troublemaker and social renegade who now lived on the reclusive edge of her family's wealth. Her father had owned the house since 1955 when it was passed to his only daughter upon his death in '61. The records showed her to be a single woman.

Rose saw two young men walking up the curved driveway. Neither she recognized, so she flicked the ash off her joint, snuffed it, then slid the rest under her hair and into the crease above her ear with the seamless practice of years.

"Good afternoon, ma'am," said Guy.

"Whatever it is, I can't afford it…Or I can afford it, but don't want it."

"I believe I know you. And you've met me. But it was a long time ago."

"That's original."

"My name is Guy Prince. My father was Peter Prince. And we came to this house one night—"

She had silently turned and shut off the hose valve and started up the driveway to the front of the house. Not a word, not a look, not a gesture.

Guy trailed along behind her.

"We brought a girl to this house one night. Her name was Teresa Vinci. She'd just had a baby—"

The woman opened the front door and closed it behind her and in those brief seconds Guy and Dean could see the stone fountain in the atrium, and the hand-carved crucifix on the far wall.

"It's here," said Guy to Dean, who was just coming up alongside of him.

"What do we do now?" said Guy.

The door reopened partway.

"Maybe nothing," said Dean.

"Leave the property," said the woman.

"I'm not trying to scare you. Don't you remember, ma'am. I was standing in that atrium and you walked past with the baby and you gave me a kind of funny look and said…'You're bleeding.' I had this cut and—"

She eased her hand out from beneath the poncho. She did not look the type that would carry a gun. But she was.

"Being concerned for my safety," she said, "I will take extreme measures."

"He's just trying to find his father," said Dean. "Can't you—"

"Let him try elsewhere." Then, she slammed the door.

Standing by the car and looking back at the house Guy said, "She knows."

Dean had already reached into the car and taken a notepad from the dash and scribbled something. He tore off the page and folded it and walked to the house and slipped the folded-up paper in the mail chute. He caught a glimpse of her looking through a slit in the shutters. If only the light had been enough for him to read her emotions he'd have seen the heartbreak of her past had come back all grown up. A sorrow that stings the inside of your throat, warning you that you are about to cry, and it will be deep and long and painful for all the might-have-beens that had not.

CHAPTER 39

In a drawer was an old photo she rose from the dead. The Summer Eve Dance at the Davenport Club. Vic Damone on the patio singing *Some Enchanted Evening.*

Rose had danced with a man in cool summer clothes at the edge of the pool under strung beads of light.

"I heard a rumor about you, Mister Prince."

"You mean that I'm in the rackets. I'm afraid that it's true."

She smiled and ran the tip of her fingers through the edge of his hair.

"So am I…" she said, "…in a way."

To love in secret was a pleasure they both understood, and then one night at the big house on Hanford she confessed she was pregnant.

Peter and his wife could not have a baby. Whatever the reason, it didn't really matter. He appealed to Rose to forget an abortion and carry instead the child to term while he'd make up a lie for his wife.

In part it was love, in part pure rebellion. To have the experience seemed like a challenge you both walk away from when you were done.

Things that you do when you're twenty can prove to be mad when you're forty and fatal by sixty. She delivered the child in San Juan, Puerto Rico, where she handed over the baby to its mother and father, and alone, got on a plane for places unknown.

She never saw Peter again, or the boy for that matter, until that night he stood in the atrium with blood trickling down into his eye.

And yet, here I am, again, she thought, looking at the stranger who had come out of my body. If I could have foreseen this moment, I would have run every impulse out of existence.

She went to the mail slot and retrieved the note. Dean had written his name and his phone number and this short thought:

My late mother used to say—God is always working in your life. Think of the good you can do.

She put the note with the photo and set them aside as she knew all too well that the good you can do is a double edged-sword.

• • •

"I think as of now, you and I know how all this links together, better than everyone," said Dean.

"Except maybe for the poncho queen," said Guy.

They had driven back down Shore Road toward the Bronx. They stopped at the inlet by Gray Mare where Guy got to examine the last known landing spot on this earth for his old man. You'd never have known this was a scene of such violence. There were just a couple of beer drinking fishermen with a transistor radio turned to the *WMCA Good Guys*.

"The Crabs performed abortions," said Dean. "That old janitor confirmed it."

"They didn't perform one on Teresa Whatever-her-name-was—"

"But she was at Twelve-twenty-one River Avenue. So what changed?"

"Maybe she was having the screws put to her, to have the abortion," said Guy.

"What were they going to do with her after? She was underage, after all."

"That depends on who got her pregnant."

They stood side-by-side with their backs against the Chevy. They were smoking and drinking the beer and Jack Daniels they'd picked up at a deli up from the Poncho Queen's house.

"Your father being involved puts the Carpettis right in play."

"Yeah?"

"Gino maybe…or his kid?"

"The girl told me she was sixteen. Chris Carpetti was about what, eighteen, then? Either him or his father, it's rape."

"The task force would love to get hold of that," said Dean.

"Did they know? Do they know? Maybe that's why they were so hot for my father."

"You think the Carpettis meant for your father to kill the girl? Somebody brought her to that place. Did your old man turn on them?"

"My father must have been connected to it. The phone call says it."

"From the Crabs to your father?"

"Dicky Palazzo's house."

"Did Palazzo know the Crabs?" said Dean.

"No idea."

"We should ask him."

"You mean confront him."

"If that's what it is."

"He's a fuckin' rattlesnake when he wants to be."

"What are we? Well wishers?"

"We could be stepping on a mine. You should just know."

"Now I know."

"What about the Poncho Queen. What's her story?"

"She feels like a fifties freak who is now slightly over the hill," said Dean. "You know...Barbie gone AWOL."

They both laughed at the emotion of it. Guy threw his arm over Dean's shoulder. They stood there like that drinking.

"She's got blood in the game," said Dean, "that's for sure. She took the girl and the baby."

"The way she and my father talked, they were tight with each other."

"You think he was fuckin' her?"

"I heard my father wasn't exactly faithful, even when my mother was alive."

"Whatever the poncho queen is, she's our edge. We don't speak of her even to Gardner."

"Do I look like a fool?" said Guy.

Then a voice out of nowhere says, "The perfect couple."

They turned. Here came two fisherman with their gear heading toward the shoreline. Older guys. The world is black or white types.

"What was that?" said Guy.

"The perfect couple...it means what it says."

Guy slid his arm from Dean's shoulder.

The man who had spoken, pointed his fishing rod. "Jack Daniels and beer. The perfect couple."

The two youths knew bullshit when they heard it. It had been a stick it in your ass slight 'cause of Guy standing there with his arm draped over Dean's shoulder. Guy took it in stride. Dean was a little less convivial.

He walked around the front of his car. He caught their private smirk reflected in the windshield. A moment later, he had taken his revolver from the glove compartment and…voila…he was striding toward them saying, "*As the World Turns*…In today's episode, alleged fag approaches two low IQ shitclowns and orders them to jump into the Sound…Jump!"

Dean aimed the gun. Man, did those fishermen panic. They were trying to protect themselves from being shot hiding behind their fishing gear. Did that redefine stupid.

Guy got his arms around Dean and demanded he put the gun down. Dean wasn't having it. The fishermen were backpedaling and then they took off.

Guy was stronger than Dean and he couldn't break loose. The fishermen were speeding out of the lot, yelling how they were gonna call the cops and Dean shouted back, "We have to do this again sometime!"

CHAPTER 40

GUY LET DEAN GO. "What's the matter with you?" he said. "They'll call the cops."

"I bet they don't even know how to use a phone. Doesn't it piss you off? I had to hear enough of that at Spofford."

Guy went and picked up the pint of Jack Daniels he'd dropped on the ground. "I got a phone book worth of grudges and unresolved moments." He took a drink. "I got a couple with you."

Dean stood there with the gun still in his hand, realizing, he tossed it back in the glove compartment.

"Did you hear what I said?"

"Where we going with this?"

"How come you never answered one of my letters?"

"Not back all the way, are we?"

"I was living in Albuquerque and you show up after ten years. And here I am. What does that say? I ask myself. You owe me an answer. I sent you a letter…and then I sent another…"

"You sent six and then the seventh…The Lord rested his case. I read them."

Guy took another drink of Jack Daniels. He was overwhelmed with emotion. "A couple of words. Even just 'go fuck yourself.' Why didn't you say anything?"

"I was ten years old, that's why. I was being incarcerated. And you drop that on me. Get real. I was a kid."

Dean got out his car keys and tossed them to Guy. They landed at his feet. "Take the car. Drive back to New Mexico. I'll have it picked up. I'll take this from here."

He started toward the road.

Guy shouted, "Take it where? You wouldn't be this far without me."

Dean stuck out a thumb to try and bum a ride back to the city.

"You're fuckin' priceless…even when you're not."

• • •

143

Guy just stood there wracked with distress and once alone he understood it was not just about his feelings for Dean. Feelings that had not diminished with time but had only grown more substantial. It was being at this place, where his father had met some unknown fate, that led him to death or to some secret escape.

This was a place where Guy was intimately connected, yet a complete stranger. Everyone has places like that in their lives. Where part of their life map is missing. Where longing and loss reside in mystery. He came to see how it was through these feelings that Dean and Peter Prince were inextricably linked. They were the life that was, and the one that was yet to be.

He walked the inlet and slugged down his Jack until he had a good buzz on, one that really tore loose the emotions and then he shouted, "Do you have any idea how much I love you?"

• • •

Dicky Palazzo was deeply stoned when he answered his front door up there on Shrady Place. He was holding a joint and riding a beautiful high, and after a moment of pure shock, realizing who was standing there, he said, "Am I hallucinating or what? It's like you're come back from the dead."

Guy Prince walked in. He looked Dicky over. He was wearing expensive haberdasher slacks, a funky tie-dyed T-shirt that said—GOD IS DEAD—and sneakers. Always fuckin' sneakers.

The house was flooded with partyers and the hi-fi was hitting it. You could hear the music all the way down Shrady, but none of the neighbors had enough dick to wrestle with Palazzo.

The crowd was a mixed set. Middle class ginzo and young hippies. Drugs, booze, food, and all the usual precoupling craziness. There was a chick standing on the couch jumping up and down. She was also topless. What the fuck that was about was anyone's guess.

Dicky swept through the crowd with Guy in tow and he got up on the coffee table and kept shouting until he had everyone's attention. He could hardly be heard over the music.

"This is a longtime family friend. His name is Guy. He's gay. And if he don't mind being gay, none of you should mind either." He jumped down from the coffee table. "How was that for an intro?"

"You're a real sweetheart."

Dicky Palazzo didn't pick up the sarcasm. Too stoned. He handed Guy the joint.

Guy whispered in his ear, "You got trouble."

"Good trouble or bad trouble?"

"I got taken off the street tonight at gunpoint."

Palazzo took Guy by the arm, led him through a pretty crowded kitchen then down a back hall to a pantry where they were pretty much alone.

"What's it got to do with me?"

"The murder at Twelve-twenty-one River Avenue."

CHAPTER 41

HE TOLD DICKY PALAZZO HOW HE'D TAKEN IN A MOVIE at the Valentine over on Fordham Road to burn off some excess anxiety. He'd been drinking Jack pretty hard all day and after the movie, when he was getting into the car he had been driving, a young turk came up to him flashing a revolver and asked for the keys.

Then one turk grows to two, and Guy was sitting in the back with a forty-five from the shotgun seat bearing down on him.

They were toughs, young, not exactly a matched set. One was Puerto Rican, the other could have been a mutt.

"How's Dick Palazzo?" one said.

"I haven't seen him in years..."

"Bring your head forward."

Guy did as they ordered. They covered his eyes with some rag they'd brought. The last he'd seen, they were on Boston Road by the Hutchinson River. The two had this shadowy manner down pat, like this wasn't their first time.

They drove for a while, and it seemed like short streets with many quick turns. Guy asked nothing. He was keeping silent as a show of indifference, composure. But he was shaken.

They came to a stop, and the one in the shotgun seat got out. Guy heard a chain rattle, then a gate on rollers was opening. The Chevy pulled ahead, and the gate closed behind them.

They got Guy out of the car. It was dead quiet. He thought for a moment he heard the faintest ripple of water.

"We're on a dock at the river's edge," said the one who had been driving. "And this..." he banged knuckles on something that sounded metal and hollow, "...is a fifty gallon drum. Which you will fit into very nicely."

They then started to question him about River Avenue and the Crabs. And in particular about Dicky Palazzo.

"I've been out of touch with everything here for a decade," Guy said to them.

"How well did Palazzo know the Crabs?"

"No idea."

"Why didn't he go with your father that night when the Crabs called?"

"I was eleven fuckin' years old. Ask him."

"We're gonna put you in that drum and we're gonna hammer the lid shut and drop you from the dock, and you will either suffocate or the drum will leak and you will slowly drown."

They then started another round of questions about Dicky Palazzo.

• • •

"How did you get loose of them?" said Palazzo.

"Better you don't know," said Guy.

"I get it," said Palazzo.

"Do you? You may have some visitors, Dicky."

"Fuck."

Palazzo wasn't so stoned anymore. He went to a cabinet in the pantry. There was a pistol residing there on a shelf. Palazzo was notorious for having guns everywhere in the house.

"What is River Avenue about?" said Guy.

Dicky Palazzo was checking to be sure the gun was loaded. "I should have gone with your father that night," he said. "That's what this is all about." He slipped the gun into his pocket. "Then maybe Peter Prince wouldn't have slicked everyone. But that was your father.

"But I won't say more and you won't say more. Plausible deniability. Whatever your father did, he did. I don't know, you don't know. You're in trouble. I'm in trouble. I don't know yours, you don't know mine. Fuck the universe."

Guy left after that priceless riff. By the time the stoners and the drunks, the party crashers and deadbeats had gone their way and Shrady was the lifeless dead end it had always been, the street got itself quite the wakeup call. Dick Palazzo had himself a shiny red XKE, and an explosion blew the car so high by the time it slammed back down, it was no XKE anymore.

CHAPTER 42

DEAN RODE THE SUBWAY TO BROOKLYN, his body still on some kind of high alert thanks to all those new doors and old pitfalls. He smoked the last of a joint as the train slammed through the bowels of dear old Brooklyn. He had every intention of confronting the Poncho Queen again, but this time without Guy.

He found his way out to Union Street. The three story building Elise lived in was just up from the Gowanus Canal. He had been to Brooklyn a few times as a boy. Mostly to Court Street, where his father did work for the Gallo Brothers. Eddie Teranova's job back then was to remove furniture from the businesses before the places were torched and they scammed the insurance company. Eddie Teranova was considered a Picasso when it came to torching businesses.

Elise had invited him out. Her film class was going to shoot scenes for a dramatic short, and also a documentary. He could tell which old brick building it was from the lights on the roof, and the people milling about.

A girl with a clipboard at the front door said, "Cast or crew?"

Dean answered, "Convict."

Elise did not believe he'd show. She already had him tagged as too much of a loner for scenes like this. Then there he was coming up the stairs through a crowd of crew members to the landing where she stood.

"You look surprised," he said.

"I figured you wouldn't come."

"I figured you figured I wouldn't come, so I did, just to spite you."

They kissed the way people do after they have slept together and aren't quite sure how to act with each other.

She brought Dean up to the roof where scenes for a drama were being rehearsed against a backdrop of Brooklyn rooftops. Elise whispered, "We're shooting in Super 8."

Dean had no idea what the fuck Super 8 was. All he knew is what he saw. Everyone there was his age and fueled with this creative alertness and intensity, this stressful tone of crazy in constant motion, all exuberance as they experienced and invented.

It was cool to watch, to be near, because it was not contaminated with the dark genies that were present deeply within him. The hardness of being, the proximity of corruption.

"What's wrong?" said Elise.

She must have read something in his expression or the coiling of his silent body. She took him downstairs where they were filming the documentary. He was drinking and getting pretty loaded as he watched. She explained she was one of the producers, whatever that meant, and went off to do her thing.

He watched and listened from a quiet corner, as youth after youth took a few minutes before that Super 8 to give their take on the world, on politics, Vietnam, sex, dreams, drugs, freedom, and change. It was a snapshot of an emerging America riffing their passions, and that made his decade of incarceration all the more painful in counterpoint.

During a lull in the filming, someone in the room called out to Dean, "You want a turn?"

Suddenly people were looking at him. He just realized trying to be inconspicuous had made him all the more conspicuous.

"Elise says you're a writer," said one of the crew. "That you published a story in a magazine."

Dean nodded, "Yeah. *True Crime*."

"About how you killed a boy, right?"

"About how I killed a boy, yeah."

Now that Super 8 had him in its sights. And it frightened him, as if it had the power of a judge.

"How long were you in jail?"

"Nine years. Since most of you were in around the fourth grade."

Someone back among the faces said, "Shit."

He stood frozen and consumed by the silence around him. Then said, "Being incarcerated that young you don't learn how to talk to, or with people. Really talk. You…barely know who you are."

"Who are you?" said one of the people who had been photographed just minutes before. Dean looked at the faces around him. He felt naked and ashamed. Like Adam after he had his ass booted out of Eden.

"I don't have any insights on the future. I don't have an inside track on the future. I don't even know if I *have* a future."

There was silence and a nervous titter or two. Dean did not realize he was being filmed, and had been being filmed.

"What are you doing with your life?" said someone. "I mean, what is your life about?"

Dean was unexpectedly absorbed in some long arcing moment, past the camera, and the stares, and the little room he stood in.

"I'm hunting for a man," he said, "a racketeer, really. A criminal. Who has disappeared. And who, it turns out, might have done one good deed... to redeem himself. At least I hope so. I—"

He walked out. Just like that. Like a phone that just suddenly stopped ringing.

Elise was calling to him from an upper window, but he was just an outline by then, a figure passing under a streetlamp. There, then gone.

CHAPTER 43

THE MURDER OF C.C. CARPETTI WAS ALREADY IN PLAY. The same day Dean had driven with Guy to find the house in New Rochelle where Peter Prince had brought the girl, there was a gay rights rally at Gramercy Park. It was sponsored by the Mattachine Society and several other homophile organizations as a fund raiser.

C.C. and Gardner had gone together, while Gardner's boyfriend, Charlie Merwin, was there to give one of his political speeches.

One of the earliest battlefields for the gay movement had been the bars. The right to drink. In New York, bars could refuse to serve anyone they deemed homosexual. Letting a "queer" drink in your establishment was asking for a police raid. That was how the mafia and C.C. Carpetti got a foothold in the business. They could bribe the cops, and they could obtain liquor licenses.

Then came the first "Sip in" where three men went into a bar, admitted they were gay, and then ordered a drink. They were, by that act, incorporating the social tactics of Gandhi and the Civil Rights Movement—effect change to unjust laws through civil disobedience. Provoke reactions, make the system respond.

Vietnam, the women's movement, the sexual revolution, the massive onslaught of media—all were provoking responses and making the American culture respond. The Gay Rights movement joined this caravan of social change. The past was trying to drag the future to its death. But the past was becoming badly outnumbered. Even the New York State Liquor Authority was softening their criteria regarding gays and bars. The bars— the gay bars—were as one cynic called them: *The canary in the coal mine. And the forecaster of the coming degradation.*

C.C. and Gardner both knew this shifting change toward social freedom would expand and enhance their personal lives, but also bring about diminution, if not the outright demise of their control on their bar business. The edge they had through her mafia lineage, when it came to liquor licenses and police payoffs, would now demand more punitive actions as the restrictions against gays and gay bars diminished. Which meant embracing violence, drugs and prostitution. And that was not a road C.C. had any intention of traveling. She understood she was not a bastion of morality, nor was she her brother.

As for Gardner, he could read the proverbial writing on the wall. Gino would look to take advantage. And C.C. only had one trump card against her brother—Peter Prince.

C.C. was watching the crowd around the speaker and that spread all up and down the street. Some of the gay men in makeup and full drag, women arm-in-arm, a crew on motorcycles, all in full pride of their flesh and being.

Looking around, C.C. said, "This is gonna come across as weird, but I feel like we're outlaws in some old western who realize their days are numbered.

"*Ride the High Country*," said Gardner. "Remember that movie?"

"Remember. It's one of Mama's favorites. She had a thing for Randolph Scott."

"And what about Joel McCrea. Tough."

"She made me see that movie twice with her. She wept at the end. A fuckin' western."

"Greatest last scene in movies ever," said Gardner. "Joel McCrea there dying, gut shot. Scott beside him, 'Good bye, friend,' says McCrea. And then Scott stands and he says…'I'll see ya' later.' And he walks off. 'I'll see ya later.' Too much."

"And McCrea is there and dies alone," said C.C.

"Someday they'll make a movie like that, and both guys will be gay."

"Not in our fuckin' lifetime."

"Hey, you…Bitch."

C.C. and Gardner turned to see who had shouted.

"Yeah, you…mafia whore."

It took a moment for C.C. to remember. The girl had been a bartender who C.C. caught scamming the till and dealing to customers. Her name was Chella Martinez. She was young and came across straight up, but she was a walking albatross wherever she went.

"This chick is fuckin' mafia," she was yelling and pointing. "She's all about bribery and payoffs. And any chick who doesn't sleep with her gets the ax."

Gardner got between the two women 'cause C.C. was telling the girl, "You better shut that down."

"Take a walk," said Gardner. There were photographers around getting film on the rally. Chella was naming off C.C.'s bars at the top of her fuckin' lungs. A photographer came over and at ground zero started grabbing stills.

• • •

That day would bury itself into Gardner right up to the hilt. That day, and the days and weeks ahead that built to C.C.'s brutal slaying…'If I had just read the signs'…There they were at the rally, talking about a movie. That movie of all movies to talk about. When this albatross of a drugged up angry siren appears out of nowhere…*I should have felt its meaning if nothing else. Some deeply rooted instinct regarding this should have had me on guard. Forgive me, girl. Forgive me for failing you…*the narrative of C.C. Carpetti's murder had been written, the antagonists chosen, the drama played out to the crowd, and framed by a random photograph. Now, all that was left was the killing.

CHAPTER 44

AFTER A COUPLE OF ROUNDS OF LOVEMAKING, Gardner and Charlie Merwin were in the kitchen smoking weed and satisfying themselves with crème de menthe sundaes. They were in robes and barefoot, and the hi-fi was tuned to WNEW FM. Charlie was going about his usual ethics pitch, but he wasn't so strident after being laid and stoned.

"There's a world for attorney's opening up. Gay rights…transgender rights…sexual rights. Leave C.C., put your social conscious suit on, and—"

"If only that radio was on louder!" Gardner said.

"You saw that crazy chick today. That's a shot over the bow of the world…The triumphs of society are quite often their acts of corruption. I forget who said it, so I'll steal it."

The sound of a growling car engine pulled into the driveway.

"The boys are home," said Charlie.

He was being sarcastic, of course. Gently sarcastic.

A minute later Guy stood in the kitchen doorway alone. He looked the scene over. "Think of the commercial this would make."

"Where's Dean?" said Gardner.

Guy shrugged.

"Wasn't that his car?"

Guy held up a set of keys and shook them. He noticed a joint in the ashtray.

"That joint looks like it needs immediate lighting."

"Don't we all," said Charlie.

Guy pulled out a seat, swung it around, and sat with his arms draped over the back. He cut some melancholy figure. He lit up and started toking.

"You haven't got him out of your system yet," said Charlie. "Have you?"

"Is it ever annoying, to be you?"

"My heart's in the right place," said Charlie.

"Maybe I'll use it one day," said Guy, "for target practice."

He smoked. He swigged a little crème de menthe from the bottle.

Total shit, ice cream or no ice cream.

"I've tried not to love him…I've tried…For years…How I've tried… I've tried to hate him…But he even bested me at that…Because he's decent…He's got character…Heart…" Guy raised his bandaged arm. "He kept me from being burned."

He took a taut breath. The lines above his eyes furrowed. He looked mature for his years, battle tested, but with the hurt of a boy.

"He is like a part of me that escaped from me somewhere way back when…And when he's around I get it back…I'm connected…I'm the Guy Prince I remember…I'm at one with him…I'm…fucked. If there ever was a case of desperate love…I got it."

The men kept themselves in check. They were giving Guy's mood a chance to settle out. They went back to their weed and desserts. Guy just sat there…a perfect image of the *'Lonely Boy.'*

Then on the hi-fi came this slick rocker of an instrumental.

"Remember that song?" said Gardner.

"Apache," said Charlie.

"Great song. Big hit in…'60. Huge. Remember who sang it!"

"The Shadows," said Charlie, "And one of their guitarists, was he a sex dream?"

The song was twangy and street, with cool upbeat and just enough steely edge to really catch you.

Trying to lighten the mood, Charlie got up on a kitchen table chair and started in performing like he was God's own guitarist. Gardner got up and flipped off the kitchen lights and opened the fridge door and there was Charlie backlit by colorful shelves of leftovers. And man, did Charlie cut a ridiculous figure, with his robe flailing open and his hairy genitals slapping left and right against his skinny thighs, like some insane life form.

When the song was over and Charlie was all exhausted out, he sat back down, breathing heavily. He was not exactly your athlete or exercise type, but he managed to say to Guy, "So dear…how was your day at the office?"

It was a good punchline…for Charlie. And Guy, totally straight faced, answered, "I killed two men. They took me at gunpoint to the Hutchinson River. But I outfoxed them. Then I stuffed them in a fifty gallon drum and sunk their bodies."

And just like that he got up and strode out of the room. "I'm gonna take a shower, then crash."

Once he was gone, Charlie looked at Gardner who was staring at the empty kitchen doorway. "He's fuckin' with us, right?"

. . .

The street was asleep when Dean returned home. Guy, it turned out, was sitting on the front steps nursing a beer.

Dean came up the walk bathed in the light from St. Lucy's Grotto. Both men were uncomfortably silent, until it was Guy who said, "I'm sorry—"

"Me, too," said Dean, cutting him off.

"That was pretty bloodless," said Guy.

"It's best that way, isn't it?"

"Where have you been?"

"Brooklyn."

"*Her.*"

"Yeah."

Dean could hear the phone in his room ringing.

"It's been like that every ten minutes," said Guy.

"You going in?"

Guy stood.

"What did you do?" said Dean.

"I scared the dick off Dicky Palazzo. And then I blew up his XKE. Only he doesn't know it was me."

Dean didn't miss a beat, didn't question, didn't disbelieve. "That must have fucked him up."

"I sure do hope so," said Guy. "I'll tell you all about it upstairs. After all, Dante, I got the idea from you."

. . .

Guy was sitting on the couch in Dean's apartment, his legs stretched out and feet upon the coffee table, relating all that went down with the two young thugs and the fifty gallon drums dumped into the Hutchinson River, but with one slight twist—it was all a lie he'd told Dicky Palazzo, a scam, a ruse. The only thing real—Guy had snuck back to the house and ragged the XKE gas tank and blew that fuckin' Jaguar into the air like it was a playing card.

Dean stood there with arms crossed. His heart took to racing. He understood, 'cause he understood Guy. He knew how that sly and deadly head worked.

"You were fucking with him," said Dean, "to drive him out into the street."

"You know what he told me when I asked about River Avenue and that night? He said he made a mistake and should have gone with my father."

"He *knows* what this was all about."

"Except we know more," said Guy.

"You did just like we did when we were incarcerated and wanted to get into someone's head to fuck them up. You whisper you overheard a rumor someone is out to get them...and you watch them unravel. You watch them expose themselves."

"That's your Spofford training, Dante."

"And the XKE...?"

"Was dessert."

Dean started jabbing an animated finger at Guy to tell him he was right on.

"Back in Albuquerque," said Guy, "when I was in the hospital and you told Gardner you were going to confront the Carpettis, I freaked you'd be killed. But you were spot on. Instinctively."

Guy got up now. He was emotionally on the move. Dean could feel the dark power of life and death in his talk. "Some, like Ross," Guy said, "want my father alive so they can get him to turn state's evidence. Someone tried to kill us...me...in Albuquerque...Why? Maybe to try and lure my father out of hiding. Or put the fear of Christ in him. But it all reinforces what you've been saying—"

"He escaped that murder attempt on Shore Road—"

"—in a car Gardner had hidden away."

"It's River Avenue."

"The girl...the child."

"A rape charge."

"It sure feels like..."

"If it's Gino Carpetti and proof is unleashed—"

"Does he turn state's evidence to save his ass?"

"He'll be assassinated first," said Dean.

"Even his own mother will do him in."

Dean nodded, then said, "You took the fight to them tonight that's for sure."

"Right, Dante. And with the radio blasting."

CHAPTER 45

WHATEVER EACH OF THE YOUTH CARRIED INSIDE THEM—the personal histories, lost details, desires, nameless moments of experience, shocks, tragedies—all the bricks in the wall that become the being, the being is. Together the youths were more than the sum total of their parts. Even if they could not understand the flow of it, they could feel its existence. And it made them immune to peril and blind to consequences.

"We're being watched, you know," said Guy.

"What?"

"There's a blue gray Rambler. Sometimes it's parked on Bronxwood just down from the grotto. Other times it's over on Mace. One man…city payroll type."

Dean went to peek out the window that fronted Bronxwood.

"It was on Mace an hour ago."

The phone began to ring and ring, and Dean just let it go on as he went to another window, and Guy said, "You gonna answer that?"

Dean looked at the ringing phone. "I'm not sure."

"It's been ringing like that all fuckin' night."

Dean took a private breath. He answered the phone.

"God is not always working in your life."

He recognized the Poncho Queen's voice right away.

"I have one request, before we meet," she said. "You are to say nothing about this to Guy Prince. Not a word. I will explain when we meet. Don't fail me. Do you understand?"

"Yes," he said, flatly.

He did not even dare glance in Guy's direction for fear he would give himself away.

"Yes," said Dean, "Yes…" He got a scrap of paper and pen from his desk…"Yes"…He scribbled a bit…"Yes"…Then a bit more…"Yes… Yes…"

He hung up and slipped the paper into his pocket crumpling it as it went. When he turned, he made damn sure he was expressionless before that stare.

"The girl in Brooklyn?" said Guy.

"Yeah."

"You sounded like you were making an appointment to go to the dentist, for Christ's sake."

"That's my seduction technique."

"Works for me."

Guy knew how to make a statement to get at you all kinds of ways at once. Dean grinned like you would when you give someone a friendly middle finger. He walked over to his desk, rifled through the papers where he'd been writing, hunting for his cigarettes. He found a pack, tapped one out, and lit it. He was staring at the papers where he'd been writing about all this.

"The truth of the matter, said Dean, "the only person I've ever been able to talk with about what really matters…is you."

Guy looked up from the couch and his solitary pose, surprised, to say the least.

"No kidding," he said.

"As a matter of fact, when I was incarcerated, I used to talk to you all the time."

"No kidding."

"When I needed to think something out, get something out…I talked to you—"

"No kidding."

"In all this time the only person I've ever been able to connect to…to really be comfortable with…is you."

"No kidding."

"How many times in a row are you gonna fuckin' say 'no kidding'?"

He told Guy about Elise…filming a short movie…the documentary…being questioned…and how he ran out.

"It was getting too real," he said. "And how could I tell them about Spofford? About being held down by my fellow inmates who took turns spitting in my ass to lube me up before they did the deed. I can't get it out—"

He pointed to his desk. "I can get it down on paper…because I can hide there. You're the only one I have the emotional ability to talk to."

Guy came over and clutched Dean's arm. "Words are shit," he said. "Plain old fashioned information. But what you see in a face, or how the words feel when they hit the world, is something else."

"I have jail stories," said Guy. "And worse yet from the Army. I bury them. Or run them out of my head. I'll fight that fight later. Right now we have…right now to deal with.

"You know what freaks me most?" Guy added.

Dean shook his head no.

"Not that my father is dead…but that he's alive. And when we catch up with him, how does he explain throwing me to the wolves. It feels like I'm living with a hand grenade in my chest."

Dean looked at the phone. The goddamn call.

"I'm scared about that, Dean."

CHAPTER 46

THE NEXT DAY GUY ASKED GARDNER to quietly get hold of Ross' home address. Gardner did so reluctantly, and without question asked a gay officer he knew who worked in human resources for the Bronx Police Department.

It turned out Ross left a trail of short stints at dumpy apartments behind him. He seemed to have a penchant for conflict with his landlords and neighbors and was now holed up in the shitty basement of a house at the corner of 56th Avenue and 137th Street in Flushing, about a block from Booth Memorial Hospital. His uncle, who owned the building, lived across the street at 5603. Ross had been warned by his uncle to keep on his best behavior, otherwise it was the street.

Ross returned late that night drunk after plying some morose clerk who worked for the DMV with enough booze to try and get her to spread her legs. Luckless and lonely and struggling with his keys, he had no idea that two shadowy figures had slipped down the driveway and broken in hours before.

He flipped on the long narrow hallway light—nothing. Cursing he made his way along with arms grabbing at the air like a blind man. Reaching the open space that was his living quarters, he felt along the wall until he found the next light switch—again nothing.

"Whaaaaaat is this shit?" he shouted in a wasted uproar. He cursed his uncle for being a cheap, miserable spendthrift.

He tried to reach for where the lamp should be and kneed a table. He hunched over in agony. He was either blitheringly loaded or the table had moved.

Bent over like an ape, he shambled about the dark slowly and tripped over an ottoman. Flat on the floor now, feeling, feeling, he found a lamp cord and pulled it and the lamp slammed down on his head. He was rattling off obscenities like some aggrieved madman. He got hold of the lamp and flipped the switch—nothing.

He thought the fuses had blown again until something in that befuddled brain of his registered.

Across the room on a table where he ate, the lights of his RECORD-O-PHONE were on. If the power was out, why was the light on?

It was one of the first reel-to-reel answering machines. An expensive item, he had five fingered it when he and O'Gorman busted the home of a drug dealer. He crawled his way over to the table, got up on a chair. He saw from the light that he had messages. He turned the play dial and waited through a few scratchy seconds.

"Mister Ross…Don't know if you remember me. I'm sure you won't recognize the voice…It's Guy Prince. Me and a friend stopped by tonight—"

Dean's voice cut in, "How you doin', Ross?"

Teranova, he recognized. Ross' head seemed to recoil from the answering machine as if it were toxic.

"We left a proposal for you," said Guy.

"Your joint needs a cleaning, dude," said Dean. "You live like a fuckin' hobo. Not cool."

"It's in the refrigerator," said Guy. "It's a legal document."

"Don't let your rage outrun your common sense," said Dean.

Ross did not wait for them to shut the fuck up. He made his blind, inflamed way toward the vague outline of the refrigerator. He actually used the worn down hum of the motor to guide him. He yanked open the door, shouting back at the voices on the answering machine. He was suddenly bathed in light. He realized the fuckers had broken in and killed specific lights and he saw in the refrigerator there was an envelope and beside it a piece of notepaper propped against an open orange juice container which he ripped off. It said:

We urinated in your orange juice.

He flung the paper aside and there he was, a nauseated, incensed, adult man sitting on the floor of a dingy rathole he called home. Humiliated, he grabbed the envelope and tore it open—

• • •

Gino Carpetti had offices in what was known as "The Haight" district of Flushing. He'd bought up a good deal of property there from College Point

Boulevard all the way to Van Wyck and Flushing Creek.

This was warehouse country, big equipment, lots of industrial buildings, dingy storefronts and apartments.

It was perfect for his needs. He'd gone into business with what he called the "Chink Brigades," the Chinese who dealt in narcotics, illegal imports, chop shops…and weapons. He saw that they were the future.

They had that first generation will to succeed.

It was also the cause of great conflict between father and son. Christopher Carpetti hated the Chinese. He hated Orientals. Period. You'd have thought it would have been the father, who had served in the army and fought the Japanese, but it wasn't.

The father's offices were in an old stone building painted white, at the corner of Fuller and 41st Avenue. It had been built in a sort of triangle with one flat side to accommodate the railroad tracks that had at one time run along Fuller Street. The offices were up on the second floor, and the only way up was through the private men's club on the first floor known as Castaldi's.

There were always a couple of dagos hanging out front or relaxing in chairs. They looked like casual enough loafers, but they were completely tuned in to the street.

As Dean crossed the street and approached the building, he drew the interest of the men mingling there. But as he reached the sidewalk and was striding toward the front door, he drew their full attention. They cut off his approach with unadorned physical contact. A hand right to the chest, one bearing down on his shoulder. Suddenly it looked like the defensive line of the New York Giants was before him.

"Private club here, boy."

The kid who actually said that was about his age.

"I'm here to talk with Mister Carpetti."

"Sure you are."

"Ask him."

"And who are you?"

This came from a gent who was sitting and had yet to get up. Middle-aged, a diligent stare, and wearing a classless suit. He was the man in that crowd.

"My name is Dean Teranova."

"Which will mean what?"

"Just tell Mister Carpetti the guy he tried to kill would like very much to discuss the matter."

CHAPTER 47

THIS WAS NOT THE USUAL FARE, and it caused the man to rise from his seat. He stood reluctantly.

"Watch this strunz," he said.

He went inside, shaking his head.

The characters around Dean said nothing. They were in full stare mode and they looked at him like he was a filthy pair of undershorts.

"Nice day," said Dean.

"You fuckin' with us?" one of them said.

"Come to think of it," said Dean…"Yeah."

The door to Castaldi's opened. The man waved Dean in. Once he cleared the doorway a pair of hands had him around the throat.

Another man hit him in the stomach. He crumpled and was kicked by another. He was choked. He was slapped. He was forced on the floor flat, arms out. He was kicked more, punched in the kidneys, frisked and kicked some more, then he was hauled up to his feet. He was wavery. He had to be held up.

"For a moment there," he said, "I thought I was back in Spofford."

This got him cracked across the face again. A nice clean stream of blood ran down his lips.

As he was led upstairs he got a quick look at the place. A few card tables, easy chairs, a couch, a bar of sorts with booze and espresso maker, a couple of televisions, a hi-fi, a lot of chintzy framed photographs of the usual glad handing…and the occasional shoulder holster.

The second floor was a huge triangular office. Gino Carpetti sat at a desk. He was a better looking version of his son.

As Dean walked in the first thing Carpetti said was, "Spofford, huh?"

"Yeah."

"How long?"

"Nine."

"Shiiiiit. That'll prep ya."

He pointed to a seat. Dean went and sat.

"Teranova…you Guy Prince's boyfriend?"

"We're friends, yeah."

"You live with that fag attorney my sister hangs with."

"I got an apartment there."

"Just so I get this straight. How did I try and kill you?"

Dean went through the New Mexico episode...then Guy's story...and finally the bombing of the XKE.

Gino Carpetti listened without once looking Dean in the eye. When Dean was done, he said, "If I meant to kill someone...I did a very poor job, didn't I?"

"I might be able to convince Peter Prince to negotiate some kind of truce with you."

"Peter Prince is shit. And I don't have any business with him."

"Then I'm sorry for bothering you, sir."

Dean got up. He started to leave, then hesitated. "Do you know a restaurant called The Old Mill? It's out on Staten Island."

"Was...on Staten Island."

"Yes, sir...Was."

"Why?"

"I thought you might remember a waitress who worked there back in the fifties...her name was Teresa Vinci."

He was not looking at Dean, he was looking right through him, with the poisoned eyes of a shoddy despot. "You remind me of a boy I knew growing up. My closest friend. He had a real knife for a mind...He died young, too."

Carpetti listened to Dean's steps descend the stairway with a measure of amazement. The man who had ushered Dean in entered the office.

"Guess what," said Gino.

"I'm a blank, Mister Carpetti."

"It seems we have a new generation of trouble in town."

• • •

Carpetti thought back to the day he had created this moment. If there had been a warning sign, he certainly had not seen it. Nothing like being blind to what's in your own head.

He had been sitting in his Cadillac that day across from The Old Mill Restaurant. Peter Prince was in the car with him.

"I appreciate you meeting me here," said Gino.

"No problem," said Peter.

They had never really spent time alone and were not genuinely comfortable with each other.

"I am, of course, counting on your discretion."

"You have it, Mister Carpetti."

"My mother trusts you," he said. "So I know I can discuss with you this very private matter. I can trust you, can't I?"

"Of course, Mister Carpetti. Trust is my business."

"I have a job that needs to be done. And I need someone who I can not only trust, but someone who must have…finesse, I guess is the word. Or as we Italians say—sympatico."

Peter nodded. "I understand sympatico…I'm Italian, Mister Carpetti."

"I thought you were a Jew."

"Italian Jew."

"No kidding?"

Gino reached for a pack of cigarettes on the dash. He seemed school boyish suddenly.

"There's a girl who works over there as a waitress. She's a decent, lovely girl. Alone. No family. She's sixteen…and pregnant."

"I see."

"You don't see. Not yet, anyway. She should be coming along directly, and I want to point her out to you, so you know her on sight."

He offered Peter a cigarette, but Peter declined. Gino was intently watching the road. Peter wished he wasn't in the fuckin' car.

"I want you to get friendly with her. So she can feel safe with you. Get her trust. You know…be parental. I've already mentioned you by name."

"Have you?"

"I want you to find someone to take her. Somewhere out of the way where she can go through these last months of her pregnancy."

Gino leaned over and opened the glove compartment. As he took out an envelope and handed it to Peter, he said, "That's her—"

She looked like a plain, everyday teenager. Almost docile in a quiet way as she walked along. She wore her waitress outfit and white socks and saddle shoes. Her hair shined from the sun. She wasn't showing yet, that was for sure.

"You have a son," said Gino.

"Yeah…Guy."

"I see you and him when you come over to see my mother. You and he are close…tight."

"Yeah. The kid's a pain in the ass. But I don't know what I'd do without him."

Peter gave Gino this hard grin. You know, one of those fake fronts of toughness that you can see right through.

"No…I can tell," said Gino. "He's your life. The kid worships you. He follows you around."

"The kids' got no taste whatsoever."

"It makes me kinda jealous," said Gino. "Christopher and I…Well… It's no secret. I'm not in good standing with his mother. So, I'm not in good standing with him. The bitch has seen to that. What's your secret?"

"My secret?"

"The bond, man. What's the secret to that bond?"

What could he answer? Nothing really nails it. "I try to remember," said Peter, "that his happiness and well-being is more important than my own."

Gino put his head back. Blew smoke out his nostrils.

"I failed that. Fuck it."

He flicked the cigarette out the car window.

"You watch over the girl until she delivers the baby. She thinks she's gonna be set up in a place for us. When she delivers the baby…I want her killed. If the baby is a boy, I want it taken to the place I've set up. Everything you need to know is in the envelope."

"And…if it's a girl?"

"Kill it," said Gino.

Peter opened the envelope, taking an extra moment for this to settle in. With all the money was a page of handwritten instructions.

"Everything understood?" said Gino.

"Understood, Mister Carpetti."

CHAPTER 48

MISSUS CERASO WAS TAKING TWO HEAVY BAGS of groceries from her car for Missus Carpetti when a young man swept in alongside her.

"I'll take those."

She looked up. "Oh my god," she said.

The elder Carpetti was in her office on the phone reading someone the riot act. Even at her age and permanently confined to a wheelchair, she was an elder statesman of ruthlessness. When she saw this figure of a man staring at her through the French doors—with a sudden coolness, she said to the person on the phone, "I'll have to call your sorry ass back."

She frantically waved Guy in.

"Remember me?" he said, coming through the doors.

"For a moment," she said, "it was ten years ago and your father... Come to me...Come...come."

He leaned down beside her and she kissed his face with a merciless affection.

Missus Ceraso closed the door to the office to insure their privacy. Behind the office was a small, cozy den where Missus Ceraso would remain until called by her employer. The one wall that separated the office from the den contained the original bookshelf. In its plankboard seams there was a crack where Missus Ceraso had, over time, come to realize if she remained very quiet and still, she could overhear virtually everything spoken in the office. Unless the parties whispered. But there wasn't much whispering in that office.

So she sat in a chair she had positioned close to the shelf and she sat there knitting and listening as she had done for the last forty years. She knew, more than anyone, the history of their crimes.

The older woman and the youth talked. They talked about his time in juvenile hall, his serving in the army, the medal he was awarded. He listened to her about her health, her bittersweet memories, her adoration for her grandchildren.

Missus Ceraso heard the woman laugh more in that hour than she had in weeks upon weeks, as Guy was the closest the old woman would be to the wildness of her own youth. She also missed Peter Prince, and this gave her a chance to be close to something that was part of him. Missus Ceraso was sure Peter Prince had been the son she never had.

Guy made a turn in the conversation. He told her about what he believed was an attempt on his and Dean's life in New Mexico. And the fraudulent story he'd made up around Dicky Palazzo. The old woman hated Palazzo and said so in a long string of vulgarities.

Then Guy flat out came to the point. He and Dean were about the business of finding his father, sure as they were that he was still alive. And did his disappearance back in 1957 have anything to do with a young waitress at the time, who was pregnant?

• • •

Missus Ceraso could feel the current running through the silence that followed that question. Of course, she knew the truth. The old woman and her son had clashed in that room over that girl. Man, had she laid her rage into him.

"You disgust me to no end," she'd said to Gino. "You should be castrated, the goddamn lot of you. You think nothing of women because you think nothing of yourselves."

"I'm sorry," Gino had said, bitterly, "that my life hasn't stacked up against yours."

"I've heard that shit," she said, "from every kind of hardon there is. And it sounds more piss poor the older you get."

"I want a son. That's no crime."

"You have a son, or didn't you notice?"

"I mean a real son. A son who is mine and not the image of that smarmy bitch."

"You married her, boy. The fault lies at your feet as much as hers. You're such a…failure. Like my father would say…You're an envelope with nothing in it."

"You'll be dead one day," Gino had said to his mother, "so there's always the possibility of good news."

"We have one thing in common, Gino. We both have sons we despise. You can be charged for rape, by the way. And there's enough task force people out there hunting—"

"Peter will take care of it."

"What?"

"Peter Prince will see to it."

"You solicited him?"

"I thought it—"

"Don't be surprised, Gino, if one day you get fucked right in the heart."

Gino had no sooner cursed his way out the patio doors, than Missus Carpetti called out, "Missus Ceraso…I need you in here, please."

That afternoon Missus Ceraso was driving her employer in the family stationwagon to Manhattan. A meeting had been called. Peter Prince was to join C.C. at her bar The Light Switch. Missus Carpetti talked to herself as they drove, and nothing could quell her displeasure.

The bar was empty, as it did not open until six in the evening. It was empty except for a kitchen worker vacuuming the carpet and the bartendress doing setup. Johnny Mathis was singing *Chances Are* on the stereo in a rather low and soothing tone. It was a strange contrast to the conversation at hand in C.C.'s upstairs office.

"He already told me he wants to see bodies," said Peter.

"Gino will pick the place," said Missus Carpetti. "He won't come. He'll send people."

"He means to kill you," C.C. said to Peter, "because of your relationship with my mother and me."

"He knows the wrath I'd bring down on him," said Missus Carpetti, "but he might take that risk anyway."

"This is about me. Let's be honest," said C.C. "He and Christopher want their dyke relation dead. I don't like to say this, Mama, but after you're passed on, they don't want to contend with someone like me."

"My Will, will have something to say about that," said Missus Carpetti.

CHAPTER 49

Missus Ceraso heard her employer say to Guy, "What do you know of Blue Mountain?"

It shocked her, for sure, to hear the words 'Blue Mountain' be mentioned. It was something the old woman had never spoken to anyone about.

"Nothing," said Guy. "I mean, I know where it is up on the Hudson. Woods…hiking…that kind of crap. Never been there."

"Never heard it mentioned by Gardner…or C.C.?"

"No," said Guy.

"Not from your father, I'm sure of that."

"No."

"Beyond silent and loyal, your father was smart. Blue Mountain proved that. Give me a cigarette, Guy, will you?"

Missus Ceraso waited in that other room, holding her breath, while Guy got out a cigarette and lit it, thinking all the while what that old woman was about to lay on the youth.

"I'm going to speak of it now…Blue Mountain," said Missus Carpetti. "And I have my reasons, which I will explain after I'm done."

• • •

Blue Mountain was about thirty miles north of New York City along the Hudson River. Not long after that meeting in C.C.'s bar, Peter made the call that the girl had delivered the baby, and both were dead. Arrangements were made for him to drive up to Blue Mountain and follow directions to a fire road near Lounsbury Pond.

He did not drive his Lincoln. He had picked up a hot car with tricked out plates that could be abandoned. He had a pistol on the front seat, and he had taped a stiletto to the inside of his belt along his right front pocket.

Blue Mountain was a friggin' wilderness. Woods so dense they were straight out of Rip Van Winkle. Forget finding your way at night. But night it was. He was to meet two men there who worked for Gino, and they would take "chain of title" to the bodies. Sometimes Gino fed on that kind of sarcasm and it made Peter all the more nervous. He was sure a grave had been dug somewhere in those woods to accommodate three.

What he couldn't know was there were not two men waiting, but there was also a third. A manchild christened Christopher Carpetti. Barely fifteen, this night was to be his "rite of passage." He was under orders by his father to put the coup de grace shot into the head of Peter Prince.

Once Prince got off the main road around Montrose, his headlights looked like smoking, lonely eyes trying to see through a wild matted landscape.

You think it can't get any darker and more dangerous, but it does. In his rearview, it was as if the world was closing in behind him, except for movements of dust spewing up from his tires.

He drove and he drove, and the going grew slower and more silent and more black, and he was sweaty even though the windows were open and the air cool from the trees and the road got more narrow so the branches scraped the car doors and then somewhere ahead…a flicker. A tiny firefly of light through a dense palisade of trees.

He was coming to that moment, where whoever was best at being furtive would survive the night.

When he saw a parked car ahead, he pulled off into the indifferent dark. He took a moment before turning off the lights to survey what awaited. Two men were getting out of the vehicle, but he thought what looked like the black outline of a head and shoulders in the back seat that did not.

This had all the signs of bad news.

He went to reach across the seat for his gun when the windshield near his head spidered from a bullet. The shot had been silent.

"Just keep it calm in there."

The men were closing in. One on each side of the car. Peter Prince could see they were young, which usually meant they'd favor aggression over caution.

He was ordered out with his hands raised. He was made to face the car. He was frisked by one man as the other removed the pistol from the car.

"Bodies," said the man behind Prince.

"Where do you fuckin' think they are?" said Peter.

He was shoved toward the trunk.

"Show me," he was told.

The three men stood over the trunk.

"Keys," said one of them.

"The trunk is open…genius."

The man reached for the lid. As he did, Peter slipped his fingers over the stiletto taped to his belt.

As the lid clicked, Peter pulled lose the knife. The trunk lifted. There was a body covered by a tarp beside a filthy spare tire, all except for a bare foot and leg.

"Where's the baby?"

"Pull back the tarp, man."

The man reached down. As he pulled away the tarp there was an explosion. The tarp was torn to flaming shreds. Peter pressed the blade latch on the stiletto. The blast from a shotgun had hit the young man straight in the face and chest lifting him from the ground and sending him back into the roadside weeds.

A moment of singed air, a scream, and smoking blackness. Before the one with the gun trained on Peter could react, Prince had swung about and driven the long, narrow acuminated blade into the man's throat with such force it tore through the trachea and scored an artery.

By the time C.C. had labored out of the trunk where she had been hidden with the shotgun and got her bearings, Peter had grabbed up the dead man's gun and was sprinting toward the other car.

"There's one more…in that car," he said.

Whoever was in the car ducked down. Peter fired at the rear windshield. There were two small explosions of glass and a voice called out, "Don't shoot…I'm not going to make a fight of it."

"Get out of there," Peter shouted.

The back door opened, a youth stumbled out.

"On your hands and knees," said Peter.

The youth went to his hands and knees. C.C. came rushing up alongside Peter and there in the pitch of light from the car interior she saw who it was—

"Christopher," she said.

He looked up. He was deathly afraid.

"You shit. My brother sent you to be—"

Christopher was looking up into two stark heartless stares.

"Man, if your grandmother knew you were part of something like this—"

He took to pleading. His aunt wasn't buying it.

"This is a sorry ass performance," said C.C. "Shoot him, Peter."

The kid froze mid-word. You talk about a look like death had reached down in his throat and manhandled his heart. Christopher was there.

C.C. lost it. She charged forward and got in half a dozen kicks until Peter dragged her off him.

Then Peter stepped forward, the gun pressing in on Christopher. "Did they have the grave dug?"

"Yeah…yeah…" He wiped the blood from his mouth where he'd been kicked and then pointed toward a section of trees.

"Shovels?" said Peter, "Where are the shovels?"

"In the car."

"Get your ass up, boy. You got bodies to bury."

Christopher got to his feet and started for the car, all slumped and looking back like they would just up and shoot him.

"Wait until I tell my brother what a candyass you were."

"You kill me, my father will go to war with you."

"What do you think tonight was?" said C.C.

At gunpoint, Christopher hoisted the bodies one at a time over his shoulder. His clothes got nice and bloody and when done, Peter made him lay down with the dead. The kid looked up at the gun and the stars beyond and when Peter fired, Christopher would hear the shot for years.

Getting a taste of that kind of fear makes some men wiser, while others crash and burn without ever knowing.

On the ride back home in an uncertain silence, C.C. finally said, "We should have killed him."

"Sorry, kid," said Peter, "but that's something your mother would have to sign off on."

CHAPTER 50

"Guy...I told you all this for a reason," said Missus Carpetti.

She sat in her wheelchair, her arthritic fingers held the cigarette that she stared at. Those eyes had seen and survived endless conflict.

"Sometimes," she said, "we must take a chance with our judgments. Gamble with what our eyes don't tell us."

"I'm sure," she went on, "my son or grandson, alone or in a conspiracy together, mean to see you and your boyfriend dead...They want C.C. dead also. So...I'm giving you my blessing to kill them, if the need or opportunity arises. If you should want my advice or council at any time, I am here."

She inhaled and Guy just sat there quietly.

In his mind this was a scene he would replay and remember, replay and remember, whose meaning would endlessly change.

"One flag," she said. "Nothing is to happen to my grandchildren. They are still young enough to be saved and then groomed."

She wagged her knotty fingers at him. "You killed in the army. And that Teranova boy did the same in the Bronx. Real power is how the mind operates when it's cornered or caged."

"Yes, ma'am," he said.

"Do I shock you?" she said.

"Nothing about you ever shocked me, ma'am."

She laughed at that. She stubbed out the cigarette, shaking her head. "Never tell a woman that. Every woman wants to believe she has the power to be shocking. It flatters their vanity. In my case, my immorality precedes me. Now come here and give me a kiss."

He got up and came to the desk and she put out her arms and he leaned down, and she kissed him and whispered, "You know our secrets, now. Your father's secrets. You join us in our secrets. Are now, a part of these secrets. And of this, you say nothing to Gardner or my daughter."

• • •

The police had cordoned off Shrady Place that first night. The bombing of the XKE was pretty much amateur night. A gasoline soaked rag stuffed down the throat of the gas tank, a flash from a cigarette lighter, and—voila—three thousand pounds of ruined steel and fine leather.

The police had searched the house that first night. They'd found pot, jars of bennies and yellows and other mind altering goodies. A half dozen unregistered weapons. It was a Christmas list of misdemeanors. Palazzo was questioned the next day and the day after with his attorney at his side.

Near evening of the third day, he got off alone. He walked down Sedgwich then along the Jerome Reservoir. Over at Fort Independence Park a bunch of teenagers were partying to The Temptations on a car radio.

Off in the quiet of dusk was Chris Carpetti.

"How is it up there?"

"When it smells bad, it attracts vermin," said Palazzo. "And it smells bad."

"You didn't tell them about Guy Prince?"

"Guy Prince does not exist as far as all this is concerned. But, man. Something is happening and—"

"I know where you're going."

Christopher shoved his hands down in his pockets.

"I think your father means to do you in. I think all this is about doing you in."

"He's a fuckin' master."

"He used you, man, to try and reel in Teranova. To get to Peter Prince through his son."

"Of course he did," said Christopher.

"Then someone tries to off those two fags in New Mexico," said Palazzo.

"And now the incident here in the Bronx with Guy Prince. Him being questioned about me. If Prince killed the two that nabbed him, who took out my car? This feels—"

"Don't try and outthink my father. That's a prescription for doom. He's got a military head. He'll throw feints with his left hand, while he slits your throat with his right. But he's the one who goes down for rape. And this isn't what it's all about anyway. It's his sister. He wants her dead. And me blamed for it."

"You think he might have gotten wind of what you're plotting for C.C. and—?"

Christopher glared at him.

"Not a word more…Sorry."

"Yeah…if it all goes bad, he means for me to bear the heat. But he's not the only one who can feint with one hand, but slit a throat with the other."

Then who should come walking out of the shadows of the trees?

"Well, look at this," said Christopher.

It was Dean Teranova. Carpetti's driver and bodyguard rose from a nearby bench where he'd been watching. Carpetti told him it was all right.

"Well," said Christopher, "How is it you're here?"

"How…isn't important. But why is."

"You found Peter Prince?"

"It's not gonna be easy to kill us. You can mention that to your father."

"Where does that come from?"

"New Mexico, for one. You or your father fucked up. The two punks you sent after Guy the other night. You fucked up. We don't die easy. We're gonna make a fight of it, man. And we'll see who gets the most reckless."

"I feel myself wobbling from the threat," said Christopher.

"Look around," said Dean. "I'm not protected."

Not thirty feet away, one of the kids by the car was up on the roof doing his finest impersonation of The Temptations, mimicking their dance steps to "*My Girl.*" He was a piece of work, loaded as he was, and he slipped off the roof and landed on the trunk on his ass.

"That's what you're like at this moment," Christopher said to Dean.

"Guy had something he wanted to tell you."

Christopher didn't say anything, because he knew he was gonna hear it no matter what.

"Blue Mountain," said Dean.

Palazzo saw the remark landed. Suddenly the youth wasn't just a footnote to something much more deadly. Dean said no more and just walked away.

"We should have had you go with Prince that night," Carpetti told Palazzo. "Should have forced it."

"You mean the night of the call," said Palazzo.

"Yeah…it would all be settled and done."

"What's Blue Mountain mean?"

"It means Prince might well be alive. It also means there's someone else who can feint with one hand while they slit your throat with the other."

CHAPTER 51

WHEN MONSEIGNEUR LOMBARDO BUILT SAINT LUCY'S GROTTO back in '37, he also constructed an underground catacomb of stacked stones, like the very grotto itself. It was a long and winding passageway of alters and homages to the saints and the Lady herself. And where one could light a candle in the hopes of having their most fervent or desperate prayer answered.

It was an ironic setting, to say the least, for a meeting between an assistant district attorney from the Bronx named Heller and Gardner Flynn, to discuss the letter of immunity left in Ross' apartment. A letter addressing the terms of blanket immunity for Peter Prince, if he would come forward and turn state's evidence against Gino and Christopher Carpetti. The letter also detailed a story of an as yet heretofore unknown rape, and the solicitation to murder the mother and child of that rape.

Ross was stationed at the gateway to the catacomb, O'Gorman at the street entry to the grotto itself. Ross was ordered to be on his best behavior when it came to Teranova and Prince.

Guy was across the street in the front yard, smoking and watching, when O'Gorman spotted him and waved him to come over. Guy was reluctant, of course, assuming bad blood. But he went, nevertheless.

O'Gorman, on the other hand, broke into a smile as the youth approached, and it surprised Guy quite thoroughly. O'Gorman was shaking his head and smiling and came right out with, "'We urinated in your orange juice...'" He repeated the statement with more acidic humor, "'We urinated in your orange juice...' Do you have any idea how bad you fucked with my partner's head? Now he gets a couple of drinks in him and he's frothing like a mad dog to anyone who will listen."

O'Gorman had Guy laughing now.

"All that aside," said O'Gorman, "you better stay sharp. There's leaks in the department and word of this could get out to Carpetti. That's why the meeting is taking place here."

* * *

Dean came walking out of the house later. He was all tweaked up, shaved, favoring a blue blazer and neat jeans, even a dreaded, hated tie. Guy came down the walkway and looked him over.

"Gonna give me a clue?" said Guy.

Dean lied. "I'm connecting with Elise." He did not like himself for this lie. But it was mandatory.

Guy pretended he was a manservant with a whiskbroom and brushed Mister Teranova down.

Guy didn't have an inkling he'd been lied to until hours later when a girl got off the bus at the front of the house and stepped into the dusk of the front gate with a shoulder bag. She came sauntering up the walkway like she owned the place, all hips and smile, to where Guy was sitting on the front porch steps swigging a beer.

"I know you," she said.

"Yeah...Who am I?"

With a cool eye she answered, "You're the competition."

He sat back snapping his fingers. "Elise...film major...NYU... Brooklyn...documentary...And not short on charm."

"Very good," she said. "Where's Dean?"

"Last I saw him, he said he was going out to Brooklyn to see you."

"He told me he was gonna hang around the old plantation tonight. So I thought—"

"It looks like we've both been—"

"Yeah," she said. "Doesn't it." She took a joint from her shoulder bag and held it up. "What do you think?"

• • •

The Davenport Swim and Tennis Club was having its Annual New Rochelle Chamber of Commerce Dinner Dance. This is where Dean was to meet with Rose Berghich. An invitation was awaiting him at the gate.

The Club was on the Long Island Sound, and an orchestra had been set on an expanse of lawn, as had rows of dining tables, each with candled bowls. The lower veranda of the Clubhouse served as a dance floor beneath a scaffolded heaven of beautifully colored lights. The evening was highlighted with all the details of middle class pomp. Dennis James, a resident of Davenport and a television personality, introduced the singer Jerry Vale to a rousing, yet gentle applause.

Dean found a place where he could be easily seen. With drink in hand, he waited. As he watched the people, many near his own age, he wondered what his own life might have been like, but for the flaws of time and place. Of course, he'd come to feel that it was a lie. Worse than a lie. Because it left out the fact of himself. The fact that he burned with conflict.

"Are you really sure God is working in our lives?"

Dean turned to see this was not a frumpy woman in a poncho with a joint in one hand and a hose in the other watering a sad-ass garden. This was a looker in a sleek summer dress with cool Nancy Sinatra boots that were made for walking and a Twiggy haircut.

"Why don't you and I wander off?" she said.

"Yes, ma'am."

"Ma'am…? Don't frighten me with such a word."

They walked past the orchestra and the dining tables and down to the black and shiny waters of the Sound. Each had a drink in hand. She also with a cigarette. She would, on occasion, look back, as if expecting someone.

"I read your magazine story."

He was surprised. "How did you—?"

She pointed to his arm. "I noticed the tattoo on your arm. Spofford. I'm a professor of Social Sciences and Political Science. I know people through my work and my family. My calls get answered."

When she spoke, there was real inflection in her voice. It was a soft voice but one pearled with emotion.

"There are two things I am going to tell you, Mister Dean Teranova, and they will have a profound effect on Guy's life, and probably your own. I can only hope God is working overtime."

Dean felt his heart constrict.

"His father?" said Dean.

"Yes."

"He survived that night?"

"Yes. The shooting at Gray Mare inlet."

"How do you know? I mean—"

"I was there."

"You?"

"In a waiting car."

"So…there was a waiting car."

"Yes."

CHAPTER 52

"I WAS TO DRIVE THE CAR," ROSE SAID. "Peter was against it, of course. But I was adamant. It turned out to be—"

She dropped her cigarette on the lawn and stubbed it out with the heel of her boot. People were passing, some walking down to the shore, some coming back. Every now and then, one said hello to Rose. She was very careful in how she spoke to not be overheard, as she related to Dean how she drove to the inlet a little before dark. Once the last of the few remaining cars left, she'd backed into the trees. The undergrowth was so dense it literally folded back in over the hood.

So she sat there into the dead of night, not even allowing for a cigarette for fear of giving herself away. Few cars came and went along Shore Road, their headlights sweeping down into the dip and curve of the inlet to then sweep on.

Rose checked her hands every now and then to see if they were shaking. She kept her mind quiet, but it was a shock to the system when it finally happened. A startling burst of whitefire up Shore Road and then another. Gunfire…it had to be. She could hear tires now swerving over the asphalt. Then what was shotgun fire. She could hear the hulking sound of the weapons coming even closer.

She summoned all the *Roses* she ever imagined within herself for a tense brief moment of time to keep her fear in check. Then she saw his Lincoln bottom out as one tire blew and it sideswiped the entry gate with a sedan chasing along behind it. The Lincoln raced toward the water with a bare rim kicking up sparks from the rocks it scored, and Peter swung the wheel and braked and jumped out as the sedan rammed his car.

Peter was sprinting toward where her car was hidden while he fired at the sedan which had come to a crashing stop when it hit the Lincoln. The flashes of gunfire were pure demonry. The driver of the sedan must have been shot because he was slumped over the wheel and the sedan engine kept revving and driving the Lincoln toward the rocky shore.

Peter was shouting for Rose to bring the car on. She realized she had forgotten to turn on the ignition. She was existing on pure adrenalin now.

Everything happening at once and so fast it was beyond her comprehension or description.

Seeing him in a rush of headlights so quickly she almost ran him over. He was shouting as he pulled open the shotgun door and jumped in. What was that other shadow mysteriously shambling out of the dark? Something grabbed open a back door. Then the explosion of a pistol just inches from her head. The concussion so loud she blacked out for a moment. The car swerved. She hit her head against the door window. There was blood from her nose on the glass. The back door winged open. A figure was trying to climb in. Peter leaned over the seat and fired again. You could hear a body thud as it went under the chassis. It was being dragged along the gravel and then the asphalt. You could hear it crumple as they swung up onto Shore Road and then it cut loose and the door swung shut.

They were speeding along in silence now.

"Are you all right?" said Peter.

Rose was fixed on the road. On the lights streaming past the sleepy homes, the closed shops. Anything to help her get past it.

"Rose?"

She had begun to cry.

"Are you hurt?" she said.

Peter looked down. He was bleeding from his right side. He lied to her. "I'm fine."

She was so unnerved she drove past Leland Avenue then turned instead up Centre Avenue passing the gray stone towers of Isaac Young. She then swung onto Hanford.

Teresa was in the window, watching and waiting as they had planned out. Rose pulled into the long, curved driveway then into the garage where the door had been left open. Teresa was hurrying along. She was to close the garage door. Rose was to get the lights on. By the time she did, Peter was out of the car and she saw there was blood all down his right side.

"Are you shot?"

"The steering wheel snapped off when the car got hit and speared me. I'll be all right. Help me inside."

As Rose got him draped over her shoulder, Teresa screamed out. She was pointing toward the car's back door. It wasn't quite closed and there was a grisly horror to be seen. A hand had been caught up somehow under the seat and part of bloody arm hung down from it.

• • •

How much more Rose would have confided to Dean, she was cut short by one of the club members asking her a few utterly mundane questions about dinner and who did the floral arrangements. It was obvious to Dean she was one of the directors in charge of this affair. It was, they both realized upon glancing at each other, a strange collision of realities.

"Peter got away, though," Dean whispered.

"It took a few weeks for him to recuperate enough. And then he was gone. You should know. I've put out word. It will take a while…if he answers, at all. I have to do it by a personal ad in a newspaper and—"

She turned suddenly as the orchestra took up the first strings of *Stranger in Paradise*. Jerry Vale leaned into the microphone, his white tuxedo coat shining with candlelight as he smoothly began to sing…*Take my hand…I'm a stranger in Paradise.*

Rose seemed to have drifted away, disappearing into some private realm. Dean had no idea she was living out a lifetime in those moments until she said, "I met Peter here. It was at this very dance all those years ago." She looked up at Dean now. "Would you dance with me? Just for a little bit."

He looked back up the lawn, past the orchestra and Jerry Vale, where the couples danced under that heaven of colors.

"Here will be fine," she said.

"I don't know if—"

"It will be all right," she said.

She took his hands and then there they were together, dancing slowly, going through this ancient, beautiful ritual, of strangers, yet connected by the unsolved mystery of their lives.

It was for her, he would find out, an excuse to cry. To remember and relive. He could feel her pain against his heart where her head rested. "You're young," she said, "but you need to understand. Time is running away. It is always running away. No matter how we try to catch it and hold it and adore it, it is running away. And sometimes our worst crime was not having tried."

He just let her sob, then she whispered, "I have one more thing to tell you." She was looking up at him now, and he down at her. "I am Guy's mother," she said.

CHAPTER 53

You would have thought they'd known each other all their lives, Guy and Elise. They were camped out in Dean's apartment, outrageously stoned, singing oldies like *Ragdoll* and *The In Crowd*, *Wooly Bully* and Dylan's *Subterranean Homesick Blues*.

"We're out of our fuckin' minds," she told Guy. "You know that?"

"Who are you?" said Guy. "How did you get in here?"

She had gotten out her Super 8 and was getting him to talk on camera. About his life, his incarceration, his time in the Army. This dude stripped it bare. No matter how down and dirty the details.

"You don't have a 'bunker complex,'" she said.

"What's that?"

"It's what Dean has, when it comes to talking about himself."

"I only have it when it comes to telling Dean how much I love him. I keep that to myself. I don't wanna…freak him out."

"You mean lose him."

"Yeah…that's what I mean."

"You two are up to something, right? Can you tell me? Is it…even legal?"

"No…no…and no," he said.

They could hear the bear throated engine of Dean's car pull up into the driveway. "How do we play this?" said Elise.

Dean came up the outside stairwell and through the patio door to find Guy sprawled out on the couch watching television. He was sporting a joint and a smile. "How did it go with Elise? I can't wait to hear."

Dean wished Guy wasn't there. He was carrying too much for this.

"Fine," he said. "It was fine."

"Fine…fine is something fuckin' parents might say."

Dean came around to see Elise there in the bathroom doorway. She was filming him with her Super 8.

"Check out the dour look on his face," she said.

"Put the damn camera down," said Dean.

"Is this what comes from getting busted?"

188

He didn't wait for her. He swiped at the camera.

The vibe coming off Dean took on its own message. Steer clear. "Go home," he told Elise. From his pocket he took out all the cash he had on hand. "Here," he said. "Take a cab. Consider me sorry."

He went over to the counter where he kept the booze. There was a little bourbon left in one bottle, a little less of Scotch in another. He poured them both into the same glass. "Fuck it," he said.

He drank and he looked about. Stares of judgment and concern.

"I'm sorry," he said. "What do I do? Keep saying it?"

"Try meaning it," said Elise. "And unacceptable impulses are not charming. You are not some formative celebrity. Comprende?"

She got her stuff together and walked out, giving him the finger as she went.

"I don't know if she bought your little drama," said Guy, "or was just letting you be, because she cares for you. But I sure didn't buy it."

"Because you can see into all those dark and stoic corners."

"I can see into yours. And I don't get sucker punched by unverified information. Something went down tonight. I mean…you even dressed for the occasion."

"I dressed, but not for the occasion."

He drank the Scotch and bourbon. It left a lot to be desired. But he didn't care.

"It's a bad place to survive," said Dean.

"Where is?"

"Right here."

"Right here?"

"Right here…right now."

"Right," said Guy.

"We made a mistake," said Dean.

"Which one…There have been so many."

Dean drank again. Rotten. He went to the fridge and got out some ice. Like ice was gonna make it taste better. It certainly did not.

"Go back to New Mexico," said Dean.

"Where the hell did that come from?"

Dean said, "Time is running away." But he was talking mostly to himself.

"You're standing next to me," said Guy. "I see you there in the flesh.

But where the hell are you?"

"Do you believe that you chase and you chase, but time is running away? And what you chase, you can't catch. No matter what."

"What happened out there tonight? Suddenly you're Mister Memorializer."

"We should go on with our lives."

"We are."

"It only seems that way."

"I don't like what I'm seeing. I don't like what I'm feeling. In other words…I don't like. Something is lurking in there"—He jabbed a finger into Dean's chest—"and I want to know what it is."

Dean slapped his hand away.

"What is this," said Guy, "fuck your best friend night?"

"Get out of here," said Dean. "I need to crash."

Guy just stood there confused, hurt, a slow anger building on contradictory emotions.

"What am I speaking, Chinese?" said Dean.

He gave Guy the slightest shove, and man, that little action hurt him on so many levels.

"Are we descending down into the pit or what, Dante?"

Dean walked over to the hallway door. "This is a door," said Dean. "I intend to close it. I want you on the other side when I do."

"I hate to steal a line from a movie and vamp it, but…I wish you'd put the gun down and then I'll leave."

"What?"

"I'd like it to be my idea."

Guy started for the door. He walked past Dean, but stopped. "You gonna come out with a little honesty or what?"

"I'll stick with 'or what' for now."

"Suddenly you're that little section of that map, Dante, that says… Unknown."

Guy actually wrote the word in imaginary letters across Dean's chest. It was one of those moves that was just aggressive enough they unleashed on each other.

They could fight. They had kicked ass and they had had their asses kicked and they weren't being heroic or inspirational. This was purely street. They crashed into the hallway walls as they grappled and wrestled.

They were serpentine and shedding blood as they devolved into barroom brawlsters on the floor. Guy was bigger and stronger, and kept getting the edge and would have probably beat Dean down ultimately, but for Gardner storming out of his bedroom, and standing over the two in his pajamas and reading them the kind of riot act that would stop a subway train.

He was a hurricane of disgust, ordering them off each other and warning them he'd call the cops and have them both arrested. Once the two of them had calmed and were sitting with their backs to the opposing walls, Gardner went back to his room.

In the hostile quiet that followed they each got a good look at themselves and it was a regretful statement to say the least, and they both knew it. Then Guy, reaching back through all those years said, "Fuck the Del-Vikings."

Dean remembered and got it. The cabbie that day of the fight against the Pirates in that filthy sump. When they were—one. He nodded.

"Fuck American Bandstand," said Dean.

CHAPTER 54

"WELL," SAID GUY, "do you want to tell me what this is really all about?"

Dean was feeling his sore and bloody face.

"We talked once," said Dean, "about what if your father were alive."

"Yeah…"

"And you had one question."

"Why didn't he take me with him? Why did he just—"

"Yeah."

Dean saw how anxious Guy began to look.

"I saw how you got back then," said Dean. "It's just how you look now. Except…less bloody."

Guy wiped at the blood streaming from his nose.

"The phone call the other night. I just let you think it was Elise. It was Rose Berghich."

Guy began to rise to his feet, using the wall, sliding up it.

"She wanted to meet."

"*Wanted* to meet?"

"Yeah."

"You met with her?"

"That was what tonight was about."

"She met with *you*, but not me?"

Dean's non answer was the answer.

"Why you…and not me?"

"Maybe she felt…under the circumstances…I'd be calmer. Or less—"

"You didn't—"

"That was her call."

"You should have told me anyway."

"That was my call."

"Is he alive?"

"He was alive. At least the last time that she talked to him."

"He got away that night?"

"He got away. And there *was* a car waiting at the inlet."

"You were right about that, then."

"Yeah. And she was driving it."

"You had no right to go there without me. You cheated me."

"That train has left the station."

"What else?"

"She contacted him about us."

"About us?"

"Us…you. It will take a week or so. It seems she has to go through a personal ad in a newspaper."

"So we wait."

"Be prepared. He may not want to meet…with us…or you."

"She said that?"

"Yes."

The young man was crashing on the rocks of the years of loss he carried around inside him.

"'You chase and you chase,'" said Guy, repeating what Dean had said. "'Time is running away.' That was her talking, right?"

"That was her talking," said Dean. "She shook me up. I got to thinking, what if he didn't want to meet…Not us. Okay. But you. After all the years."

"I never thought of it that way."

"Maybe it would be too painful for him. I mean. He'd have to face his past in you. All grown up. The years. I think *she* felt this."

"You were preparing me, weren't you, Dante?"

"I didn't want you going off crazy. Better you're pissed at me."

Guy walked over and put out a hand so Dean could grab it and get up. They stood in the half dark hallway. Two young men on the verge of whatever comes next.

"You got any other secrets you're carrying around that I should know about?"

Dean thought of what Rose had told him about being Guy's mother, so Dean would understand her actions. Yet demanding his silence on the subject until she deemed otherwise.

"Yes," said Dean. "I'm afraid I do."

"You're a marvel of friendship, Dante. You know that. Even when you're not telling me the truth, you're telling me the truth. That's rich."

"It kills me to hurt you," said Dean. "You understand that, right?"

• • •

Son and father met. There was always a level of tension between them, but on this day, there was a quiet, poisonous shadow across their lives that had only been matched by the catastrophe at Blue Mountain.

As they sat in Gino's dining room, alone, father and son, having coffee, a beautiful sunscape upon the Sound that their dining room looked out over, father and son each believed the other was a lying shit.

"Let's review what we're facing here," said Gino. "Someone goes after that faggot Prince kid. They question him about Palazzo. Then Palazzo's car is blown. What does it mean?"

"I don't know," said Christopher.

"What do you think it means?"

"That's why we're here. To—"

"What do you think a reasonable man, not one who has to stick his head out the car window when he drives to see where he is going, might think?"

"Someone might think one of us is behind this. If there isn't an outside force—"

"And what does that do?"

"Do?"

"What does that fuckin' do?"

"You tell me…"

"It puts us in further conflict with each other, doesn't it, Christopher?"

"Further conflict… How much further is left?"

"Right. But…if there's an outside force working at this—"

"Simplicity," said Christopher.

"Simplicity?"

"I'm looking to see what confronts me."

"And me."

"You?"

"I'm looking to see what confronts me…yes. And you know what I think, Christopher? This is Blue Mountain all over again."

Christopher stood now.

"I won't let you take me there," said the son.

"You're always there, skulking around the billboard sized failure of yourself. No? Prove me wrong. Every father waits for the moment his son proves him wrong."

Christopher had an immense desire to crush his father's skull.

"Christopher, here's where we're at from all you told me…I believe the facts…I just don't believe the story."

Christopher had had enough, and as he just walked out on his father, Gino said to him, "Did the thought ever take you, it might be my sister behind this? That she's setting us against each other?"

• • •

Missus Carpetti knew the meeting between her son and grandson had not gone well from the way Christopher walked past the house without stopping, even for a hello, or for not waving to her. He was trying to be invisible and that need to be invisible was to her a sign of weakness or guilt or worst of all, treachery.

Missus Ceraso entered the office carrying a tray with the woman's lunch.

"I've failed as a parent," said Missus Carpetti. "My son has no character, and it is a lack that he has passed down to his own son."

"C.C. doesn't suffer from that," said Missus Ceraso.

"Maybe there's just something in her that I cannot take responsibility for."

While Missus Ceraso set out lunch the old woman called her daughter. C.C. answered and the two women chatted away on all standard issue triviality. But C.C. picked up something in her mother's voice.

"What's wrong, Mama?"

TWO YOUNG MEN
AT BREAKWATER

CHAPTER 55

After talking with her mother, C.C. called Gardner. "I'm thinking about moving to Florida," she said. He knew what that meant and the urgency it carried. An hour later, they were in his private office at the house.

"Better bring Guy and the other one down here," she said.

Dean was at his desk. He had been up most of the night writing of all that had gone down. On the page where he described about learning from Rose that she was Guy's mother, he just stopped. It was suddenly too real, seeing it there. Talk about a clue to the future. It would be left to him, he knew. The words would have to come out of his mouth. He tore up the page.

There was a knock at the door. It was Guy. "We're wanted downstairs."

When Dean stepped out into the hall, Guy saw how in a matter of hours, Dean's scuffed up cheek was already discoloring.

"You apologize," said Dean, "and I'll fuckin' shoot you."

When all four were in the office Gardner got up and handed Guy a sheet of paper with a few handwritten words on it. Guy read it over and then handed the sheet to Dean. Gardner had turned on the office radio. Classical music played. He set the volume just loud enough to cover their talk. He then went and closed the office door.

What was written on the sheet of paper:

There is a chance this office, maybe even the house, is bugged.

Gardner had them all squeeze in around the desk where C.C. began to talk in a little more than a whisper.

"My mother feels my brother might be getting ready to make a move against me. So…she'd been putting out feelers…There is a rumor that secret negotiations might be in progress to lure Peter Prince back to testify against Gino on a rape charge." She looked at the men around her. "There's blood in the water, boys. But you both knew that already."

When Guy and Dean walked out of the office they stopped in the hall-way and studied each other, because all this was no surprise. They'd pushed for the limits and now the limits were pushing back.

"Time is running away," said Guy.

Dean didn't need a translation or an explanation, he knew what Guy meant.

"I'll call her," said Dean, "but not from here."

"Give me your car keys," said Guy. "I want us to take a ride."

Dean called Rose Berghich from a pay phone at a luncheonette on Eastchester Road. The news was not good, they picked up some coffees and Guy took the Parkway out toward City Island. Dean drank his coffee and said nothing.

"You know where I'm going, don't you?" said Guy.

"I know where you're going."

"I got a favor to ask, Dante."

"Ask."

"When we get there."

Guy turned into the Orchard Beach Parking lot. It was a weekday and cool and near the end of the season so there wasn't the usual crazed mob.

As they parked, Guy said, "I think we're being followed."

Dean looked back over the seat.

"Maroon Cyclone...Sixty-four."

"What makes you think so?"

"I watch all the time now. I spotted it on Eastchester Road."

Dean saw the Mercury had slowed and was trolling across the lot. Dean reached under the seat and got out a revolver. "Here you go," he said, and he slid the revolver across the dashboard to Guy. He then saw Dean take a second revolver out from under the seat.

"Full of surprises, aren't you?" said Guy.

They tucked the guns away and Dean followed Guy down the Promenade toward Twin Island and the Breakwater at the far end of the beach.

They came to that rocky barrier in silence. The waves jetting against that long reef of stones.

"You said you needed a favor?"

"In a minute," said Guy.

Guy was off in his own moment, staring into the light. "This place is important to me," he said.

"I know."

"And you know why?"

"I know why."

"I've come here a few times since I got back."

"I guessed as much," said Dean.

"Did you ever come here, Dante?"

"After...I was released from Spofford. I came by once."

"I'm glad. I thought about this place a lot when I was incarcerated. And when I was in the army."

He looked at Dean. His mood deepening. "If something happened to me...okay...*if*...something happened. I want you to take my ashes—"

"What? Is that what you brought me out here for?"

"I want you to take my ashes to the edge of the Breakwater."

"You can't be fuckin' serious!"

"—And spread them across the water."

"It's not good to have thoughts like this."

"Will you do it?"

"You bad luck yourself."

"Will you give me your word?"

"You got to vacuum your mind of this. You don't want to bad vibe yourself into—"

"I had Gardner write something up."

"Great."

"Will you do it? I need you to tell me you'll do it. It's important, Dante."

There was no sidestepping, no turning this into some personal footnote you can envelope and slip away in a drawer somewhere. This was down to your most mortal presence.

Dean nodded, "I'll take care of it."

• • •

The hard part for Guy was past. He grew more relaxed looking, he even grinned a bit.

"You look like you just ordered chop suey somewhere," said Dean. "Let's get out of here. See what's happenin' with that Mercury."

They started back up the Promenade. Guy glanced over at the bench on the walkway by a triangle of trees.

"That first day," said Guy, "right there. I saw this man watching me. I was pretty sure I'd seen him before around the Kennedy Home."

He told Dean how not long after that, he had snuck off the grounds to have a smoke and a can of beer he'd copped from a janitor's locker. He was on that 'spanse of grass between Stillwell and the Parkway.

Well, a car pulled up and a man got out. Same man. And he called out to Guy, "Hey…you know where the School for the Blind is?"

He was starting right toward Guy, at a real slow innocuous pace.

Guy said, "You can practically see it from here, you dumb shit."

Guy pointed. The man didn't look back and Guy knew. He jackrabbited out of there a second before the man charged him.

Guy flung the can of beer at him and sprinted back toward the Home. The man was full grown and in good shape, but Guy was like a fuckin' missile darting through gaps in the trees, slipping eel-like into the underbrush, ducking low hanging branches. He leapt the tracks and was up a gravelly slope and over the fence behind Linden Hall, just out front of a reaching arm.

Guy turned to face his pursuer with just six feet of chain link separating them. "*Too fuckin' late, old timer.*"

Gasping for air, the man said, "You got lucky today, boy."

"Suck my dick, loser."

• • •

The Mercury was still cruising the lot. They could just make it out as they were coming up from the promenade. It slowed dramatically as it passed Dean's Chevy.

"I don't like the looks of that," said Guy.

"Let's see what we can do about it. You go that way…I'll go this way."

Dean took off at a run. Guy did the same. They were heading for the exits to cut the car off from getting away. Dean was closer as the car was heading in his direction. It had its windows shut so there was no telling who or how many were in it.

Someone must have spotted him or Guy racing up through the rows of parked cars because the Mercury took off, its tires scoring rubber.

Dean and Guy were fanning out, their shadows fleeting across the asphalt. The Mercury picked up speed and went sweeping past Dean, swerving to keep as far from the youth as possible.

Then Guy saw Dean pull the gun out from under his shirt and thought, Holy Christ…right here in the fuckin' parking lot. He was gonna yell but it was too far.

Dean fired two fast shots at the car. Pop—pop. One of the shots must have struck because Guy saw sparks flying off the side of the Cyclone chassis. Then it swung out into the street and was gone.

Guy caught up with Dean. Out of breath, he said, "What the fuck were you thinking?"

Dean looked down at the gun. "Something just took hold of me…I thought…we need to put the fear of God in them…before it's too late."

CHAPTER 56

IT WAS NEAR MIDNIGHT AND DRIZZLY and the pavement was all shiny where the streetlight pooled, and there, in the dark of the grotto entry, was Dicky Palazzo. He had a ski mask and gloves in his hand and when he crossed the street the two men with him waiting out front of the Parkway Apartments, also, crossed the street. They were putting on gloves and ski masks and the three jumped the short sidewalk fence fronting Gardner's house. Silently they disappeared into the shadows of the driveway.

Palazzo and Christopher Carpetti had met earlier that day in the Howard Johnson's parking lot on Bruckner Boulevard. It was a sunless, humid afternoon for plotting out their treachery.

Christopher had lied to Palazzo making a point about his father's growing disenchantment with the man. The veins in Carpetti's temples were fleshed out and the skin there sticky white as he kept feeding Palazzo the threat that his father was becoming. He wanted Palazzo to fear for his survival and that his survival rested with the son, the son who was already seeding the assassination of his own father, and if necessary…his grandmother.

Neither Guy nor Dean were at the house. Only Gardner was there, upstairs, with his boyfriend Charlie Merwin, so the three men in the ski masks entered with the ease and silence of seasoned professionals.

Palazzo could hear them upstairs getting all talkish and laughy, and he had one of his men turn off the downstairs lights and stay on guard there while he and the other man ascended the stairs.

The shower had been turned on and things had gotten quiet and the second floor hallway was dark but for a stream of lamplight from the open doorway. Palazzo edged along until he could see into the bedroom to the bath and through the shower doors where the two men were having sex. Charlie had his hands braced against the wall tiles while Gardner held him about the waist.

Seeing that boy girl fag shit acted out disgusted Palazzo, and he approached the bathroom with stealth while the lovers were lost in their cries and grunts. Palazzo waited until they'd orgasmed and their bodies got all soft and slippery before he charged in and shattered the glass shower doors with the barrel of his handgun. Charlie Merwin screamed out and then recoiled and Gardner just froze there in space, arms out. Palazzo ordered them, demanded, they shut the fuck up, and he hit the other shower door with his gun barrel shattering it.

Charlie had begun to whimper.

"Which one of you is the attorney?"

"I am," said Gardner, placing himself between the weapon and the bundled up figure of his boyfriend on the shower floor.

The water was still running and raining out through the broken glass where Palazzo reached in and grabbed Merwin by the hair. He pulled the bleeding excuse of a man through the shard edges of the door.

Charlie Merwin was getting all cut up—his arms, his hands, his legs. Palazzo forced him to get down on the bathroom floor on all fours like a dog and he kept him there.

"Where is Peter Prince?"

"I don't know," said Gardner.

"Peter's son...and that queer friend of his?"

"They don't know. No one knows."

Palazzo made Charlie crawl on the glass. The pathetic son of a bitch was practically bleating. His knees were bloody, his shins, the tops of his feet, the palms of his hands. They were all torn open as the water rivered across the tiles turning them pink with Charlie's blood.

"Where is Peter Prince?!"

"Do you think I wouldn't tell you...?"

"Where is he?"

"...that I would just stand here and let this happen?"

Palazzo pressed one of his sneakers against Charlie's face, forcing it down on the glass then grinding it. The low roiling agony coming out of that pathetic creature was too much. Gardner was begging now, that he knew nothing.

And then, as if that were not enough, Palazzo pressed one of his sneakers against Charlie's ass until he was flat on the floor. He then put all his weight on Charlie so his groin got good and cut up.

Palazzo kept demanding and he kept getting the same useless answer and no amount of threats or torture or taunting of their manhood turned the trick.

Then the other man who had come upstairs with Palazzo whistled. Palazzo turned. The man in the hallway was pointing and animated, and it looked like he had something.

• • •

The personal ad that had been decided on years ago read:

Dear Stranger in Paradise, Be a Stranger no more.

Every time the phone rang, Rose's hopes were hijacked by disappointment. She waited all night, the house dark, listening to the old songs on the hi-fi that had been part of their time, only to wake to another day of waiting.

Every bleak thought passed through her mind and the phone became an ugly instrument that filled her with resentment.

You cannot mask a truth that haunts you, and she wondered if maybe he did not want any part of what that personal ad hinted at, as it had been years and who cares to dig up one's fateful history.

It was better to be careful and safe and maybe Peter Prince had a wife now and a family, and he didn't need the fallout. She wouldn't blame him, but the old feelings lingered. That was the worst. You can tamp down the hunger because the person you hunger for is gone, but when they are at the edge of possibility.

"I should have never let you go," she said. "I should never have let the boy go. Never. I didn't know all those years ago I'd be plagued by such self inflicted aloneness."

How many times had she said this to the dark, preparing for if that chance came when she could confide this to him and to his face? How many times had she whispered herself to sleep saying it?

What was worse were the dreams. He would be there suddenly, a shadow on a city street, a stranger passing in the night with just a hint of his profile she chased after, someone in a lonely bar back in the dimness of a booth alone that she did not recognize at first but then this overwhelming presence of him took hold.

She would walk to the vacant darkness of the living room with its vaulted ceiling, and there—

She gasped.

A dream took on depths and became the monochromatic outline of a man, his features filling in, as he leaned forward and into that passing moonlight through the long windows.

"How you doin,' girl?"

"Is it you?"

"I needed to make sure it was safe. So I've been watching."

She came up from the couch like a cat and had her arms around Peter crying into the shoulder of his leather coat, her emotions being so exposed.

She held his face to the moonlight. "Let me see you," she said. "Let me really, really see you."

He still looked young for his age, even with the deeper run of lines, and his hair was just as thick, but he had a widow's peak now and it was streaked with gray. He wore a moustache that made him seem so much of the times, yet absolutely outside it.

"Is it unfair of me to tell you how much I've missed you? How much… I wasn't sure you'd come."

He pushed her back a bit.

"I didn't want to come."

He opened his coat and took a semi-automatic from inside his belt and set it on the table.

"I'm not sure I even should have. Or if I will stay."

CHAPTER 57

THERE WAS A POLICE CAR AND AN AMBULANCE out front of Gardner's house when Dean turned the corner at Mace. Guy jumped out of the car, sprinting up the walkway and was stopped by an officer at the open front door, when a voice called out, "Let him in."

It was O'Gorman at the top of the stairs.

Charlie Merwin was sitting on the edge of the bed in a bathrobe. The paramedics were attending to his endless cuts. He was silent, exhausted and well beyond angry listening to Gardner lie.

He stood by the bathroom entry in trousers and nothing else, the floor tiles covered with glass and watery blood, him explaining to the investigators how three men in ski masks had broken in. They were looking for things of value and they beat up Charlie and him.

Ross stood off alone like he was taking notes, but he knew this was all crap, a lie, a cover, a dodge. He understood what Gardner was doing, that the last thing they needed was the *Daily News* flashing an old photo of Peter Prince to the world.

Dean joined them at the doorway to the bedroom as Charlie was explaining to investigators in a wiped out voice how one of them beat and kicked him and used his sneaker to grind his face into the glass on the floor.

Ross pointed to Guy, then to Dean, and motioned they follow. Out in the hall he said to Dean, "Is this your homestead, cowgirl?" pointing to the apartment door across the hall.

"I live here," said Dean.

Ross entered the apartment with Dean right behind him to show that the place had been ransacked. Piles of notes from his desk were now missing, others were strewn about all over the floor.

"I see you're deep into secret thoughts for your boyfriend."

"Kill it," said O'Gorman. Then he went on. "We all know what went down here tonight. These were Carpetti's people. Do you have any idea who they might be?"

Neither Guy nor Dean answered.

"And you," O'Gorman said to Dean, "any of the papers that were taken, did they have anything that could help the Carpettis get to Peter Prince?"

"They couldn't get what doesn't exist," said Dean.

"Liar," said Ross.

"We're trying to make this work out," said O'Gorman. He was trying to be conciliatory. "Show a little faith in us."

"What I told you…is…"

Guy wasn't so sure.

Ross walked out. "They know where Prince is. And I don't know why you bother asking them anything. The whole lot of these fags can finish each other's sentences."

O'Gorman followed after Ross, telling the two youths, "They didn't kill anyone tonight. But they're gonna, and you're on the list."

Once alone, Dean headed for the refrigerator. "I need a beer."

Guy was right on him, half whispering, "I saw what you'd written up and—"

Dean put a hand to his mouth for Guy to shut the fuck up. He opened the fridge door to end up face-to-face with a note attached to a beer bottle.

Dean pulled it loose and read it. He broke into a grin and handed it to Guy. "Words of wisdom from Ross."

The note read:

Fuck you, screamers!

"That's rich," said Guy.

• • •

Gardner went in the ambulance with Charlie. Once the investigators had all cleared out and the house was dark and the night had closed back in on the neighborhood, Dean grabbed a flashlight and said to Guy, "Come on."

He headed out through the kitchen and crossed the driveway and went down into the garage through the back door.

He flipped on the flashlight. The garage was filled with crap. Decades of legal filing cabinets, old furniture, and endless, forgotten junk.

In a dusty corner spotted with rat shit Dean started pulling boxes off a styrofoam ice chest. He knelt down and removed the cover. He aimed the light.

The chest was filled with papers, notes, Dean's notes that Guy recognized from the quirky handwriting.

"I stash it all down here," said Dean. "Now you know why they got nothing. What I leave up there is practically gibberish...just in case of a situation like this." He shut the light. In the dark he said, "Now *you* know."

CHAPTER 58

THEY SLEPT TOGETHER THAT FIRST NIGHT. She was still intently alive to him, as he was, she felt, alive to her and she wondered, were they past the time for possibilities.

Peter stood looking out the bedroom window and into a quiet New Rochelle morning. Being here again, in the house, with her, brought back the years, his youth…his son. It was more painful than he'd imagined and he strangled on the thought…I can still escape. Desires be damned.

All the things she had wanted to say to him, that she had prepared to say to him, she saw that to try and just step back through the years was courting disaster. And what did not yet exist would disintegrate before her eyes.

She explained how Guy and the other boy found her, and why they approached her. For him—immunity—meant one thing. But for the girl? The violent risks?

"Is she all right?" he said. "Do you even know?"

• • •

There was a Schraffts Restaurant up on Main Street. It had a side entrance on Centre Avenue where there was a counter and tables and a quiet lounge where ladies came in the afternoon to luncheon, talk, and get politely loaded.

Rose was a regular there and knew the waitress who approached the darkish booth where she and Peter Prince sat.

When Rose saw Peter and Teresa Vinci get their first look at each other, there was a stilling shock that guises and time cannot overcome. Truth betrays all, more often than not.

She was older now, twenty-six, her hair short and curly and blond. And he was still the man she remembered who had denied death from having her. They clasped hands almost instantly. He could feel her nails digging into his skin.

Names had been changed over time, so it was left to Rose, "Dawn

Booth…I'd like you to meet Mister Goldberg. His friends call him Goldy."

Before going on, the young Dawn Booth had to excuse herself. She was in the bathroom crying and crying, when Rose entered. "I've imagined this day," Dawn said in a choking voice. "I imagined it like God must have imagined heaven."

About a block down from the restaurant was Blessed Sacrament Church and just past it, at 145 Centre Avenue, was a once formidable mansion with four tall Greek columns along its lengthy front porch that had long since been sectioned off into apartments.

This is where Dawn lived with her son on the ground floor in the front apartment and had for all those years, as it was Rose Berghich who owned the property.

They sat in her tiny apartment with its second hand furnishings, and talked about a possible immunity agreement and her coming out of the shadows to testify about the rape and how could her safety be assured against what would be inevitable attempts upon her life.

"I'm afraid, that goes without saying," she admitted. "But less for me than for…*him*."

She pointed to the window where Peter saw a young boy hurdling over the front hedge and sprinting up the walkway. He came through the front door with the boundless energy of a ten year old before stopping short. He knew Rose, but not the man.

The kid was wearing sunglasses and a Beatles t-shirt and was carrying a baseball bat and glove. He stood there in silence until his mother said, "Peter, this is a friend of Rose's. His name is Mister Goldberg."

"But my friends call me, Goldy." He put his hand out to shake.

"Hey," said the boy. But instead of shaking the older man's hand, he slapped him five.

"Sign of the times…So, your name is Peter?"

"Yeah."

"I named him," said Dawn, "after a man who saved my life when I was a teenager."

Everything Peter Prince had missed, or had been lost or tossed away by him, merged in that tiny apartment living room. This boy, he thought… Peter…was practically the same age as Guy had been when I abandoned him. That was the word—abandoned—at least it was the word as Peter Prince now saw it. And no wishful maneuver was going to come out of nowhere to change it.

Later, when they got into his car, Peter Prince covered his face and rested his head against the steering wheel and began to cry.

Rose did not need to ask why he was crying so, she had lived the same years.

Leaning over she got her arms around his shoulders and rested her head on his back, and she just let him cry it out.

"I abandoned my own son," he said. "What kind of a man am I?"

CHAPTER 59

SOMETHING WOKE DEAN.

It turned out to be Guy sitting on the couch breakfasting on a beer.

"I know who ground Charlie's face into all that glass."

Dean sat up. He stretched. Guy took to staring out the patio windows and into all that gritty Bronx sunlight.

"You gonna tell me...or surprise me?"

As they came downstairs they could hear a shouting match going down in Gardner's office. It was a one man show, and Charlie Merwin was the show. He was demanding Gardner cut C.C. and her mother out of his life. Color them gone. Like yesterday. Or it was gonna be thank you, fuck you, and see you.

Gardner was pleading his case, and there's nothing more pathetic than one of those "end of" emotional appeals. But Gardner had no intention to cut and run from C.C. or the old woman. Not happening.

Charlie saw where all this was heading, and he couldn't have been more emphatic in his ultimatum and he had the wounds and the stitches to express it. This was the immoveable object against the irresistible force. This was a straight from the heart good-bye. No fringe, no side dishes, no compromises.

"At least get those two world wreckers out of your house," said Charlie.

"What are you talking about—"

"They're dangerous. And they wear that fact like it was a badge of honor."

"That's ridiculous."

"They're good looking bad asses who served time for murder as boys and will most likely end their lives bleeding out. No matter how good their intentions."

"That's a little extreme, isn't it?" said Guy.

Charlie turned. Guy had heard enough and was shouldering the doorway.

"I didn't mean for you and Dean to hear that."

"It wasn't murder," said Guy. "It was manslaughter."

"See what I mean," Charlie said to Gardner. "Here they are…outlaws walking out of the smoke and bearing finality," he said of the two youths. "*The Pirates of Pelham Parkway*. I read your fuckin' magazine story. Manslaughter…all right. I don't know how much good you think you're doing since you returned here, but not much in my opinion so far, if last night is an example. Am I wrong? I don't know! I hope so.

"You're both dangerous. You probably don't even realize that about yourselves. Quite how dangerous. Maybe it's just who you are. Maybe that's the attraction between the two of you. Maybe each one of you can't exist without the other. I don't know.

"Maybe you're part of this new generational empire of violence who fed on too many gangster movies and cowboy shows. The 'gunfighter nation' borne of bummed out wars and bad vibes. I don't know. Can you tell me? No answer?

"I wonder…maybe you are America, and none of us will get it until later, or until it's too late. I don't know. I had hoped that the modern gay man, as he attained selfhood and took to the battlefield, would be a better breed of man, but I guess I might have been wrong. I don't know. Am I?

"Maybe you are a better breed. Maybe you're what comes next, like Darwin says. The stripped down man ready to fire up and die doing some badassed stuff. I don't know.

"I look at you both. Standing there…the Don Quixote's of Fordham Road. You righteously frighten me because I know this will end in blood. *That*…I know. And it can't be otherwise, and do either of you know why?

"You don't have to look up to the sky or see into the future or as far as God to know. It's because you've come hunting for it. You might even be grateful for it. Be defined by it. After all, you've been weaned on America. Gardner can tell you that much, because part of him is almost as mad as you are, or you wouldn't be here."

• • •

When Dicky Palazzo opened his front door he was wearing a ginzo t-shirt, boxer shorts and filthy, untied sneakers. Guy and Dean shared a glance after checking out the sneakers.

"You're a real fashion statement there, Dicky, you know that," Guy said. Then he jerked a thumb toward Dean, who was standing just behind him. "This is Dean Teranova. He wrote the magazine story. You mighta heard Chris Carpetti talk about him."

"Sure. We kinda met. Come in. What are you doin' here?"

"Got something we need you to pass along."

"Sure."

If Palazzo was shaken or distraught at Guy and his boyfriend just showing up like that the morning after, he was totally cool about it. They followed Dicky into the family room where three guys were playing poker.

"How deep in are you?" said Guy.

"The four of us started last night after dinner."

One of the men at the table—Guy remembered that morose looking stare. He was the motherfucker who had tried to kidnap him over by the Kennedy Home all those years ago. The man didn't recognize Guy, though. Not until Palazzo said, "This is Guy Prince and Dean Teranova. These cats are gay. And if they don't mind being queer, we don't mind them being queer."

Guy grinned and saluted a hello and made like that pinched faced wop who'd tried to take him down was a total stranger.

Guy went off with Palazzo and Dean kicked back in a sloppy old lounge chair by the bar where he was out of the way but could see everything.

In the kitchen, Palazzo asked Guy, "What's up...?"

"You hear about last night?"

"No."

"Gardner Flynn was tagged by a couple of men wearing ski masks hunting for my father."

"No shit."

"It was ugly."

"You were there?"

"No. But Ross and O'Gorman were. I think they picked up something. I got the vibe when I got home, and they started hitting us up. Listen...I need you to pass along something...My old man would like to cut a deal."

"You talk to him?"

"No...but he got word to me and Dean."

"How?"

"Ma fuckin' Bell, genius...Go to Chris or Gino or both. Me and Dean don't want to get between the two."

"What does that mean?"

"It means what it says. Dean and I don't want to get between those two. You know how they can get."

Guy was doing his best to poison that place in Palazzo's head where he kept his crazy thoughts.

Dean could sort of see into the kitchen. The conversation from there didn't look like much. Dean was minding his own business and watching smoke rings he blew float across the room. Then, one of the men at the table said, "What's it like being gay?"

Dean knew what this was. The question hung there like a smoke ring. This was a sleight of hand stick it to him and let's see how he deals with it. "You must be shit-assed bored asking that."

"No...serious..."

"It's like being an astronaut," said Dean.

"What?"

"Astronaut. You know what a fuckin' astronaut is, right?

"Yeah."

"As an astronaut, you got to get used to having a rocket up your ass."

This turned it. The men took to laughing. Even the one who'd asked the question. Then one of the men said, "I take book for this fag priest who's got some wicked sense of humor. I tell him this and he will shit in his cossack, or whatever it is they call it."

Guy came into the room with Palazzo trailing behind him. Dicky looked a little glossed over with uncertainty.

"Let's rock and roll out of here," said Guy.

As the two youths walked out, Dean could hear one of the men say, "Fuckin' astronaut."

CHAPTER 60

"How'd it go in there?"

"I fucked with his head enough to fill a ten gallon hat. And hey...one of those characters at the table. Tall...pinched face...black shirt..."

"Yeah."

"He was the cretin who tried to nab me off the street back at the Kennedy Home."

"No shit."

"Yeah. But I made like I didn't recognize him."

They got into the Impala. Palazzo was still standing in the open doorway. Guy leaned out the window and waved. As he did he quietly said, "We're gonna take you down, scumbag."

Palazzo waved back, then closed the door.

Dean turned on the ignition. He went to shift gears, but Guy grabbed his hand and stopped him.

"Check this out," said Guy. "There's four men in that house. I say Palazzo brought two with him to Gardner's. The last one was left here to watch the fort in case someone came by, or something happened on Shrady. For cover. Now all four have an alibi for last night. That they were in the house playing poker."

"Very slick. You get this from your father?"

"I used to sit at the top of the stairs in the house on Independence and eavesdrop the old man and his people as they would plot out their business. I'd digest all the chitchat as they talked about their crimes and the maneuvers around their crimes to keep from being busted. It was like going to school, only—"

"Deadlier," said Dean.

"Yeah."

This was the country they were in now, where you're just a misstep from catastrophe.

"I'll tell you something else," said Guy. "Those boys are not done yet."

"What are you saying?"

"The four are still hanging out. This breed does not do 'hang out' together, unless there's action on the docket. Otherwise they'd split. Go chill in their own smarmy corners. I saw this with my father and the people he ran with. I can't justify what I'm feeling any better than I watched this play out as a kid."

"All right…what do we do with it?"

• • •

What they did was find a place where they could watch anyone who went in or out of Shrady.

The three men in the house with Palazzo were Ernest Cerussi, Kurt Greenwall, and that spidery creep, Robert Pavlica, who had tried to kidnap Guy. Cerussi and Greenwall had long records for assault, armed robbery, and distribution of narcotics. Pavlica had done time for attempted murder and child molestation.

Guy had been correct in his feelings. The four had remained together because the killing of C.C. Carpetti was set for that night.

The three worried that Guy Prince showing up the morning after the break in and assault at Gardner's might be a warning. That maybe Carpetti should be cued in about this. Palazzo wouldn't hear of it, because he knew Carpetti wouldn't hear of it. The break in and the beatings had proven to be a bust. The papers they'd taken from the house had also proven to be a bust and were already heaped in the trash and burned. Not going forward was out of the question.

That was their way of thinking.

• • •

They hovered down on Kingsbridge Terrace, on a flight of stairs to a shabby apartment building where they were hidden by the trees and could look across the street and onto Shrady. Dean came and went every now and then, hitting a pay phone to see if there were a message left from Rose Berghich.

"I wish you wouldn't keep doing that," said Guy.

"If I don't call Gardner's, how will I know—"

"He's not coming. He's not ever coming."

Dean saw Guy was getting tight.

"You're frustration doesn't make that so."

"You're not gonna go collegiate on me, are you?"

Dean let that pass.

"He got the word," said Guy. "My father put on his best lawbreaker hat and considered the options. Just like those shitbags up on Shrady. And he banked the odds."

"I'm unfuckin' swayed," said Dean.

"Are you trying to piss me off? Because if you are trying to piss me off, you're—"

"He'll show up," said Dean. "And I got that from a good source."

"What source?"

"Me."

"That's buying into slow death, Dante. I refuse to keep buying into slow death. I've lost enough principal *and* interest."

"He'll show up," said Dean, "because he's like you. And you're like him. And you'd show up."

"I wouldn't have abandoned my own son."

"You might," said Dean.

"What's that mean?" When Dean didn't answer, Guy grabbed him by the shirt and shook him hard. "…I'm talking to you."

Dean used an arm to sweep loose. "Maybe you haven't noticed, tough guy…but the streetlight has turned red."

They might have gotten into it. Dean knew Guy was suffering and it was a dirty wound because there was the son, fighting for a father he had not seen in a decade and now knew he wasn't dead. Here was the son playing the paladin, waiting on word would he see him again.

Then Guy got turned by something he saw.

"Check this out," said Guy.

Down Shrady came this aqua Chrysler 300. Cerussi was behind the wheel, with Pavlica in the shotgun seat, his arm dangling out the window, his hand tapping against the car door like he was in beat with the radio. They took off up Kingsbridge. Greenwall was a pretty short guy, and could have passed for a slight chick and could barely see over the dashboard.

"What do you think?" said Dean.

Guy pressed the knuckles of one hand against his lips. He looked back up Shrady.

"It's your call," said Dean.

CHAPTER 61

THEY FOLLOWED THE CHRYSLER PAST THE RESERVOIR and up through Van Cortlandt Park with the radio off and keeping it cool. It was evening when they turned onto Katonah Avenue.

Woodlawn Heights was a neighborhood of small apartments, two family homes and lackluster storefronts. At the corner of 239th Street was a delicatessen carved out of the front of a clapboard dwelling. Where 239th slanted up from Katonah—a girl stood smoking, and when the Chrysler showed up she flicked away the butt and jumped in the car.

She was a wild looking thing wearing a buckskin coat with fringe. And she was wild looking in that overamped, unhealthy kind of way.

"What's the matter with that picture?" said Guy.

It was the first he'd spoken since they'd started following the Chrysler.

The car then made its way down into Manhattan. And in no hurry. All the way to the Village. That's when things got strange.

They let the girl out, and she walked up the street and entered a bar called HERNANDA'S HIDEAWAY.

"Hey," said Guy, "that's one of C.C.'s bars."

A couple of minutes later the girl was being 'escorted' out by a bouncer and two bartendresses. And she was all bad attitude.

About ten blocks later, the Chrysler pulled over and she got out again and started up the block and entered a bar called THE TEA ROOM.

"I don't like this," said Guy.

"What?"

"This is also one of C.C.'s bars."

A few minutes later, the girl was hauled out and she was in a spectacular rant.

This scene repeated three more times. All were C.C.'s bars. Then the Chrysler cruised back to Woodlawn Heights where the girl got out at the same corner. Only now Pavlica was going with her. They walked up 239th Street and through a beat up gate behind that clapboard building, where she used her key to enter a ground floor apartment.

As the Chrysler pulled away, Dean said, "Did you notice anything?"

"What?" said Guy.

"She wasn't wearing the buckskin coat when she got out."

"I better call Gardner and let him know all about this," said Guy.

When Guy got back to the car after making the call he was rather pale.

"The paralegal who answered the phone said Gardner was at a deposition."

Dean saw Guy was suffering through the uncertainty.

"What else? What's the matter?"

"The Berghich woman wants us in New Rochelle...like now."

It was happening, and you didn't need to be struck by lightning to know.

"You think he's there," said Guy.

"Just keep your act together."

"He's there. Otherwise, why have us—"

"Fuck otherwise. Just keep your act together."

Dean grabbed the stick shift and was about to put the Chevy into gear when Guy got a hand on Dean's and stopped him.

"Wait...Take a beat. About when we were back at Shrady—"

"If we keep it honest with each other," said Dean, "we'll be all right."

"You sure?"

"The untold story is...I'm sure of you."

"The untold story, Dante, should include...I'm not so sure of me."

"Keep the self-inflicted wounds to a minimum and make the other guy pay."

CHAPTER 62

ROSE WAS SITTING ON THE FRONT STEPS of the house on Hanford, her arms draped around her pulled-up legs, a cigarette hanging from her mouth like a character out of a Cagney movie, a portrait of anxious intensity. A set of headlights swept into the circular driveway and flooded over her.

She stood as the car doors slammed. "Gentlemen," she said, after taking the cigarette from her mouth. She pointed at Guy, "Take a walk with me." To Dean she said, "You hang out. Go make yourself a drink. Watch the television."

"Is he here?" said Guy. He was looking from window to window, to the open doorway with its fountain and crucifix he so well remembered.

She didn't answer. She came over and took Guy by the arm.

"Is he here?" said Guy.

"You want an answer you don't like," she said, "or no answer?"

Dean watched from the doorway as they walked off in the direction of Isaac Young. When Dean went into the house he felt as if he were carrying the baggage of his and Guy's whole life with him. It was quiet in there and dimly lit with just a few candles. The place felt timeless in a way. As he peered into the shadows, he heard a voice say, "I read your magazine story."

His head snapped around. Across the long living room with its over coffered ceiling, Peter Prince stood in the doorway to the family room, where there was a pool table and bar.

He was smoking and partly in shadow. He was totally present and in full command of himself.

Dean could just feel that, even across the room. Yet he was not what the youth had expected. He was more the gentleman, maybe with some touch of the rough. But this was a man who came across as a corporate executive, a stockbroker maybe, or someone weaned in the bureaucratic hallways.

"The car keys," said Peter. "That was very clever on your part. Very observant of detail. And thinking things through."

Dean crossed the room slowly.

"You're not at all what I expected," said Dean.

Peter Prince laughed. He opened his leather coat. There was a pistol holster clipped to his belt. "Does this do it?" he said.

"I didn't mean it…that way."

"I know you didn't, son."

Dean put out a hand to shake.

"Well, well. And a gentleman. Want a drink?"

"Not now, sir."

Peter went into the den. There was a drink already on the bar waiting for his return. He took the drink and put out the cigarette, then went and sat on the edge of the pool table. Dean stood quietly in the doorway waiting.

"You come up with the idea about the car keys, then project that to me having a car tucked away at the Gray Mare inlet. You learn about River Avenue…you approach my son. And step-by-step, you end up here. The two of you have done more to track me down than the half dozen men they brought to find me and kill me. And that," said Peter Prince, "is a compliment."

"Yes, sir."

"You could have done very well for yourself in army intelligence, Mister Teranova."

"Never thought of it, sir."

"Can't blame you. You don't seem…the conforming type. Neither you, nor my son."

He took one of the pool balls and began to roll it across the table so it made a triangle before slowly coming back to him.

"How is my son?"

"Hurt…angry."

"Very clearly stated. Does he believe I abandoned him?"

"Did you?"

"That must be the writer in you."

"Did it come across as—"

"I would say, yes, I abandoned him. Depending how you define abandoned. And yet here I am all these years later. But for how long?"

He had not once looked at Dean all this while.

"I hear your father is a seasoned hustler," said Peter Prince.

"He's a conman…a scammer. Very low rent."

"I gather you and he aren't close."

"I've only seen him once since I got out."

"Be careful…he's going to come back into your life."

"What makes you say that?"

"Because, at some point, they will use him to take you down."

Peter Prince was looking at Dean now.

"They're closing in, you know."

What he'd said spooked Dean. It sounded so formidably sure. So utterly fated.

"You've been asking for it, of course, through your actions. Haven't you?"

"Yes, sir."

"Whatever prompted you and Guy to hunt me out?"

"You're a big part of both our lives. They even extended our incarcerations to try and get us to tell where you were…"

"Even the score…make it all come out right…and attain manhood along the way. Sound about right?"

"Yes, sir. I think so. All of the above."

"Dean…fathers can do two things. They can raise their sons up or they can take them down. Sometimes they do both in one lifetime."

Peter finished his drink in one long slow continuous swallow. When done, the flesh around his cheekbones tightened, the eyes narrowed. These were eyes that had seen things, done things. These were the eyes of a perpetrator of crimes.

"How do you think I handle this with Guy?'

"I don't know, sir. You're his father."

"You're his boyfriend."

"His friend."

"Even when he was a child I knew Guy was gay. I had many gay people in my life. C.C.… Gardner… in the war. My older brother, God rest his soul, was gay. Toughest bastard that ever breathed. Marie Carpetti could tell you stories. Guy doesn't know any of that. Guy was like my older brother. It sounds like he still is."

"Are you going to see him? Talk to him?"

CHAPTER 63

C.C. HAD BEEN MEETING WITH HER ACCOUNTANT in the Village. They combined dinner and a work session at his apartment on Hudson Street. Dicky Palazzo had gotten word of her whereabouts that night from Christopher Carpetti, whose people had been informed by a bartendress who worked for the younger Carpetti as an informant.

It was nearing midnight when C.C. said goodnight to her accountant. The accountant would later testify that C.C. had had a few glasses of wine and smoked a joint, and when she left, she was talking about opening a discotheque and was feeling utterly free and alive.

The murder of C.C. Carpetti—assassination—if you prefer—would be coined by the *Daily News* as the *Garden of Eden Murder.*

C.C. was parked on Christopher Street just off Hudson. She was a short ways from the corner where there was a wide alley between two apartments. It was, in fact, more than an alley, as it extended well back into the block between the buildings.

There was a patio partway down a few steps, and beyond the patio there were trees and a garden where residents came to hang out and catch a few rays during the good weather. On the walls of the buildings that framed the garden, artists had done their rendition of the Garden of Eden. Only in this Eden, Adam was with another Adam, and Eve with another Eve. The snake was still the snake.

C.C. was unlocking the car when she caught sight in the door window of a figure charging at her. She thought it was a woman in a buckskin coat, wielding a knife. That one moment kept her from being killed right there. The knife strafed the flesh along her neck but penetrated her shoulder.

She tried to escape into the alleyway, her purse fell to the sidewalk, the car keys were left dangling there in the door lock. She was reeling backwards, trying to fend off the slashing blade. She screamed out as the knife cut deep into her forearm and had to be violently pulled loose.

She was defenseless and tried to run, holding her bloody arm, making for a fire escape ladder, trying to scale it, the knife blade slashing down her back.

Falling under the weight of such brutality, stunned, her body in the throes of shock from loss of blood, this sinister harbinger of death now leaning over her, desperate, she gathered herself, to keep alive she rose up to attack her attacker.

Tearing at the woman's face, the knife blade cutting through her cheek, the blade grating her teeth. Crying out in agony and futility, she faced a distortion of shapes in a buckskin coat in the half light from the apartment windows above.

She got a hand on the woman's hair as she was falling, only it was not her hair. It was a wig. And it wasn't a woman she was fighting, but a man.

She staggered across the brick patio, leaving a blood trail for every year and month and day, tumbling down the brick steps, collapsing, then crawling, only to collapse again, fighting the death hunting her, this thing using her back as a sled, opening her flesh again and again until she finally gave in. At the edge of the garden grass she lay, trying to grab a breath, a horrid, gravelled sound coming from her failing lungs where nothing's left, just feelings getting smaller, getting further away, disappearing from the edges of her sight, until there was only those images of Eden painted on the apartment walls beyond the fingery length of branches floating on the dark night breeze. There one moment and then gone.

It was the blackness after that. The blackness one sees but never knows, can never speak of or recall, the blackness you will travel through forever, and that little matters.

Her killer was gone by then. Just another faceless stranger melting into the streets, to be picked up in a car about a block away that then silently slid into the Bleeker Street traffic.

C.C. Carpetti's cries were never answered.

She would lie there another half hour. She had completely bled out by then. When residents were later questioned, some claimed they thought it was a neighbor's television, or a fight between lovers, maybe even some whack job flipped out on acid. It wouldn't be the first time. This was the Village after all. Home to stoners and freaks, and a bastion of social aberration. All poor excuses for what was their act of simple cowardice.

CHAPTER 64

GUY WALKED WITH ROSE in the shadow of Isaac Young and its gray stone towers, along the wrought iron fencing. Its high black iron gates in the wash of a streetlamp is where she stopped.

She could get a good look at him there. They had spoken very little, really. She wanted to take it all in with the time she had.

"I went to this school as a girl. When all my dreams were before me."

"You and my father had a thing going."

"More than that."

He picked up the absolute tenderness in her voice.

"Sounds like you still have a thing going."

"I hope sometime you will know—how much there is between us."

"He didn't take you with him either."

"The history we share."

She took to just watching him.

"What?" he said.

"Would you mind if—"

She reached out. He saw she wanted to touch his face. It was, he thought, a strange request, but it seemed to mean so much to her.

She ran a smooth hand slowly down his face as if trying to capture something of him. She thanked him, then looked at her wristwatch.

"We can go back now."

Walking into the entry, past the fountain and that sculpted crucifix the size of a man hanging on that wall—the crucifix which had been so enormous once. Guy was that boy again on that first night, his whole life now weighted down on his shoulders.

Guy stood at the edge of the living room with his hands in his pockets, and there was Peter Prince with Dean at the arched entrance to the family room. Dean walked past Guy and joined Rose and the two disappeared into the quiet of the house.

Guy approached his father slowly and in silence through a river of candlelight and looked the man over like he was a member of some strange sect that he did not know. All emotions on the rise, all contradictions

228

sharpening, no past to cling to, no chance for perspective, not with so many lost years to cross is so short a space and time.

Peter Prince was older, the merry slickness and the smile and all that easy charm which came to him as easy as driving a car, wore now the shadow of years. But the way he stood and the way he stared had not changed one bit, and the youth felt a measure of amazement. Time does stand still in fits and spurts before rushing on.

The father gestured in the son's direction.

"You know what I thought when I saw you walking through that door. It was my brother…you're Uncle Chet. Too bad he died before you got a chance to know him. Did I ever tell you how he got his name…Chet?"

"No," said Guy. He was only a few feet from his father now and could view him better in the lamplight of the family room.

"It was a nickname from the war. His favorite record back then was *Chattanooga Choo-Choo* by the Modernaires. You probably never heard of it."

"No," said Guy.

"It was a big hit…He played the record all the time. Driving me and all his friends nuts. So we started calling him Chattanooga…then just Chet."

"What's this got to do with me…With us…Why we're here?"

Peter went to the bar, reached for another cocktail he'd made. There was a lit cigarette in an ashtray that he puffed on. He was, thought Guy, taking his sweet fuckin' time.

"That," said Peter Prince, "is exactly how Chet would have reacted. And it didn't always serve him well."

"I get it," said Guy.

"Do you? Chet was the toughest man I ever knew. Way tougher than me. But he came looking for a fight sometimes before it was even necessary. Like you, walking across that room."

"What a pitch," said Guy. "You're working me. This little riff about your brother is a bank shot." He made a flashy move, sweeping an arm toward the pool table.

"Did you walk in here and expect I would apologize," said Peter. "That I'd be overcome with remorse. That I'd ask, plead, beg forgiveness for abandoning you. Well…I won't insult your intelligence. And I sure won't demean mine.

"And I don't need a bank shot," said Peter, "to make a point. I made a choice years ago not to kill that girl and her baby. I did it because I had a moment when I really saw myself. When I was forced to review my personal bloodstained history.

"And then I saw that if I didn't kill her, I could extort Gino with regards to his sister and Gardner. And I knew leaving you with Gardner was best.

"I was known for being able to make cold-blooded decisions. Decisions are filled with risk, and with risk comes repercussions that you cannot foresee. That poor kid dying in a nothin' fight. The task force trying to exploit your incarceration.

"And unless I'm totally fuckin' blind, one can see you and Dean survived it. One might even say, you show signs of thriving. Who knows, without all this going down you two might have grown up to be a pair of self-serving douche bags the world is so fond of."

Peter reached for his cigarette. "I'm talked out," he said. "It's your turn."

CHAPTER 65

IT DIDN'T SURPRISE PETER THAT HIS SON WALKED OUT. Just turned and flat out walked. Like he was tearing up his birth certificate or something. "That kid is a tough one," is what Peter told Rose when they were alone.

"He's not a kid," said Rose.

Dean caught up with Guy out in the driveway.

"I guess you heard," said Guy.

"I heard."

Guy put out a hand. "Let's blow out of here."

Guy was gunning it up Centre Avenue. Not exactly the street for it. They shot past 145—the old mansion turned into nothing apartments where the girl lived. Past Blessed Sacrament where her kid went to school. Past Schrafft's where she worked. They had been that close to her and with no idea.

"What did the two of you talk about?" said Guy.

"Pretty much everything."

"No shit."

"Right down to Palazzo...the whole thing...Even blowing up his XKE."

"How'd my old man take that?"

"He gave me a look that weighed about five thousand pounds."

"I know that look. I carried it around with me for years."

They got to Main Street. It was the usual dragway of an era on the way out. A Loews Theater, an RKO, a couple of record stores, a Woolworth and Grants...and a pub.

"There," said Guy, pointing to Chumley's Pub.

"It was an offshoot of Chumley's in Manhattan. Faux cool, faux class. Favored the Iona College crowd and the College of New Rochelle. Too civil really for a couple of characters with bad thoughts on their agenda.

"He's not gonna do the immunity thing," said Dean.

They were hunched up at the bar like conspirators.

"He tell you that?"

"It's not him. It's the girl. She's afraid. And besides, she doesn't want it out there the kid's father is some mafia scum who raped her. Then there's the shit the mother would have to endure…if they don't kill her. It's like they did in the Luizzi murder. You read about that? They called the victim a whore, a druggie. Your father says Carpetti will have guys coming out of the woodwork that say they humped her."

"He talked to her?"

"He said he did."

"What'd he come for? When you get right down to it?"

There was too much Johnny Mathis on the jukebox. Too much Dean Martin, and Barbra Streisand singing *Second Hand Rose*. Music you can drift into a coma by.

Guy's father was the question that couldn't be answered, and the whole thing left the son charged with a live or die feeling. He needed to move on from this kiss-ass bar.

When he got tired of repeating his father's riff, he called the bartender over—"Do me a favor man, give us the names of the most rowdy bars you got in this rest home of a town.

"You see…we're from the Spofford Press doing a review of bars." He asked Dean to flash his tat.

"Spofford," said the bartender, "isn't that a jail or something?"

They checked the bars off that had been written down on a napkin as they got blasted at one after another…*THE CHURCH KEY…THE BEECHMONT…BUZZY AND DICKS…THE BARGE.*

None of it was doing any good. Guy kept wanting to know why his old man had come there. Why do that whole riff?

They had drunk all the way to The Barge which was on the dock at the entrance to Hudson Park, and Guy sat at the bar like some brooding statue.

"Nothing like being a portrait of drunk contemplation," said Dean. "It's a real, fuckin' mood booster."

"The two people I loved most in the world," said Guy. "My father and you. One I loved who left…and the other I can't get to love the way I'd hoped."

"If you think I'm gonna sit here and let you nosedive into melancholy like some bad movie, you are out of your mind."

Guy would have taken action, he was just too loaded. But the stare—

"Look at that stare," said Dean. "That's your father, man. You stare like him, you look like him, you walk like him, talk like him, you are fuckin' him. It's some kind of genetic voodoo. Now…to answer all your questions, all you have to do is start thinkin' like him."

Talk about a statement that went straight down all those neural pathways. Guy started wagging a finger at Dean. Next thing, he got up and literally hoisted the bar stool on his shoulder and started to walk out with it. From across the bar, someone yelled, "Where the fuck are going with that barstool?"

The Barge was just rowdy enough that no one tried to stop someone walking out with a barstool. If something crazed was gonna happen, this crowd was for it.

Guy got outside and set the barstool down on the edge of the dock. He sat and got himself nice and comfortable, crossed one leg over the other, lit a cigarette, and took to staring out toward the Sound.

That was it. He looked totally out of place and quietly nuts. Of course, if you stood back far enough, he *was* a picture of drunken contemplation.

Dean came outside to watch. So did a couple of patrons. Dean heard one laughing drunk say, "There's something wrong with that mother fucker."

After a while the patrons went back into the bar totally bored. Every now and then one of them would glance out a window like Guy was something growing in a petri dish. After about two cigarettes worth of contemplation, Guy took to staring into the water, at his own reflection there in the black murk of the harbor.

"Let's talk," he said to himself quietly. "Why did he come back at all? Laying on you that cold blooded riff is no answer. Not into immunity or being a state witness…Why bother to come out of the closet…so to speak.

"But that's not the real question…Why you are still here in Dick Van Dyke country instead of back in the Bronx? Why didn't you blow? That is the real question."

He stared into the watery grave face that was his father, once upon a time, staring back. "Unfinished business…that's why he's here. And why you're here. You have unfinished business. He has unfinished business. He's yours…you're his.

"And he didn't need to apologize. His being there was the apology. An apology that put him at risk. Just like mine would be."

He looked down the dock to where Dean stood nursing a beer and waiting.

"Unfinished business," said Guy.

"What?"

Guy stood and wobbled his way toward Dean. "Unfinished business. Just like his own unfinished bus—"

He didn't even get the rest out of his mouth before he shambled himself right off the dock and into the water.

Dean watched him in the water, flailing away. A couple of people in the bar came rushing out. One of them said to Dean, "I don't think your friend can swim!"

"He's not my friend," said Dean. "I don't even know him."

CHAPTER 66

JUST A FEW DOORS DOWN FROM THE ALLEYWAY where C.C. Carpetti was murdered was the Theatre de Lys. Playing that night was *Sergeant Musgrave's Dance*. A drama that symbolically became more fitting and pertinent to the murder as the times and facts changed. At the show that night was an AP reporter who came upon the sickened and panic stricken crowd at the entrance to the alleyway just minutes before the police arrived.

By then, one of the tenants, whose apartment overlooked the alley, had taken a photograph from a fire escape with his flash of the butchered girl with the mural of a gay Eden behind her. This photograph would make the cover of the *Daily News* morning edition. As many of you New Yorkers must remember, this became one of the newspaper's most despicable and popular images and fanned the flames of the public's conflict concerning gays.

Very quickly the victim was identified. Events and scenes steamrolled after that. Phone calls went out like a contagion of madness. At least two witnesses claimed they saw a suspicious looking woman with dark hair and a buckskin coat hurrying toward Hudson.

Through a source, the AP reporter got Missus Carpetti's direct phone number out at College Point. Complaints had already been reported that a former employee of C.C. Carpetti, by the name of Chella Martinez, had been making the rounds of lesbian bars Carpetti owned, with talk she was a victim of sexual harassment and violent threats.

A squad car made its way to the Martinez home address over on Katonah. The apartment door fronted a filthy garbaged yard. No one answered the doorbell but one of the officers peered into an unwashed window to see the shadowy image of a woman sprawled out in a chair.

Breaking in, they discovered what looked like the murder weapon, a bloodstained buckskin coat, and the body of Chella Martinez. Death likely from a lethal overdose of heroin, as the needle was still in her arm. The officers also noted the dead woman had bruises on her face and shoulders, and assumed these were made during Carpetti's death struggle.

Gardner was working late, trying to keep at bay the loneliness of Charlie Merwin walking out of his life, when his private line rang. He thought it might be Charlie, and he got this huge emotional boost, only to hear a man he did not know identify himself as an AP reporter…"Mister Flynn…C.C. Carpetti was murdered tonight in the Village. It is being described as a 'lesbian slaying.' Do you have any comment?"

When Gardner spoke, it was with the voice of a stranger in a vacant body. "If true…this is a terrible family tragedy…and a deeply personal tragedy…C.C. was a fine young woman and loving daughter…And, may I add, the best of friends."

While he spoke on the one phone, he was dialing another. Missus Ceraso spent most of her nights now at the Carpetti house. She had a private suite at the end of the hall and Gardner thought, hoped really, he could forewarn her to unhook the phones before some reporter got through. He was too late by minutes.

A distraught and exhausted Missus Ceraso explained how she had been awakened by screams. She had hurried as best she could to Missus Carpetti's suite to find the older woman collapsed on the floor by the bed, the phone off the hook beside her.

She was rocking back and forth, a hobbled figure broken with sorrow. "They've killed my baby," she said. "…They've killed my baby…They've slain her with a knife…in an alley…in an alley for God's sake."

She held her wrinkled and birdlike hands to her face. Missus Ceraso eased down beside her, and the one woman took hold of the other. Missus Ceraso herself was now awash in agony over C.C.'s death. An agony she had not experienced since her own son was killed by a car bomb.

They rocked together on the floor, and Missus Ceraso thought her friend, so dear to her, would die of a heart attack or stroke from the way she wailed away with pain.

"They've killed my baby…They've killed her. They've taken the pride of my life from me."

By the time Gardner arrived at College Point, the street around the two homes had been cordoned off. The block was an infestation of newspeople. Missus Carpetti refused any form of sedation to calm her. Her sense of total despair at her daughter being butchered was now being matched by the part of her that was a revenge seeking missile.

She faced the endless questioning with Gardner at her side. Ross and O'Gorman were there to observe and take notes. The strength the woman showed under the circumstances would make her a most terrifying adversary.

Later, when all were gone but one lone patrol car guarding the street, the family gathered in the living room to grieve together. The grandchildren, Christopher's wife, Gino and his wife, Christopher had been notified in Albany where he was on a business trip and was already now returning home. Gardner was there and Missus Ceraso.

The old woman said not a word about what she was truly feeling, what she sensed, but prayed was not so. It was Missus Ceraso, who when alone with Gardner, whispered, "She knows it was Gino or Christopher."

"Did she say that to you?"

"She doesn't need to say it with words, she is saying it with her eyes."

CHAPTER 67

GUY HAD TO BE FISHED OUT OF THE SOUND. He stripped down and put on the Impala's heat full blast. He closed the windows and placed his clothes over the vents to dry them. The inside of that car was a friggin' sauna. They were down in Hudson Park, and Dean got out and retrieved his jean coat from the trunk and went and crashed on the beach.

Lots of reveling youths, drunk and speeding out of the parking lot blowing car horns and leaving rubber, killed any chance of sleep.

Laying there, Dean was hoping he and Guy could make things right. He'd remember this, 'cause right about that time, C.C. Carpetti was being wheeled into the morgue.

• • •

In the morning they drove to the house on Hanford unannounced and knocked on the door. Rose answered. "He's been expecting you," she said.

They entered, all polite and unassuming.

"You haven't read the newspapers, have you?"

There was an ominous tone to her voice.

"He's in the breakfast room," she said. "With news.

A somber looking Peter Prince was sitting at the table having coffee, the newspaper before him, when the two youths silently entered. They saw right away something wasn't right. He might even have actually been crying, his eyes were red that way.

"I've been sitting here for hours thinking about us all…and how deeply connected the crucial events in your life are…even before they happen. As if they were an obvious progression." He glanced at Rose leaning against the doorjamb, then at the two boys. "It can almost make you discount chance, and good fortune. But it shouldn't."

He slid a copy of the *Daily News* across the table.

The youths squeezed in next to each other. The cover of the paper was the photo of C.C. on the brick patio at the edge of the garden with its revisionist mural of Eden. She'd died with her eyes open. The headlines read:…

UNDERWORLD DAUGHTER SLAIN…MURDERESS COMMITS SUICIDE…and the most brazen of all…SOME SAY IT WAS LOVE…

The facts, as written, of course, did not match the details that Dean had confided to Peter Prince when they were alone that first time.

"They have no idea," said Dean, looking up from the newspaper.

"Who ordered the killing?" said Guy. "It's the father or the son. Palazzo on his own…No chance."

"I knew that girl since she was twelve years old," said Peter, his voice hushed and half stunned. He remembered—

She had been a Girl Scout, all gangly and youthful. Her troop was having what they called a backyard campout. Tents were set up behind Missus Carpetti's house down to the water. The girls played games, ate on the lawn, were awarded badges for merit. At night Missus Carpetti led the troop on a midnight hike around the neighborhood.

The girls had taken extension cords and run them from the den down to an open area between the tents where they'd set up a record player and speakers. They did their own version of *American Bandstand* and they danced together within a ring of lanterns.

Peter was there with Missus Carpetti. It was not long after Peter's older brother had died in the employ of the woman, and she didn't want Peter to suffer his grief alone.

He was in the den with her playing Briscola when here came C.C., out of breath. "We need more records, Mama."

Before she started off to her room to get the records, she said to Peter, "I'll bet you think this is all just silly girl stuff."

She started off again to her room but stopped. "Oh…Mister Prince. I'm sorry about your brother."

All those years later Peter sat staring at the sordid headlines thinking how the old woman must be suffering at this moment. His eyes clouded, his cheeks marbled. He began to cry, "I've come back to this—," he said.

The boys did not know what, if anything, to do. Rose could have come forward to comfort Peter, but she knew it must be Guy who seized the moment.

"Guy," she whispered.

Just saying his name made him understand. He reached out and took his father's arm.

"I'm here, Pop. And there's no bad blood between us."

Peter nodded, and wiping at his eyes, he stood. "Both of you. Come with me."

The two youths followed him out back and across the yard to the garage where they entered through a side door. Peter turned on the light, and there was the Mercury that Dean had fired at.

CHAPTER 68

"Look familiar?"

"How long have you been here?" said Guy.

"It's not important. Here's what is…We're in a home brewed range war. Father…son. It doesn't matter who started this. Maybe both. The old lady is gonna scorch the earth to find out who killed her baby. Then she's going to torch the guilty."

"Did we put them over the edge pressing Palazzo like we did?" said Guy.

"This has been a decade coming, and it is gonna blow out of control. Me and the girl were the reason they were kept in check. Too late now. Missus Carpetti is getting old. She's not in good health. Gino and the kid both have to know the old lady was gonna leave the power of her estate to C.C. This drama is as old as the Bible and the evilest of dreams.

"What you said you saw, is what is…Greenwall, Cerussi, Pavlica and Palazzo. Palazzo gets the order from on high and relays it to his players. He's the firewall.

"And he won't give up the Carpettis. Even if they get to him. He'll have more moves than a rat at midnight. He'll claim the other three went off on their own to get in good with the son…or the father. The Carpettis will have witnesses saying he was swimming the English Channel when the killing went down."

"You think it's the son?" said Guy.

"I think he's most likely to succeed at fucking up a wet dream. But that doesn't mean the father didn't have a hint of it and just let it happen."

"What if they corner Palazzo and offer him immunity?" said Dean.

"He'll be just a different version of me and he doesn't want to be a different version of me. And I don't blame him. I had the advantage of the old lady in my corner. She wanted peace. She's got people on the inside and everyone connected to last night is wearing a death sentence. And don't think Missus Carpetti doesn't suspect her own might be plotting her demise."

"You think?" said Guy.

"One generation is always looking to put the other in the ground. It's natural as taking a breath." Peter grinned at his son. "Even you and me."

"What about us?" said Dean.

"You mean, what do you two do now?"

"Yeah."

"That's where I've been steering this conversation."

• • •

There were news trucks outside the Gardner Flynn house on Bronxwood, and a police officer stood guard on the porch by the front door. There were unmarked cars parked in the driveway. The youths recognized one of them belonging to Ross—or O'Gorman. They parked the Chevy down on Mace, so they could sneak up the outside stairwell to Dean's apartment without being spotted.

They could hear a conversation coming up through the floorboards. They made sure to walk quietly, open doors even more cautiously. They could hear a shaken Gardner struggling to answer basic issue questions in the wake of this shocking murder.

They hung back on the second floor hallway.

"Shall we go down?" Dean whispered.

"Give it a minute, Dante."

Guy got out a cigarette and lit it. The hallway was dark and Dean cupped his hands around the match so not even a spec of light might get noticed.

"I was thinking back to the day we shot those four rats then went over to the pond, if your retard enough to call that sewer water a pond. And took over the raft—"

Dean started riffing the song…*Baby, The Rain Must Fall.*

"Yeah," said Guy. "I'll zip it. It was just that I got thinking…"

"You should have kept your mouth shut and played it cool and not got yourself incarcerated."

"But look what I'd have missed."

They were both thinking about what Guy's father had told them. Warning them of the consequences if they went forward. They passed the cigarette between them.

"Well," said Dean, "there's no time like the present to get on with lying."

Dean started for the stairs.

"Hey, Dante…you know I love you, right. That I'll be there to the end."

"Yeah…I know."

CHAPTER 69

THERE WERE FOUR MEN IN THE OFFICE WITH GARDNER. Two investigators, Ross and O'Gorman. It was quite a surprise when the two youths came sauntering in.

"Well," said O'Gorman, "we've been wondering about you."

"That's what happens when we're not around," said Guy. "It sends shockwaves through the system."

Gardner got up. Shaken, he said, "I've been trying to find you both. You know, right?"

"Yeah," said Dean. "We know."

Guy went around the desk and hugged Gardner…"We're here now, my man," he said quietly into Gardner's ear.

"Where have you two been?" said O'Gorman.

"Upstairs," said Dean.

"You know what he was asking," said Ross.

Dean went and sat in that chair in the corner, where he could be alone. "New Rochelle," he said.

"And what's in New Rochelle?" said Ross.

"Tell him," said Dean.

"Bars, bars and more bars," said Guy.

"You can prove that," said O'Gorman.

"Easy," said Dean.

"We started at a place called Chumleys Pub," said Guy. "It's your kind of place, Ross. Drippy music. It's the Glen Island Casino…1950."

Dean had taken a folded-up bar napkin from his shirt pocket. Opened it. Asked one of the investigators to pass it to O'Gorman.

"We had the bartender give us a list of joints," said Guy. "We were looking for bars that were a little more—"

"Rowdy," said Dean.

"Yeah. We like it rowdy," said Guy. Then he said to Dean, "You know what he's thinking."

"I know what you're thinking," said Dean. "So I know what he's thinking."

"What am I thinking?" said Ross.

"You're thinking we're liars," said Guy. "That we know people you don't. Hear things you don't. See things you don't. Learn things you don't. Pick up rumors you don't. Because my father was a criminal and part of all that." To Dean he then said, "Is that about right?"

"I think you summarized it pretty well."

"You have no sense of it, do you?" said Ross.

"You'd be shocked what we have a sense of," said Dean.

"Who's Rose?" said O'Gorman. He was eyeing Guy.

This caught Guy off guard. It took him a moment to put on the act. "Rose?" he said. He looked to Dean.

"No idea."

"The paralegal working here yesterday said you called twice trying to reach Mister Flynn. That it was important. If you were getting drunk, why did you need to reach him?" said Ross.

"At the same time the paralegal said you had gotten a couple of calls from a female named 'Rose.'" said O'Gorman.

"Don't know a Rose...But...Hey," Guy said to Dean, "The chick with the camera from NYU."

"Her name's Elise."

"We get loaded, we give out this number to a lot of people," said Guy.

"We give this number out to a lot of people loaded or not," said Dean.

"The office number?" said O'Gorman. "Why not your own?"

"This is like having our own private answering service," said Guy.

"Very uptown," said Dean.

"The calls you made to this office," said Ross, "and the ones that came in from this 'Rose' were all noted and time stamped by the paralegal. And it just so happens, they fit within the time frame of when Miss Martinez was going from bar to bar looking for Miss Carpetti, and when Miss Carpetti was finally murdered."

"I fell into the Sound last night," said Guy. "I was so drunk. The bar was on the water. On the dock. What was the fuckin' name?"

"The Barge," said Dean.

"The Barge...how obvious," said Guy. "Check it out. We crashed at the park right next to the bar. Hudson Park, they called it."

"Where'd you make the calls from?" said Ross.

Guy looked to Dean.

"This isn't a tough question," said O'Gorman.

"These fags think they're the United Nations," said Ross. "And it's all on the Q.T."

"Don't go there," said O'Gorman.

"We are there."

"Guy didn't make the calls," said Dean. "I did."

"But you don't remember where," said Ross. "You stopped at super-markets, a liquor store, a gas station, but it's all a fuckin' blur. That about it?"

"That's about it," Dean said.

• • •

When the investigators left the house, and the officer on the porch drove away, and it was only O'Gorman and Ross who remained, the conversation took a decided and secretive turn.

"Do you think this will get the word leaked out?" said Gardner.

Ross was watching out the window. The news people were hounding the investigators as they attempted to get in their car. 'Beautiful,' he thought.

"Word will leak out that we don't believe these two," said Ross. "And that they might well have information regarding the murder. I can practically guarantee it."

"And we know where to drop the word in the department," said O'Gorman. "There's people there we have hard suspicions inform Carpetti."

"When we have him in our sights, your father will come forward?" said O'Gorman.

"He'll come forward," said Guy. "But not the girl. She's too frightened. The wrath of the path, you know what I'm saying."

"It isn't perfect," said O'Gorman. "Nor what we even prefer. But it's what it is."

"You understand...now that the daughter is dead," said Ross. "We got to keep it like there's bad blood between us."

"You mean there isn't?" said Guy.

"Greenwall...Cerussi...Pavlica...and Palazzo," said O'Gorman. "These are the four."

"Those are who we saw at the house," said Dean.

"There can be no leaks on this," said O'Gorman. "No fuckups. And there's something else…At some point we're gonna give Gino Carpetti a hard time. Shame him publicly. I say it 'cause you'll be out there, and who knows how he'll strike back. Or to who."

"That's something to look forward to," said Guy.

"Anything else?" said Gardner.

"Yeah," said Ross, and he aimed what he had to say at Guy and Dean. "For a couple of screamers, you're not short of guts. I give you that much."

"Well," said Guy, "coming from you, that's almost the Congressional Medal of Honor."

CHAPTER 70

MISSUS CERASO HAD A LITTLE HOUSE IN WHITESTONE on Fifth Avenue and 149th place. She had lived in that house with her late husband, had raised her departed son there. It was home to her memories and youth. She spent little time there now. She would go there every day or two to pick up the mail, make sure everything was safe and in working order. When the phone rang she assumed, as always, it was Missus Carpetti, needing or reminding her of something.

"Hello?"

"Is this Dear Missus Ceraso…who has kept the Carpetti world running all these years?"

"Yes…Who—"

"This is a friend from the old days…And a loyal subject."

The voice. It felt unmistakable. A hand went to her chest clutching the hope it was who she suspected. "Peter?"

The meeting was arranged. The two women waited at the Whitestone house until it got dark. They kept the shades drawn, the house dimly lit. They hardly talked, they were so swept up with anticipation. Missus Ceraso had left the back door unlocked, and when it opened, the two women were almost like schoolgirls as a shadowy figure stepped into the doorway.

There he was, a graying reminder of years past, of joys and times that were and were no more. He was a looming reality that gave them hope.

"Ladies," he said, "you're looking game as ever."

They were overcome with emotion. He knelt before the old woman as if she was a queen and so she did not have to stand. He rested his head in her lap, and she stroked his hair. And he spoke to them with utter fondness. Missus Ceraso kept a statue of the Virgin Mary on the mantel, and she blessed herself and thanked the Holy Mother for sending him to them in their hour of need.

Missus Ceraso wept openly.

"Did you see what they did to my baby?" said Missus Carpetti.

"I've seen."

"They degraded her in the newspapers. They degraded her for being what God made her, leaving out how good she was. You will help me find out who did this."

"I believe I know who physically committed the act."

"Who gave the order? Gino…Christopher?"

"That I don't know…But I will."

"Are the boy's all right? Guy and that—"

"Teranova," said Missus Ceraso. "Dean, I believe."

"They'll be at the church for services," said Peter.

"Good…good."

"Gino or Christopher," said Missus Ceraso. "it doesn't matter. We know what their intentions are."

"She's become my Cardinal and chief advisor," Missus Carpetti told Peter.

· · ·

Bickford's was a chain of cafeterias throughout the city that had a long history, and not just for its modest fare and frenetic service, but as a social and cultural landmark. The poet Allen Ginsburg had written about Bickford's in his famous poem '*Howl*.' And Walker Evans, the noted photojournalist made Bickford's part of his vast mural on American Life. Later Woody Allen, Andy Warhol, and William Styron would become part of Bickford's continuing legacy.

This one morning would add to that history, but in a much more infamous way, as the four men involved in the murder of C.C. Carpetti would meet at the cafeteria on Fordham Road.

Dicky Palazzo was the first to arrive, and he was not happy about being there at all. Ever since Greenwall had called him the night before and demanded under threat they meet, a vile course of uncertainty wreaked havoc on Palazzo's whole system.

Cerussi and Pavlica arrived together. It was still the midst of the midday rush. They were all there except Greenwall, and Greenwall had demanded they meet and had set the time. The men drank coffee and waited through the world of clattering plates and buzzy chatter, waitresses scurrying past with carafes of coffee.

249

Cerussi was amped up, worse than Palazzo, though Palazzo always kept his anxiety on the inside. Pavlica could not give a shit.

"He probably got busted for some half ass action," said Pavlica, "and he needs us to cover for him. And he's gonna plead or press us."

"The way he sounded on the phone. Not right. It freaked me," said Cerussi.

"He's a pansy," said Pavlica. "Certifiable."

"He's not queer."

"He's worse than queer. He's a fuckin' pansy. You made a mistake bringing him in on this," Pavlica told Palazzo.

"You're fuckin' brilliance is earth shattering," said Palazzo. "How have I ever lived without it."

"You're getting an answer to that question right now, and it doesn't look too good."

Palazzo glanced at his watch.

"You don't need to check your watch to know he's late," said Cerussi. "He's fuckin' late. And he's getting later by the minute. And you don't need a watch to know that."

"If that dickless suckshit doesn't show in ten minutes, I'm outta here," said Pavlica.

The minutes passed and as Pavlica went to leave, Palazzo warned him, "You want to end up lining a suitcase…I—You—We…are waiting."

"Wait…all right," said Pavlica, crossing his arms. "I'll just kick back and watch you face how bad you fucked up."

They did another anxious ten minutes, when over a loudspeaker they hear, "If there is a Mister Richard Palazzo here, please come to the Manager's Office."

Pavlica made this dark, I told you so laugh.

Palazzo flung down his napkin.

The Manager's Office was by the entry to the kitchen. Palazzo peeked in the open door.

"You the manager?" said Palazzo.

It was loud and hot and busy in the hallway. And an exasperated, over-worked, thick bodied gent with food stained shirt cuffs looked up from an endless stack of paperwork.

"You Mister Palazzo?"

He nodded.

"You have some ID to that effect?"

Palazzo reached for his wallet. The manager held up a sealed envelope.

"What is that?" said Palazzo.

"One of the girls said a man handed it to her. Said he found it on the floor."

• • •

Palazzo returned to the table.

"Well," said Cerussi.

Palazzo held up the envelope so they could see his name on it. "The manager said someone found it on the floor and passed it to a waitress."

"And my mother," said Pavlica, "when she wasn't busy in the kitchen, invented the atom bomb."

"You gonna open it?" said Cerussi.

Palazzo was thinking it out, tapping the envelope against the palm of one hand.

"Open it," said Cerussi.

"Not here," said Pavlica. "This says wrong."

So they hovered together in Palazzo's car. Cerussi in the back, leaning over the seat.

"You want to quit breathing down my shirt," Pavlica warned him.

When Palazzo tore the envelope open, it contained a folded sheet of paper. And what did he find when he unfolded it—Greenwall's driver's license.

And it was stained front and back with what had to be dried blood.

"We're dead men," said Cerussi.

"Speak for yourself," said Pavlica.

"Go home," said Palazzo. "Get on with your business. I'll deal with this."

"Hopefully better than Greenwall dealt with it," said Pavlica.

"That's it?" said Cerussi. "What else was there?"

Later that day Palazzo sat in his kitchen smoking a joint, with a semi-automatic pistol on standby. He was trying to get his head around all this, when the phone rang.

"Yeah," he said.

Music was playing. The Beatles *Nowhere Man*.

Palazzo hung up. About an hour later, the phone rang. He picked up the receiver but didn't say a word. There was the music again.

"I know it's you," said Palazzo.

CHAPTER 71

SAINT RAYMOND NONNATUS was the patron saint of pregnant women, children, and midwives. The beautiful gothic church, rectory and school in his name took up most of the block on East Tremont and Castle Hill in the Parkchester section of the Bronx.

It was where C.C. Carpetti had attended school, where she was baptized, received her first Holy Communion and was confirmed. It would be where the funeral service would serve to celebrate her life before she was laid to rest in the Carpetti Mausoleum in the old section of Saint Raymond's Cemetery.

The morning of the funeral was hard for everyone. Gardner had left the night before to stay at Missus Carpetti's to help with the preparations.

Dean waited for Guy out by the car. He wore a tie and jacket. Guy, on the other hand, favored black motorcycle boots and a white embroidered collarless shirt he had looted in Mexico. He had even tied a rainbow colored bandana around his head. Each got a look at the other.

"Ain't we a pair?" said Guy.

Neither had had much chance to sleep the last two nights. Dean drove to the church, they smoked. The last few nights hung in the air like a mortal presence. Guy tried to keep things up moving around the radio dial.

"My mother," said Dean suddenly out of nowhere, "used to tell me God is always working in your life. Even when you least expect it. She told Gardner that the first time they met. I wrote it in the note I left for Rose to get her to call."

Guy shut off the radio.

"But after the other night, you have your doubts," said Guy. "Is that about the drift of it, Dante?"

"That's about the drift of it."

Guy sat back and put one foot up against the dashboard. He was watching the Bronx roll by. "That's what I love about you, man. You don't hide behind theories or excuses, don't do that pretense thing. You're willful and honest, and you make a fight of it. Dante...It's doing in the bastards or the deep blue sea."

253

Dean nodded, but Guy saw he was conflicted. This cat was at war with his own sense of decency and right. How the world is supposed to work, not how it seriously worked.

"Sisyphus pushing the rock up that hill ain't got nothing on you," said Guy.

"And you should take that tie off," Guy added. "Open your shirt button, pull the collar up on your coat. Try to catch a little of that Steve McQueen vibe. After all, it's C.C.'s funeral we're going to, not a fuckin' job interview."

• • •

They were heading up Tremont about a block from the church when Guy got good and unrelaxed suddenly, his foot dropping down from the dashboard as he leaned forward and said, "Holy shit!"

They'd expected a few news trucks, a skeleton of photographers and reporters. They'd expected some members of the gay community, and those with anti-homosexual sentiments. But this was social upheaval meets Ringling Brothers Circus.

The streets were overrun with people. Cars were not only parked every foot of the way down Castle Hill, they were double parked. If you needed to get down Castle Hill, forget it. If you needed to get through on Tremont, good luck. There had been a few officers assigned to the service, but they were overwhelmed just trying to keep Tremont from turning into a parking lot.

Dean dumped the car in a lot three blocks away.

It was a growing mob scene through which they made their way. There were throngs of gay people. The suit and tie crowd, the college types, cool hipsters, hippies, chicks with sweatshirts announcing their sexuality, ladies dressed uptown, gays in drag, some done up like movie stars. There were endless placards and pamphleteers.

And for every one of them, there was a disagreer, a hater, an anti-gay placard and pamphleteer. Shouts for social change were met with threats. Dirty jokes confronted righteous indignation.

There was a burning electricity on these streets. It was a warm, clear, bright day and in the sky the clouds looked like they had been simonized just for the service.

Those few blocks were giving off a lifeforce all their own. Some could call it politically magnificent and socially mind blowing. Others would say it was tawdry and degenerated. But it was alive and true to the times. It was the times and the reality that came with it, a reality that was burning just beneath the surface of all existence.

And if you did not come to that moment and see and understand it existed, you will live forever in mid-sentence. And that reality cannot be displaced, driven out, or be done with, because a piece of it exists in us all. It was and would be another chapter in the history of the Bronx. And the Bronx of that time was on the cutting edge of America. For better and for worse.

There were security guards at the entry gates. Carpetti people. The take no shit brigade. Family and friends had to show passes to get them seated in the front half of the basilica, which had been cordoned off for them.

It was chaos around the gate all right. Get rid of photographers, haters, funeral freaks, gossip meisters. There was a character passing out black armbands with C.C.'s initials done in pink. He was wearing one as a garter and another as a choke collar, and it didn't take long before one of the security guards was guiding him out toward the gutter.

Talk about an expression of anonymous men and women in a provoked state of mind. "Total insanity…I'd like to introduce you to…true life tragedy," Guy said to anyone listening.

Dean heard and nodded.

Before they had gotten into the line to show their passes, a man cut them off and flashed his ID.

"We under arrest?" said Dean.

• • •

They were led to a car that they recognized right off, and that was double parked on Castle Hill. Ross and O'Gorman sat up front.

The man who had brought Guy and Dean over ordered them in the back, then slammed the door and walked away.

"What's going on?" said Dean.

Neither man in front spoke.

"Well…what is this?" said Guy.

"You damn well know."

The two youths glanced at each other.

"Look at these queer pricks, like they have no fuckin' idea."

"That's the way we queer pricks are," said Guy. "It's a trait we picked up so we can deal with the straight world."

"Greenwall is missing," said O'Gorman.

"Is that good or bad?" said Guy.

"Listen to him," said Ross.

"There was blood all over his kitchen floor."

"Not good," said Dean.

The two youths just sat there like stoic innocents.

"You two are about a farewell letter short of being dead men," said Ross.

"Fortunately for me," said Guy, "I can't read or write so I don't know quite how far a farewell is from—"

"Peter Prince is here," said Ross. "And here is ground zero."

"You're talking now," said Guy. "We never—"

"Greenwall was no accident. No fluke. Prince is here. And by now Palazzo knows he's here, and he's probably shitting jelly. Help us," said O'Gorman, "before we all go up in smoke."

"We've tried," said Dean.

"He won't come out. He won't jeopardize the girl," said Guy. "That's what we know."

"*How* you know is just as important *what* you know," said Ross. "As *how*...is connected to *what*."

"And *how*...is *who*," said O'Gorman. "We need to know...*who*."

"Can't go there," said Dean. "We've been straight with you about that."

"Today...right here," said O'Gorman. "We're gonna rattle a few cages."

"Carpetti," said Ross. "God bless him."

"And when we're done," said Ross, "the night is gonna come down so fast—"

"Hey," said Guy. "One funeral a day is quite enough, thank you."

CHAPTER 72

GUY AND DEAN WERE USHERED TO THEIR SEATS in the second pew. They were sitting directly behind Gardner and Missus Carpetti. Missus Ceraso sat on her friend's right, putting her between the old woman and her son, Gino. This arrangement had been intentional. It was Missus Carpetti's not so subtle separation from her son for all to see. Gino's wife and Christopher and his family took up the rest of the first row. And there before them was the sleek and beautiful mahogany casket that C.C. lay in.

Dean had never been to Saint Raymonds. He thought the church more than beautiful. Closer to a creation from ancient sources. Half a football field of pews and with light coming through a huge red stained glass window above a triptych of doorways. The walls and columns were of African marble and the interior of the church had that warm glow you might see at dusk upon the ocean. He looked at C.C.'s casket. It was so small, and in a way, it felt almost helpless beneath that vast transept with its domed ceiling.

It all made him think of his mother suddenly and of being out upon the rocks of the Breakwater at Orchard Beach with Guy. These thoughts came at the same time to claim him and he experienced a powerful sense of the meaning of eternity.

Guy whispered, "Churches give me the creeps. You know that."

"Don't know it," Dean whispered back. "Don't want to know it."

"It's all candles and death."

"My mother loved churches...the beauty and the *quiet.*"

"Is this your way of telling me to shut the fuck up?"

"I thought I was being pretty sly."

Guy quieted. He looked around the packed and overflowing church. There was a tension in the air, pronounced, troubling.

"My father's here somewhere," Guy whispered.

This caused Dean to start scanning the crowd. "How do you know?"

Just like that Missus Carpetti turned in her seat, and it was as if she had heard everything they'd said. "Because he loved C.C....and he loves me. Just like we love him. And besides that...he told me. Now...be quiet."

The service was emotional, touching, one might even suggest it was restrained. Neither Gino nor Christopher were allowed to speak. That honor was bestowed upon the two granddaughters. A black poetess named Audre recited verses in C.C.'s honor. Friends from college paid tribute. Gardner spoke, Missus Ceraso spoke. Missus Carpetti was last. She was emotional, but in no fucking way restrained.

By the pulpit a couple of microphones had been set up and were wired to four loudspeakers that spanned the width of the alter. Missus Carpetti waved and three women with guitars came forward from the baptismal font.

"C.C. once told a friend," said Missus Carpetti, "that should she die, this is what she wanted played at the service. But before these ladies begin, I have a few words to say, as I have read everything written about my beautiful daughter. I have heard all that has been said and shouted, the insults in the street, even around this church."

Someone, as if on cue, shouted a vulgarity from the rear of the church. There was a sudden rash of condemnation and more vulgarities and then a sweeping team of security guards came down the aisles and put that all to rest.

"I've heard all that, too," said Missus Carpetti. "I've had to hear my baby was struck down by the hand of heaven for her lifestyle...that she got what she deserved for being who she was. Well...to all those who wrote that and said that and shouted that and even think that...Go fuck yourselves."

What followed was a moment of perfect shock, and the silence that comes with it, and those in attendance were looking at each other with "what comes next" expressions. Even the three girls there to sing just stood dumbfounded, as if waiting for someone on high order them to begin. Then Dean felt Guy stand and he looked up and Guy said, "Put it to them, ma'am."

Dean thought—'this was straight from the heart wiseass'—and it set off more applause around the church. It started as a slow ripple that began to rise and rise, and all down the pews people were applauding and shouting support and whistling and then here came the vulgarities again. It was a scene all right, like an expanding force that was too big for that old structure.

Then the girls just suddenly began to sing, their voices echoing out from those loudspeakers. "*...We shall overcome. We shall overcome... Someday..."*

The unleashed emotions flooded out through the church doorways and onto the sunbleached and gritty sidewalks crowded with people. And the music, you could hear it all the way down Castle Hill and up Tremont... *Deep in our hearts...We do believe...We shall overcome someday...*

Maybe someday, but not that day. That day there was that unseen something that haunts creation. The overwhelming conflict that is man, or who is to lay claim to the future.

People were up on the hoods of cars now to get a better view of the craziness. Camera crews shouldered through all that human traffic like half-mechanical creatures. Gays were singing to the music and raising their arms in a surge of power as the bier carrying the body of C.C. Carpetti was being wheeled out to the hearse.

People were pressing the sidewalk from the church where the bier had to pass through, and even with security the going was getting tenuous and one might even suggest dangerous. The things said about the dead girl tested the limits of vileness and Missus Carpetti called to the boys. Dean and Guy muscled their way until they flanked Missus Carpetti and Missus Ceraso.

The Carpetti wives were enraged that the old woman had chosen outsiders over her own family. Gino couldn't have given a rat's ass personally, and as for Christopher, he would have liked to see the old bitch trampled under.

No sooner had they slid the casket into the hearse for the trip to the cemetery than Ross and O'Gorman appeared. And like that, they were around Gino Carpetti and they had him by the arm and he was being escorted from the scene over the threats and objections of his family and the security team. He put a hand up as if to say, "Let it go, it'll be all right." It had all happened in front of the mob and it brought out all the predictable reactions. And you could still hear the girls in the church through the loudspeakers...*We'll walk hand-in-hand, we'll walk hand-in-hand...we'll walk hand-in-hand—someday.*

Guy glanced at Dean. They both had the same thought. This was a moment of absolute black irony, Carpetti getting marched off to the lyrics of a protest song.

CHAPTER 73

THEY GOT GINO INTO THE BACK OF THEIR CAR, and the three of them drove off down Castle Hill all so officiously.

Gino was watching the scene at the church as they passed. There were people giving him the "'fuck you.'" Rumpled losers, uncombed protestors, dullards, blank-faced dickless bastards and fags galore. A drag queen all dolled out, grabbed his crotch and practically pressed it up against the car door windows as they sped by.

"Can you believe it," said Carpetti. "America has turned into a whore hole. And did you hear the fuckin' things said about my family? Did you?"

Neither Ross nor O'Gorman answered.

"Were you in the church? Did you hear?"

They didn't want to go there.

"We weren't in the church," said Ross.

"My dyke sister brought all this down. Fuck her in her coffin. Who's got a cigarette?"

O'Gorman took a pack from his coat pocket and passed it to Carpetti.

"Tell me something," said Carpetti. "Give me good news."

O'Gorman shook his head. "No good news. Greenwall is still missing."

"If Prince doesn't want him found," said Carpetti, "Greenwall could be lining the inside of a dog food can by now. What about Prince's kid... and that boyfriend of his?"

"They talked to Prince. He won't put the girl at risk."

"How noble of him."

They were blocks from the church, and Carpetti was still on it. The humiliation enraged him more than anything. "Some drag queen has the audacity to—"

"The two boys know how to get to Prince," said Ross.

"Prince will have too many tricks for anyone to jump the wall. Christ... he's an artist at this. He's been working it for ten years."

Carpetti smoked that cigarette down to the butt. He couldn't get that drag queen out of his mind. "Screamers," he said, "they mean to take over the fuckin' world."

"What?" said O'Gorman.

"Screamers…they mean to take over the world. They practically got a language all their own, already."

Ross and O'Gorman glanced at each other. They knew…quiet is best.

"Can you bait him out is the question?" said Carpetti.

"Peter Prince?" said Ross.

"Peter Prince."

"Not so far."

"The two boys…are they vulnerable?"

"Vulnerable?"

"Which one is more vulnerable to the other?"

• • •

Friends and family gathered at the Carpetti house after the cemetery. The girl singers at the church set up in the back yard. They were covering many of C.C.'s favorites—The Chiffons, The Shirelles, The Ronettes…Connie Francis, Mary Wells, Lesley Gore. The girls singing revamped some of the lyrics. Like Lesley Gore's *You Don't Own Me*. They changed going out with boys—to girls.

You think this didn't bend the brain of some of those in attendance. Considering many friends of C.C.'s there were gay. This was change coming right off the launch pad and into their laps. And the kids there, down to the littlest ones, were dancing to the music, to the vamped gay lyrics, like this was a new world order *American Bandstand*.

Missus Carpetti watched it all. Thought back to the days of C.C.'s Girl Scout Troop camp outs and how they'd do that *American Bandstand* thing.

There'd be no more cherished moments, no more sharing intimacies. It would all be in the silent world now, with the old lady whispering to a ghost.

She caught sight of Christopher crossing the back yard. He was making it straight for Guy, who was talking with Gardner and Dean. She wondered where a bolt of lightning was when you need it.

Christopher came walking behind Guy. "You were a fuckup in the church, you know that."

"Did either of you hear anything?" said Guy. He heard all right. He turned. Big act of surprise motion. "Oh, it's you. Your grandmother didn't think so."

"I'm not my grandmother."

"No shit. But without her you'd be parking cars somewhere. Wearing one of those pretty jockey vests and existing on tips, saying, 'Thank you, sir' and 'Yes, ma'am.'"

"You're going right over the edge, you know that," said Christopher. "And you're taking your future with you."

"Why don't you get our car," said Guy. "It's that Chevy Impala. And make sure there's no bombs under it like when you fucked up and killed Missus Ceraso's boy."

"You got an animal here," Christopher told Gardner and Dean. "And you'll end up, where he ends up."

"And something else," said Guy. "You've lived too long."

Gardner tried to lead Guy away to blunt all this bad business. "He's a little drunk," said Gardner.

"You *and* your father," said Dean. "Lived too long."

Dean tried the same with Christopher, getting him by the arm. "Let's you and I talk."

Guy broke free of Gardner. He went over to where the kids were dancing. As a matter of fact, he singled out Christopher's young daughters. They were doing the Watusi and he joined them, flashing hipster moves that the girls copied. And if that didn't utterly piss off Christopher, when Guy tossed Missus Carpetti a kiss and she caught it, that really put the knife in.

Christopher told Dean, "You gotta cut loose from him."

"I understand."

"You want this to work."

"I want it to work."

"Cut loose."

CHAPTER 74

THE WOODSTOCK HOTEL WAS ON WEST 43RD STREET, just off Times Square. It was an elegant hotel at the turn of the twentieth century that grew in stature and notoriety as the theatre world around it came into being. But by 1966, it had deteriorated into a seedy firetrap that would only worsen in the seventies. As of now, it was home to addicts, losers, reprobates, prostitutes, artists who never made it, drunks, the poor, the shoddy and the desperate. The hallways stank, the carpets were mildewed, the painting chipped, the walls cracked, the elevator rattled, the piping was a maze of rusted, leaky fittings, and the stairwell was a sometimes toilet. Did I forget to mention it was also home to a hunted murderer.

A postcard arrived at Dicky Palazzo's house. It featured an artist's rendition of the hotel in its heyday, with awnings and Pierce Arrows parked out front.

At first, Palazzo thought it some kind of sales promotion, then he flashed a look at the back of it.

It was addressed to him in a bland, childlike print. And the note—it wasn't a note really, or a hello. It was some kind of stain, or smudge mark, but it wasn't that either. Because once he took a few seconds to get it, to really get it, after staring and staring, like it was some kind of Rorschach test, he came to recognize it was a fingerprint. And the closer he held it, the deeper he looked at it, he could see it was not done in ink. It wasn't printed off one of those police blotter pads they have in every precinct house in the world, it was done in good old sturdy blood.

Palazzo shouted, "Where are you?"

"In here," said Pavlica.

He was at the card table in the den in his shorts, playing solitaire and watching *I've Got A Secret*.

Palazzo had moved Pavlica in, for the time being, even though he despised being around the child molester, so they might have an edge on Peter Prince if he tried to take them down at the house. He'd even offered the place to Cerussi, but the guy was too much of a headcase, thought he'd be safer keeping on the move.

"Where is Cerussi?"

"What do you mean?"

"Where does he live?"

"Midtown. Times Square, like."

"Hotel?"

"What else. He moved after Greenwall disappeared. I dropped him off there."

"The Woodstock?"

"What's that?"

"That the name of the place?"

Pavlica shrugged. He seemed more interested in the fuckin' television show. Palazzo tossed the postcard on the table.

"That the place?"

Pavlica put the playing cards down, reached for the postcard. Checked it out. "Might be. But there ain't no Pierce Arrows parked out front, I'll tell you that much. Why?"

Palazzo motioned for him to flip the postcard over.

Pavlica did so with disinterest. Saw the address. "What? Did he send this or—"

He dropped the postcard like it was toxic and up from the table he came. He'd seen the fingerprint, and it took reality to register in that smarmy brain of his, like instantly.

"Shit," said Pavlica.

"Oh, yeah," said Palazzo. "That got your attention."

Pavlica went to his trousers which were draped over a chair. Palazzo noticed Pavlica's underwear looked like it had not been washed in entirely too long.

From his wallet, Pavlica got out part of a matchbook cover. "His number."

He dialed the phone. The men waited while it rang. Jesus…It rang so long Cerussi could have walked all the way from Jersey and still been able to answer.

CHAPTER 75

GUY WAS STRETCHED OUT IN THE BACK SEAT OF THE IMPALA, hands behind his head, a casual buzz on, as they drove home. Dean was behind the wheel of the mothership trying to digest everything that had gone down. Gardner was in the shotgun seat and he was one stressed attorney.

"You tell him 'you've lived too long'," said Gardner. "What was that about? What were you thinking?"

"That I was a hardheaded, calculating son of a bitch who is looking down the road, and I can see reality coming straight at us, and it's fuckin' crossing over the white line…Hey, Dante…what were you and Chrissy Boy talking about all huddled together."

"We were comparing our Christmas shopping lists."

"I thought so…I could feel the excitement coming off you two. And I can imagine you decorating him up like a Christmas tree…with a semi-automatic."

"He wants me to blow you off…Cut you loose…Sell you out, etc., etc., etc."

"We were in a bad place before," said Gardner, "but now?"

Guy jumped to another subject. "You could see it in the church…at the old woman's house. The world is coming around. It's on the move and we're in play. One day we'll be just ordinary slobs that get up, go to work, live our lives and bore you to death."

"But where it counts," said Gardner, "where he who rules lives…it's still the fifties. Gino and his son are the fifties. The police are the fifties. The district attorney offices are the fifties. The FBI is the fifties. And they would all rather be in business with a Gino Carpetti, than with you and I."

At the house, Gardner lit up a joint. He kicked off his shoes and slouched down in his desk chair. He was done in by it all. Guy made himself a bourbon and coke. He was gonna drink right through to tomorrow. Dean went upstairs to change clothes and have a few minutes alone.

Guy stood in the hallway where he could shout to both. "There's something I want you both to think about. We're not gonna be able to outsmart them at every turn. And there's more of them than there are of us."

Dean could hear Guy well enough, even upstairs. Dean saw there was a note on his door. The paralegal had pinned it there. It explained—Eddie Teranova had called. He'd left a number. He wanted to get together with his son in Jersey.

"Are you both listening to me?" said Guy. "We went to a funeral today, gents. That should say it all."

The note gave Dean pause, coming on the heels as it did after such a long silence, and where exactly their lives were at that moment.

"We're gonna have to figure out how to go about killing them," shouted Guy. "Father and son. Because they are gonna do us."

Dean had changed and came back down in a t-shirt and jeans and barefoot. He sat on the stairs.

"Look where you started," said Guy. "Look where we are. We found my father, thanks to you. You got him immunity if he came forward. But the girl won't out of fear, so my father won't... Where do we go now?"

"I've been asking myself that."

"Men came in here looking for your notes. They are a paper trail to destruction. What's on those notes is in your head. You are the mortal battlefield now, Dante."

"I recognize that, too."

"The world keeps moving on, man. And you got to keep your eyes fixed on what's around every corner, so you don't end up just a casualty, but a cause for something good. That was your aim.

"You did everything right, Dante. And the better you did the deeper the hole got dug. The more threats you are under, the worse the dangers become, and the risks intensify.

"If you had completely failed, everything would be cool. You could walk away clean, but you didn't fail. Failure solves all problems. Failure is the ultimate escape hatch. That's why there's so much of it around. It's one of the deep truths of existence. I picked that up from my old man."

Gardner was standing in the doorway now. Watching, listening. Trying to get his head wrapped around all this.

"But that's not where we're at, is it?" said Guy.

"It's not where we're at," said Dean.

"We're in Madison Square Garden...And it's a smoke filled night. I say we strap up, turn the music extra loud, and come out firing. Those are the rules that are in effect. I say we ride them."

Dean stood. He was giving away nothing about what he felt or thought. And Guy understood.

"Sleep on it, Dante. It ain't priceless, but plain fact. I can always go back to being a well-heeled bum. We'll just have to get used to living with a death threat hanging over our heads."

Guy went upstairs, the clicking ice in his glass fading with each step. It was just Dean and Gardner now.

Dean knew then why Guy had confronted Christopher Carpetti as he had at the house. Guy Prince was no crazed cowboy, but a very surgical thinker. A strategist disguised as some wild boy of the road.

Gardener thought he'd picked up something in Dean's eyes, something no lawyer likes to see.

"You're not *listening* to any of that?" said Gardner.

CHAPTER 76

DEAN DROVE OUT TO PARAMUS to meet with his father at The Steak Pit. As he got out of the car and entered the restaurant, he wished he hadn't come at all. His father waved to him. It was like a bad handshake.

Eddie Teranova was sitting in the same booth in the Onyx and Gold Room as they had before. He was already working on a martini, as he had before. And it looked like he was wearing the same wrinkle-proof clothes as before.

"Mister Teranova," he said.

"You're a model of consistency, Pop."

"Is that good, or is it bad?"

"It's both…and it's neither."

"Smart people make me nervous."

No sooner had Dean sat than the waiter came over with exquisite efficiency to take his cocktail order.

It wasn't much of a conversation until the waiter brought Dean's drink, and then his father raised his glass.

"Let's drink to the fact that I was pretty much a failure as a father."

"Well," said Dean, "if that doesn't jumpstart a conversation."

They tinged glasses and drank.

"I'd apologize," said Eddie, "but you'd see right through it for the shallow ploy that it was."

They tinged glasses again and drank.

"Maybe you just should not have been a father," said Dean.

"It's true…I'm too selfish."

"Are we gonna open a chapter on the Teranova life story titled… Honesty?"

"It'll be a short chapter."

"Let's drink to short chapters."

They tinged glasses for the third time and drank.

"I never felt connected to you, Dean. Either as a son or as a man."

Eddie's look shifted. He had a tough mouth, it had a slight distortion that Dean had never noticed before. Maybe it was simply the fact that

Eddie Teranova was getting older, and the body changes to fit the man.

"Did you ever feel connected to anyone?"

"Gambling," said Eddie.

"Not mom?"

"Gambling."

"Gambling is not a person."

"Ahhh, my boy, but gambling is… a person…It's a woman and a cocktail and a fine meal and a blowjob and a good night's sleep all in one beautiful, exciting package."

"Pop, I have a sudden twinge of regret at not trying to know you better."

"And you're the better man for it, I'm sure. I read about the girl's murder. She's one of the people that—"

"Yeah."

"How is…what you're writing about?"

"It's a moment to moment thing."

"I'm sure today will become one of those moments."

"This conversation is taking on shades of conversations yet to be had."

"I hope to get proper credit for all the things I've done wrong," said Eddie.

Dean sipped on his drink. Then he leaned back and Eddie knew from the way the youth sat and how he stared, where they were going.

"I got a question," said Dean.

"How did your mother really die…"

Dean nodded.

"The tug of war of unfinished business," said Eddie.

"And I don't want the crap she fell asleep at the wheel while you were driving to Chicago."

Do I tell him the truth? Eddie was sipping his drink deciding. The truth is rotten. It's like jumping from a rooftop because some dipshits think it's the right thing to do.

Does he tell Dean he and the old lady were arguing about her precious boy and why did he never go to Spofford to see him? Because he couldn't stand him, that's why, and the fact that he was gay only played into the endless disdain, and she made some comment that finally pissed him off and he slapped her face and she lost control of the wheel. And there it was.

It could have been just as easily him that was coffin bound, but as

Dean's mother liked to say...*God is always working in your life.*

"What I told the police is true," said Eddie.

"They didn't believe it. It sounded like a story that came out of nowhere," said Dean.

"Con artists, gamblers, creeps like me...we exist on stories that come out of nowhere."

"But you did lie to the police, like you're lying to me?"

"I lied to the police, like I'm lying to you."

"How you manage being dishonest—even when you're not, displays dazzling talent."

"Just make sure I get proper credit for the things I've done wrong."

"So...Mister Teranova...Why are we here today in Paramus, New Jersey, at The Steak Pit, in the Onyx and Gold Room?"

Eddie set his cocktail down. This, Dean thought, has all been the wind up for the pitch. Then he saw his father pluck at his neck with a thumb and index finger and he knew. The tell—the old man was choking on the lie he was about to peel off.

"I'm here," said Eddie, "to present you with a financial offer to sell all you know to a private bidder."

Dean felt this massive surge of hatred. Told himself...be cool. Act like this is just another day in Spofford jail, except here a waiter brings you cocktails.

"Pop, you're not ruthless enough to get into this for somebody."

"I'm ruthless enough so I won't die for you."

"I can't protect you."

"I won't protect you."

"You could die."

"You will...as I am told."

CHAPTER 77

PETER PRINCE HAD WARNED HIM. He'd said if your father shows up, what it would mean. He had been right on.

Operative immorality—in his notes that's how Dean described his father's preferred method of life.

Dean sat on his apartment terrace and smoked and watched people enter and exit Saint Lucy's Grotto as they filled all kinds of containers with water from the shrine. Of course, the water was not from Lourdes. It was good old fashioned Bronx tap water blessed by a priest. But miracles are miracles, no matter where the water comes from.

Dean killed his cigarette and went downstairs.

Gardner looked up from his desk, when Dean said, "Where's Guy?"

Gardner pointed up toward the ceiling.

Dean closed the door behind him. "I need you to do something for me, and it's on the QT from Guy."

"Why don't I like this already?"

"Because you're a good attorney, which is what I need."

• • •

Elise had set up her camera on a tripod in the dining room. She had moved the table a bit. And placed the chair just so Dean would be sitting with a Beatles movie poster on the wall behind him. She had angled it all so that the title,

HELP
—is on the way—

would be hovering just above him.

Dean had called and asked to come over. He'd offered money to her roommates so he and Elise could have a couple of hours of well paid for privacy.

"How come," she said, "you decided to get filmed again...for the documentary?"

"Unfinished business."

"Well," she said, "I love unfinished business."

She sighted him through the lens. She thought—he looks so far away.

"Can you make a copy for Guy?"

"Easy," she said.

"I'll want you to give it to him."

"Me...?"

• • •

Rose Berghich peeked out the shutters when the doorbell rang. She saw it was Dean, and she called out to Peter. As she opened the door Dean apologized for just showing up like he did. And before he could ask to talk with Peter, she said, "He's in the living room."

Peter stood by the French doors to the patio.

"Can we talk...Just you and me?" said Dean.

Rose disappeared into that large still house and Peter went out onto the patio with Dean right behind him.

"Where's Guy?"

"I want to leave Guy out of this."

"So it's like that."

Peter sat. The sun had just edged over the patio awning and everything was just beginning to warm.

"You were right about my father," said Dean.

"I'm sorry to hear it."

Dean just stood there now in the sun. Silent, unsure. Running his fingers across the top of a wrought iron chair.

"Tell me why you're here, and we'll see if it matches with what I assume."

Dean explained with quiet anger how his father had brought him an offer, wrapped in a threat, to sell Peter out.

"You know why they picked you?"

"Guy won't sell you out. He won't sell me out. And I have the information."

"Hell…you love my son, even more than I do."

"Can you come up with a way I can kill Chris Carpetti?"

• • •

You'd have thought Chris Carpetti might have learned his lesson after Blue Mountain. But vanity overrides common sense, and pride thinks it can make a fool of prudent simplicity.

The Kensico Reservoir was about thirty miles north of New York in the town of Valhalla. There was a bar in the hills along Route 22 which followed the shoreline all the way to the dam.

It was a funky beer garden with a series of outdoor grottos on a rise that looked out toward the water. Set back in the woods, you'd never find the place if you didn't know it was there, or it was late at night when a few streams of neon snuck through the trees and were the only light for a good mile.

The bar, known as Teddy's Hall, was closed on Mondays. Teddy was a special kind of entrepreneur who could be trusted to rent the place for very prime get togethers. He was a big mouthed bastard, and there was a photo of him by the register and below it, a caption—God made people like me for a reason. Call it envy, call it admiration.

From where he sat in one of the beer garden grottos out back, Chris Carpetti saw this heavy engined Impala through the trees slowly wending its way up the gravel road to the bar, leaving a train of dust in its wake.

"It's got to be him," Carpetti said to his driver.

His driver walked to the open bar door and yelled, "He's coming. Be cool."

Out front were Palazzo and Pavlica. Being there was the source of some serious anxiety. They didn't for a moment think this was going to go as simply as Carpetti fuckin' thought.

Dean could start to see the squat rock shell of the building with its fake Middle Ages door and windows. There were two cars parked out front and he recognized them both. He swung into the clearing.

He could see Palazzo a lot better than the other one. Even at that distance, as he rolled up, he could see he was being regarded with grave concern. He scanned the edge of the trees for any sign of movement. There was hardly a breeze running through all that shadowline.

He put the car in park and cut the ignition and took a long breath. He was wearing sunglasses so they could not see his eyes, not see where he might be watching, not see he might be afraid.

CHAPTER 78

Palazzo and Pavlica flanked Dean as he stepped out of the Chevy.

"We're gonna search you," said Palazzo.

"You don't need to do that. I got a gun right here," he said, tapping his waist.

"Lift your shirt," said Palazzo.

Dean lifted his shirt. There was a pistol, all right, wedged down in his jeans.

Pavlica reached for his weapon.

"Hand it over, please," said Palazzo.

"Fuck you."

Pavlica had his weapon and was drumming the barrel against the Impala chassis.

"Hey," said Dean, pointing at Pavlica. "Pull a gun on me, and I'm back in the car and outta here. There's four of you…and one of me. I'm not walking through here naked."

Carpetti could hear an argument outside heating up. He could see from across the bar and through the open doorway to where the three men stood. He called to his driver there in the doorway, "What the fuck is going on?"

"The kid has a gun and won't give it up."

Carpetti walked up beside his driver.

"He said if he can't keep the gun he's outta here."

Dean could see Carpetti there in that phony looking doorway like some ancient Norse king. He was thinking it over. What kind of threat could some lone queer be?

"I'm here to negotiate a deal," Carpetti said, "Not to start a range war. Let him the fuck in."

He went over to a table and sat. Dean walked past the driver and into the darkish bar.

"When you're in there with Carpetti," Peter Prince had explained, "make sure you know where everyone else is in there. Where they are standing or sitting at all times."

"Yes, sir."

"Because when the killing starts…it all happens so quickly. And there is no time to think. Whoever looks like the worst threat…you shoot them first. And you hope to God you made the right decision."

Dean took a seat at the table where Carpetti sat, making sure he could see the driver and the open doorway. He took off his sunglasses, not only because it was dark in the bar, except for where the sunlight came through the stained glass windows in long smoky streams, but so as not to look or appear suspicious.

"Before we get it on…" said Carpetti, "how'd you do it?"

"Do it?"

"Find Peter Prince."

"You."

"Me?"

"River Avenue…the Crabs."

"The Crabs were dead. Was it someone close to them…who'd been living in the building?"

"Look at me," said Dean. "People will feel a lot safer talking to me than…someone like those cretins outside. Don't you think?"

"The Crabs didn't know?" said Carpetti.

"They didn't know."

"Won't Palazzo be shocked."

Carpetti leaned forward, as if to share an intimacy with Dean.

"I've got something you need to know…Because I want you alive. I want to make our business work. Our business works, I keep alive. My father…He means to have you dead. Yeah. He's already laid out hard currency with people that are as close to you as I am now. You might say to yourself…Carpetti is fucking with my head. It's a ploy, a move. That I'm dropping the number thirteen on your ass to work you. Brother, if you think that—"

For the moment Dean forgot he was listening to a witless murderer and a son of a bitch who would lie even when the truth sounded better. But there was something in Carpetti's voice. Some pedestrian fear. A shakiness that carried real weight to it, that had Dean believing him. Had him forgetting why he was there, in the dark of that bar, in the heavily wooded hills above a quiet roadway. Until a blast from a shotgun and one of the men outside was thrown back across the hood of a car, flat out, arms spread, leaving a trail of his shiny blood upon the paint.

CHAPTER 79

THE NEXT MOMENTS HAPPENED exactly as Peter Prince prophesied. It was not a time for thinking, as he'd said. Survival demanded your ability to grasp disorder almost instantly. You must change from being a thinking man, a feeling man, an understanding man, to a fierce destroying force. Killing is its own reason for existence. And you must dive into its dark, wild water willfully knowing, or you will die.

Dean came up from the table reaching for the gun under his shirt, his fingers fumbling, failing to grasp the weapon.

The driver had turned to the open doorway where two men were being slaughtered. He seemed to have forgotten Dean was there. Maybe he did not believe the youth to be a threat, and gave him no due. Maybe he just assumed.

Dean leapt up from the table out of pure fear. In that, he would not be wrong. From where he sat, Christopher Carpetti saw Dean fire. The youth had determined the driver as the greater threat. Carpetti saw the driver hit from a pittance of ten feet. The driver's whole body reared against the bar, turning, and with a second shot, he grabbed at his back.

The driver tried to run toward the open doorway, stumbling, his hands pressed against his chest, only to fall dead at the feet of Peter Prince who entered the bar behind the smoking barrel of a shotgun he carried.

Through all this, Christopher Carpetti had not moved. He had been still in a way that almost defied the science and nature of calm itself. When he finally saw it was Peter, all he said was, "You."

He turned his attention then to Dean. The dusky light from the windows lent his face a color it might not have truly had.

"Remember what I told you," said Christopher. "I hope it bleeds you to death."

"What did he tell you?" said Peter.

"His father has paid someone to kill Guy and me—close at hand. Isn't that how you told it?"

"Get out," said Peter. "I'll deal with him."

Dean turned to go.

"Hey," said Peter. He pointed the shotgun barrel at the table. "Your glasses."

Dean grabbed them off the table and like that he was gone.

Dean crossed through the sunlight to his car. The two men lay in the gravel lot like small bloody islands, lifeless. Palazzo's eyes, open, stared off toward points unknown.

In the bar Peter Prince heard Dean speed off down the hill.

"Your father…" said Peter.

"What about him?"

"Who did he bring in to do the killing?"

Chris did not speak.

"You think you're gonna break with tradition and man this thing out?" said Peter. "Dream on."

Christopher's shoulders stiffened—"I go dead…You get nothing."

Peter crossed into the light from the open doorway. The bar darkened even more, and it had suddenly grown so quiet in there one could hear the birds outside.

Dean made his way down Route 22 aiming for White Plains. The two lane road was heavily wooded all the way, and as for traffic, it came as close to none as you can get.

There was an old stone bridge of no consequence that you had to pass under. One end was gated, the other fed the service road to the dam.

Dean was just approaching the overpass when he heard a car horn behind him and saw it was Ross and O'Gorman. They were flagging him to pull over.

The underpass was a bare twelve feet high and arched and so cramped a space that two cars passing alongside each other had to almost kiss. Dean eased back on the gas just a little, and as he did Ross sped up. He had crossed the white line and was pulling up on Dean's flank. O'Gorman was yelling and flagging Dean with one arm to pull the hell over.

Dean slowed a little more and waved and pointed beyond the bridge and that's when Ross put that gas pedal to the floorboard. His car lunged and there they were racing to the underpass, the sunlight coming through a world of trees tight to the roadway and leaving bright burning patches on the asphalt.

And that's when Dean caught a glimpse, nothing more really, in his sideview mirror of what looked like a bit of shotgun barrel just eyeing up over the edge of O'Gorman's door. It was those little rushes of sunlight that gave it away. That exposed it. And just as both cars whooshed into the underpass O'Gorman brought the shotgun up to fire.

You take the moment that is about to happen, and you roll back in time to when Dean walked out of The Steak Pit with his father, following after him to where the cars were parked out back.

"Well…What's it gonna be?" said Eddie Teranova. "Do I get an answer?"

"You know what I would tell anyone who put their faith in you," said Dean.

"That's one of those questions of yours that makes me just want to walk across a mile of burning sand barefoot for the fucking answer."

"I'd say…'anyone who put faith in my father for anything has failed already.'"

"How old are you?" said Eddie.

Dean stopped. He and his father were face to face now.

"A cringeworthy question," said Dean.

"You're twenty," said Eddie.

"Look at you. You're making me feel all sentimental suddenly."

"Be careful…you don't want to end up twenty forever."

Dean turned away. "I'll call you with my answer."

Eddie Teranova had no idea Dean followed him. He was always too involved in his own manipulations and betrayals to have a broader awareness of the world around him. He also didn't know his kid had this kind of instinct. That he saw his father as strictly the short leash type.

He had also not realized how well Dean had learned the lesson from when his old man had beat him down that time in the apartment over at 1540. And his mother had angrily said, "What's he to learn from that?" To which Eddie had answered, "He'll learn how to see around corners."

About a mile down Route 4, toward the George Washington Bridge, Eddie pulled into the parking lot of a diner called Holly's. It was one of those well trafficked, old-time joints with aluminum siding and huge windows that the sun burns through. Dean had been there once before.

Guess who was taking up space in the booth Eddie Teranova dropped his sorry ass down into…Ross and O'Gorman.

CHAPTER 80

DEAN HIT THE BRAKES JUST BEFORE THE SHOTGUN FIRED. They were under the archway. The blast echoed and birds struck from the eaves in all directions. The front end of the Impala was scored with buckshot. Something in the engine exploded. Dean cut the wheel and drove it right into the sedan, ramming it against the rock abutment. The driver's side of the car crumpled it hit so hard and Ross was almost thrown clear. The sedan caromed off the gray walling and straight back into the Chevy.

They sped into the sunlight completely out of control. The left side of the sedan's tires were blown, and it spun out on its sparking metal rims and began to flip over. As it did, it hit Dean's car and drove it straight up a short incline. It was skimming trees and the hood came flying loose. One door was torn away and the chassis lifted off the ground and slammed back down and it hit a huge stone so hard the engine was torn loose from its boltings.

Moments later the world there was still and quiet as the day of creation. There was some smoke rising from the sedan which lay upside down in the roadway, and there was this sparky clicking from the Chevy engine. The driver's door creaked open in painful successions and Dean struggled out on his hands and his knees.

As he tried to stand, he saw a piece of metal door panel had pierced his side just under the ribs. There were little geysers of blood he tried to patch with his hand, but even a blind man could see it was bad.

He fought to stand, keeping hold of the chassis. He stumbled down the incline, reaching the road. Tottering, trying to breathe, he removed the handgun from his jeans. He saw his own shadow before him in the wavery sunlight until he stood before the sedan.

O'Gorman was still in his seat, the dashboard having torn him in half. Ross was pinned under the hood, exposed from the chest up. Alive, but hardly, bleeding from his ears, trying to free himself, as futile an action was ever conceived. Could he see Dean at all, or realize it was him when Dean said, "Anyone who puts faith in my father for any fuckin' thing has failed already."

What could Ross answer, if he could answer at all?

"I want you to know something…while I still can." Dean was shaking the hand with the gun. "My life was worth it."

Ross was suffering so. Every moment in one's life has two possible ends. Dean leaned down and shot poor Ross dead, to put an end to his suffering.

Dean turned to his own fate now, looking down at the blood jetting between his fingers from the wound.

A car came up the road, and Dean saw it make this screeching, wild stop. A man got out and took in the scene. Then he jumped in his car and wheeled about and was gone back from where he came.

Dean struggled along, and when he could carry himself no farther, sat down in the road. He pulled a leg up and rested an arm on the knee to try and ease the pain in his side.

He could see far down that quiet strip of blacktop where the light gleamed through the parting trees. *God is always working in your life…even when you least expect it.* His breathing told him he would shortly know.

He stared down that long road draped in dazzling light that spotted through the trees, then closed his eyes.

He went to where he could see the Breakwater at Orchard Beach. Where he was on that long jetty as the splashing blue black waters made the rocks shine under a burning sun. He went to that moment when they were together, just two boys at Breakwater in all its perfect simplicity.

He didn't even know it happened. He had no idea when he had gone. He did not know that his body had quietly tipped over. That his cheek rested on the heated asphalt or there was sun on the shoulder where it read:

SPOFFORD
Class of 66
—I fought the Law—

He did not know, of course, the road had been cordoned off. That the police were working up the scene, gathering evidence, taking pictures of his face, the wound, the tattoo on his shoulder. That he was being collected like a specimen, that an officer said, "He looks like he's resting, not dead."

He didn't know there were people now all along that gated bridge grabbing snapshots, pointing, running back and forth, refusing to be ordered away, leaning over the ledge to better see the blood, filming, absorbed to their hearts content at this vision of unmitigated violence.

He did not know he would live forever, and for reasons beyond the worst in men.

CHAPTER 81

ALMOST IMMEDIATELY the shootout on the road got connected to the killings at Teddy's Hall. Evidence told the police there was one more suspect, at least. Most of the dead at the beer garden had been taken by shotgun. And there was no shotgun discovered at either scene to match evidence at the bar.

Guy had been in Superior Court most of the day as a favor to Gardner, waiting on papers from a family court judge. But that wasn't the true reason. Gardner Flynn had made sure Guy Prince had an airtight alibi that he did not know he'd need, until he walked into the house on Bronxwood.

He heard the paralegal crying somewhere back in the house. Gardner was on the phone in his office. He was ashen, and looked as if he had been swallowed by the world.

Guy knew without a word. He knew his life was to be broken apart by the way Gardner delayed hanging up the phone after the call was over.

"What happened to Dean?" said Guy.

Gardner clasped his hands together to keep control of himself.

Guy shouted furiously, "What happened to Dean?"

"Dean was killed today in a shootout with Ross and O'Gorman on Route 22 up in Valhalla. Both agents are dead."

Guy watched as Gardner pressed his hands together even more tightly.

"There is a beer garden by the Kensico Dam, said Gardner. "It's closed on Mondays. It's where Chris Carpetti is dead…Palazzo is dead…Pavlica is dead."

Guy fought to keep from crying. To brace himself against the fact that he was breaking apart. That everything he was, was being stripped away word by word. He was shaking with agony, and he was shaking with rage. He went to the fighter within him to hold on, to keep upright, to find survival, until he knew.

"How did it happen?" said Guy. "Why did it happen?"

"We don't have much time," said Gardner. "That call was from a friend telling me the police are on the way with warrants."

Guy walked into the office. He was waiting for an answer that was not forthcoming. This set off all kinds of signals in Guy's head. Gardner was trying to legal up on how to answer.

"You knew, didn't you? This just didn't happen. You sent me to court today because—"

"Do not ask a question I cannot answer."

Guy was right on the other side of the desk. This was a young man ready to commit an extraordinary act of violence.

"No one could have outfought the two of us together. Not the whole fuckin' lot of them."

Gardner was desperate to retain his calm for what he knew was coming. "There's a lot we need to talk about before—"

Guy slammed his fists down on the desk so hard it lifted. "I ought to kill you for this. I swear to Christ. As much as I care for you, Gardner, I ought to kill you for letting him do this."

"Hold onto all that fight," said Gardner. "This is not over yet."

Police cars swarmed onto the street and into the driveway.

Gardner got up, he called to the paralegal. "It's the police. Let them in." He slammed the office door shut and locked it. Said to Guy, "Tell me that you want to hire me as your attorney in all matters."

You could hear them coming into the house, like a platoon storming a beachhead, warrants in hand.

"I want to hire you as my attorney in all matters," said Guy, "except one."

The police tried to enter the office. When they realized the door was locked, they called out. Gardner took Guy aside.

"Today could have gone down at the order of Gino Carpetti. And it may well be that now you are all that, legally or otherwise, stands between him and what he wants."

CHAPTER 82

GARDNER FOUGHT THE WARRANTS. Fought for every inch, so they know these dogs got good assed teeth. The warrants were specific for Dean's apartment, but that did not include Gardner's personal living quarters and offices. They wanted to search the garage, but it was also not included in the warrant. Investigators put the house in lockdown until they came back with amended paperwork.

Gardner knew what they were looking for. Dean's notes that might contain evidence of criminal activity by the Carpettis that instigated the murders. And, of course, a shotgun that had been instrumental in the body count.

They left Dean's apartment a wasteland, but what they got was nothing. The garage search was a filthy, dusty time-consuming waste.

Guy learned upon his release the following day that an ice chest was nowhere to be found. He also learned Dean's father was coming to the house with an attorney, a Carpetti flavored attorney.

"What for...Why?"

"For no damn good, of course," said Gardner.

• • •

The *Daily News* had scooped the other papers with their cover photos of the crime scene. No one did tasteless and crass like the *Daily News*. They had also coined the phrase that you've seen written over the years—The Kensico Damned Murders—another of their great contributions to American culture.

Chris Carpetti's violent death, coming as it did on the heels of his aunt's slaying, along with two members of a Bronx task force into crime, opened doors of suspicion as to what really happened and why. These kind of elusive suspicions rarely get to the truth, but rather create endless notions of conspiracy.

Missus Carpetti put out a simple press release through her attorney. *My family has faced one terrible tragedy after another—We will get through this with the help of God, family…and our closest friends.*

The *Daily News* was not the only paper to infer she meant there would be more killing.

It was the day after the murders that Gino and his mother met for a brief few minutes. The room was like a sealed tomb with the two of them buried there.

"Mama, is there any way we can make this right? Make it work?"

She hated when he called her 'Mama.' And she knew it was his own private expletive for her. She thought a long time, then said, "I wonder?"

"Yes?" he said.

"I wonder," she repeated, more quietly.

"What?"

"I wonder if you'll live long enough for your two granddaughters to grow up and Lady Macbeth you?"

· · ·

Eddie Teranova showed up with an attorney that Gardner knew, by the name of Leonard LaSala. LaSala looked more like an NFL lineman than a legal expert, but he was sound and he was slick. Guy was in the office and Gardner made the introductions. He asked the men to sit.

"What's the boyfriend doing here?" said Eddie.

"I believe that will become obvious as we talk," said Gardner.

"You reviewed my papers?" said LaSala.

"Yes."

"As the deceased's parent and only living heir, Mister Teranova has the right to all the boy's possessions. Particularly the papers he has been amassing for a book or future magazine stories."

"I don't know where those papers are," said Gardner. "Or who might even have them. Dean was…secretive about those."

"As you know, we have interest from a private source for those papers."

"And even that first magazine story," Eddie interrupted. "The Pirates… There's a film company—"

"This is all moot, anyway," said Gardner.

He lifted a document from his desk and leaned forward and passed it to LaSala.

"What is that?" Eddie Teranova said.

LaSala thumbed through the pages. "It appears to be a Will."

"Which Dean made out just before he was killed," said Gardner.

"This…" said Eddie Teranova, "has all the makings of a con job."

"The Will," said Gardner, "appoints Guy Prince executor and sole beneficiary of all Dean's accounts and properties… intellectual properties included."

"Cavalry to the rescue," said Eddie. "Always has a smell to it."

"You will certainly understand my questioning this document," said LaSala, "considering its timing."

"Absolutely," said Gardner. "It was witnessed by a Superior Court Judge…and a priest."

"Fuckin' A," said Eddie.

"The Will has to be validated," said LaSala. "You can't sell or lease any of the papers."

"Papers I do not have."

LaSala stood. Gardner reached for an envelope and offered it to Eddie.

He took it. "What is this?" He opened the envelope. It contained a check for a thousand dollars.

"Your son left that to you," said Gardner.

Eddie knew this made it even more insurmountable to contest the Will. "You fuckin' princesses stick together, don't you? Protect each other's dicks at all costs."

LaSala asked his client to politely, "Shut the fuck up."

They left together. Guy had kept silent as he'd promised Gardner he would, but now he followed the men out. He wanted to ask Teranova how it felt to have his son crush his grubby dream before it even got started. That he was a bottom feeder whose best laid plans got blacked out. He had a litany of barbs to scar him with, but all he said was, "You shouldn't have had that meeting at the diner on Route 4 after you left The Steak Pit. You left your ass wide open. And Dean took you…'cause he learned how to see around corners."

Yeah, thought Guy, when he saw the look Teranova gave him. Yeah, the knife went in deep and the knife went in wide, and ain't no milk and honey on the other side.

Gardner came up alongside him as the car pulled out of the driveway.

"You shouldn't have told him that," said Gardner.

"No...Why?"

"Because Gino Carpetti will find out you know way more than they ever thought, and that you might be able to drop it on him."

CHAPTER 83

GUY SAT ON DEAN'S SOFA while the sun moved across the window. Alone, smoking endlessly, listening to the music that had been him, and trying to come to grips with still being alive.

How long Gardner had been standing in the doorway Guy had no idea, and didn't bother to ask.

"Dean knew what you were doing," said Gardner, "when you told Christopher 'You lived too long.' You were working to get him to turn his rage on you."

"I *would* get hooked up with someone I couldn't outsmart."

"He told me," said Gardner, "he always felt guilty that you served time for what *he* did. That he would have lied about you being there."

"But I was too quick on the draw."

Guy leaned forward and flicked the ashes of his cigarette at the ashtray…He missed. "This time," said Guy, "*he* was quicker."

He looked over at Gardner. It is terrible to see such sorrow on someone's face. To be powerless to stem the tide of it.

"I need your car for a few hours," said Guy.

"Be careful," said Gardner.

Guy lifted his shirt to show Gardner he was carrying a gun.

• • •

There was an eight-story apartment that covered most of a block and was just down the street from the house on Hanford. It was 300 Pelham Road. Guy's father had explained to him that Guy could enter the basement at one end and walk through a long series of joined corridors and come out on the far side of the building which would make it very difficult being followed.

Behind the building was a play area for kids, and benches that faced Titus Mill Pond. No one was back there at night, and it was always dark.

Guy sat on a bench and waited about an hour before his father arrived. Peter Prince sat next to his son.

289

"I'm sorry about Dean," said Peter.

"Thanks."

"I'm sorry about everything, son."

"That's too vast for anyone."

"Do you want to know how it went down at the beer garden?"

"No."

"The kid was fearless, you need to know that."

"I can't talk about it."

"Understood…Dean brought his papers over. Rose stashed them away. Fuckin' Sherlock Holmes could never find them. They're yours any time you want."

"I called 'cause I need a favor from you, Pop."

"Ask."

"When I go to kill Carpetti, I need you to drive the car. If I get away. I also want the shotgun you used."

"That's two favors."

• • •

There was a car parked in Gardner's driveway that he didn't recognize. On the chance there was another warrant in his immediate future, he ditched the weapon he was carrying in the mailbox on the porch.

It turned out Gardner was playing host to Elise. They were drinking Manhattans. She was a little drunk and she gave Guy a salute, then she got up and went over and kissed him. He could see her eyes were red and puffy from too damn much crying.

She took him by the hand, and said, "Come…I've got something for you to see."

She led him up to Dean's apartment. There he saw a small projector had been set up on the coffee table and a white sheet tacked to the opposite wall like a movie screen.

"Turn out the lights, would you?" she said. As he did she told him, "Dean filmed this before…It was, he said, for the documentary…But it's you it was for."

When he sat, Elise turned on the projector. A little square of sheet brightened, and there was this funky dining room with a plain green

Formica table and beat up vinyl chairs that sure didn't match. And there it was, on the wall behind the chair, the poster for the Beatles Movie:

HELP
—is on the way—

Guy could hear Dean off camera talking with Elise. Then there he was, walking into frame, glancing at the poster, jerking a wry thumb at it, grinning…even singing a few bars of *Help*.

Dean made this abrupt stop. Like he'd just gotten a glimpse of what was in all probability down the road. After he sat down, the camera framed up a little bit cleaner. Then Elise said, "You're free, Dean. Go get it."

There was a pause. "Yeah," he said quietly. "Free…" He paused again. "Guy…if you're seeing this…Yeah…if you're seeing this…"

Dean sat there a few moments in silence staring straight at the camera. Guy could see, he knew the look with all its godawful honesty. Dean was somewhere down in the depths of his own being, edged with apprehension.

"I did what I thought best, partner. It was me they wanted to shake down or take down. As we well know, it was my notes they were after and what I carried around in my head. I told Gardner after the meeting with my father, when I saw that he'd hooked up with Ross and O'Gorman, I knew we were at total low tide and no time to waste. I did what we'd talked about way back…take the fight to them…" Dean took a breath. His face momentarily shaded with doubt. "…I hope I wrecked them."

There was another period of silence, one filled with what seemed to Guy, like a deep distance.

"Guy…what I wish I could have changed, was hurting you…by leaving you. You always seemed to know exactly who you were. It was different with me. I was still searching, trying to understand how to place all my feelings…One thing I knew…There was a oneness between us that—"

There was so much in his expression that Guy picked up. The open wounds, the wishes, the grasping, affection, and yearning. "It's not fair to go on like this," said Dean. "It's not right because it can't change any—"

Dean settled a bit. There seemed in him a readiness for the moment, for what was to come. "Guy…" he said, "I love you more than you will ever know…and…I'll wait for you at Breakwater."

CHAPTER 84

Sometimes murder is best plotted as a simple exercise.

After the killings, Gino Carpetti shipped his wife off to his daughter-in-law's house over in Spuyten Duyvil. It was one of those Emily Bronte ripoffs on the Hudson that had made the rounds of House and Garden. Getting her out to be caretaker for the grandkids in this time of sorrow and crisis was all smoke. Carpetti had moved three bodyguards into his place on College Point because he knew Peter Prince and maybe even Guy Prince would come hunting. And he wanted just enough fire power to bait them.

How Guy Prince got into the house, if they could even prove it was he who had, no one was ever quite sure. One plausible hypothesis came to be called the Trojan Horse theory. Only this Trojan horse turned out to be Missus Ceraso's station wagon. The one she had driven for years back and forth to the house, for shopping, for taking Missus Carpetti to the doctor or to Saint Raymonds Cemetery to be near her daughter. The theory was much discussed and debated. There would even be a feature story in TRUE CRIME, the magazine that had been the original publisher of *The Pirates of Pelham Parkway*.

The wagon was always parked in the driveway, and that wasn't but about forty feet from Gino's house. Guy Prince could have hid in the back with that shotgun covered by the clothes and drapes meant for the cleaners until night settled in.

It was Saturday and Gino always watched the show *Gunsmoke*. Matt Dillon was a fuckin' television god to him, as ironic as that must seem. Carpetti and the men with him camped out with coldcuts and beer and their weapons in shoulder holsters.

Investigators assumed from the information they could gather, that Guy Prince would have had to chance remaining hidden a good five hours in that car. They thought it too chancy, but it had actually been six hours.

Around dusk some of Carpetti's men drifted outside, drinking and talking trash, absorbed in their petty victories, all that overamped manshit. One of them even leaned against the car for quite some time talking up his love woes. Gino put in an appearance after it just got dark, and for a minute, Guy thought—'Do it now.' But that ill thought out desire got voted down by the weeks and weeks of preparing.

He lay with the cold barrel of the shotgun kissed up against his cheek, like a corpse covered with a shroud, until the appointed hour. Then, as the car door slowly and slightly opened, he slipped out into the night. The overhead door light had not gone on—a fact that investigators would come to only weeks later when they explored theories about how the killer got into the house. The bulb proved to be burned out.

As Guy made his crouched way across the lawn, keeping close to the house, Missus Ceraso watched through a crease in the blinds of a darkened bedroom. When she saw that Guy had disappeared into the stillness around the back of Gino's home, she went to the office.

Missus Carpetti sat on the sofa quietly. The old woman looked up. The light from the television streamed sharply across her face.

"He made it around back."

Missus Carpetti nodded in silence. Then she pointed to the sofa. "Sit," she said.

There was a mudroom behind the pantry of Gino's house. The door was always locked from the inside with a deadbolt. But not on this particular night.

The mudroom was dark when Guy entered. The only light shone down through the hall from the kitchen. He stood at the edge of the dark and listened. He could hear the television in the family room at the far end of the house. He knew the place well enough for what he was intent on doing, as he had been in there many times as a boy. Investigators wondered what had been the killer's point of entry, and the mudroom seemed the most likely, but there were no signs of force used.

Earlier that night, Missus Ceraso had brought over a large salad bowl of her homemade caponata—which is, if you don't know, a sort of Sicilian ratatouille. It was one of Gino's favorites, and she brought him some from time to time. He thanked her, and she offered to put it in the refrigerator.

Gino was in the hall talking to one of his men when she slipped back to the mudroom and unlocked the door. The bolt made this loud, nasty click that almost stopped her heart. She'd reached the pantry door when one of Gino's men appeared. He stood there staring at her in a cold, base way.

She pointed to the pantry, she was frightened. "I'm shopping tomorrow…I…wanted to see if Mister Carpetti needed anything."

As she crossed the lawn she had to walk past her station wagon. She was too frightened to even look at it. It was nearly eight o'clock. He had been hidden in there for hours, and there were hours to go.

In the house the men were absorbed in the television show. Guy could hear someone make an occasional wisecrack about Festus or Kitty, but no one was up and walking around.

Guy checked his shotgun. He made sure the handgun holstered to his waist was tight. His hands were gloved. He stretched and closed his fingers just to be sure he could feel and move freely enough. He took a long, deep, slow breath.

Then, just like that, he was striding from the mudroom and up the hallway where the light fell across the face of his pared down stare, eternity nothing more than now, give or take a few seconds. He passed through the kitchen, through the dining room, on a collision course years in the making, crossed the living room, and chambered a shell.

The family room was framed by a wide open set of double doors and one of those big twenty-five inch color Admiral televisions in its Danish modern cabinet took up the back wall. The men were relaxed and lounging about the room with their liquor and their cigarettes watching Matt Dillon face off against some badassed guest star.

One of the men sitting by the door, with his arm draped over a chair and a beer in hand, caught sight of something in the corner of his eye. He half turned and when he said, "Shit," Guy blew the bottle out of his hand, taking half the arm with it.

It was a bloodletting after that. Guy could not chamber the weapon fast enough. He killed them where they sat, he killed them where they tried to stand and make a fight of it. The room in that house had become a world of blue smoke and powder stench.

Gino had escaped death before and he threw himself out the French doors landing on the pavers among shattered glass. He managed to get out his revolver and rise up and make a run for it, but Guy caught him with a shot and Carpetti lunged forward grabbing at his back. He stumbled and then fell.

Guy turned on the men in the room. He meant to leave no witnesses. Wounded or dead, it didn't matter. He got out his revolver and he fired at close range. A face, a head, the heart, any movement, no movement. There would be no question marks.

Then he kicked open the broken French doors and went after Gino Carpetti.

He was still alive, and on his feet, staggering and looking back. He had slogged across his lawn toward his mother's house, toward the lit patio, the black and white images on the television screen burning through the glass doors of that darkened room.

The women had heard the shooting, they had sat in silence and waited. Missus Ceraso saw him first.

"My god," she said.

Gino was at the edge of the light, a presence with a face grim white, and on a collision course with death. The night behind him exploded. A burst of fire from the gun barrel drove him forward, arms sprawling, onto the patio brick.

There he was, not twenty feet from the office doors, trying desperately to rise. He still had hold of the gun and was forcing his arm around to fire the weapon, but Guy kicked it out of his hand. The weapon skidding along until it was lost in the dark.

Guy knelt down and hovered over Gino Carpetti. He pulled his head up by the hair, so they could be face on face.

As Gino was dying, Guy said to him, "Spofford...Class of sixty-six...I fought the law." He then let go of Gino's head. It slapped down on the brick. Guy stood, aimed his handgun, and put a bullet in Gino Carpetti's head. He glanced toward the office, and then he took off into the dark.

The two women had sat there through it all. Missus Ceraso's hands were pressed against her mouth. Missus Carpetti glanced at the clock on the wall and said, "We'll give it a minute...No...Two...Then you'll call the police."

TWO SOULS
AT BREAKWATER

CHAPTER 85

THE TWO WOMEN'S STORY NEVER ALTERED. They had heard shots, their first thought, it was Gino's television. They saw someone running across the lawn. It turned out to be Gino. A man shot him and he fell. The man stood over him and shot Gino dead. It happened so fast, the light being so tenuous, they could only describe the man as very tall, thin, long blond hair and older, maybe forty. Certainly not a portrait of Guy Prince.

After weeks of investigation, questions that could not be answered only mounted. Guy Prince was interrogated. He had no alibi other than he had passed the night in the apartment at the house on Bronxwood. Gardner Flynn could neither validate nor deny the statement, as he had been in New Jersey at Princeton University, visiting a friend.

No one was ever indicted for the crime. It remained a source of investigation, controversy and gossip. The general belief was that Missus Carpetti had her son and grandson killed as revenge for the murder of the daughter she so loved. No one would put it past the old lady to commit such an act, certainly not the newspapers, and not the Bronx task force into crime.

Missus Ceraso would defend her employer and friend to her death. Both women would be buried in the huge Carpetti plot in the old section of Saint Raymonds Cemetery. Carpetti in the mausoleum beside her daughter, Ceraso beside the son she'd lost in a car bombing.

• • •

Guy would remain at the house on Bronxwood, Dean's apartment would become his own. He would keep the urn with Dean's ashes on a table alongside his typewriter. Guy would make the long journey with a restless conviction to see that Dean's notes were published as he had intended.

Peter Prince would return to from wherever he came. No one would ever connect him to Rose Berghich and the house on Hanford or with the waitress at Schrafft's and her son. It would be two years before the woman who'd befriended Guy, who came to watch over him, confessed she was his mother.

Life, he thought learning this, just doesn't want you to sit still, does it?

On the anniversary of the day the two boys met, Guy took Dean's ashes and drove to Orchard Beach. At the Breakwater he walked far out onto the jetty. It was summer all along the shore, and everything summer is and means to a pair of young boys at the beginnings of their world.

There Guy scattered Dean's ashes upon a tide that had turned toward the sea. It was an emotional place, alone there like that. A place that can only exist for a brief moment, because the past and the future are going their separate ways.

Guy slowly went about his task, talking to Dante, remembering, reliving moments about certain times together, feeling him, reaching for him, missing him, needing him, wishing for him...loving him.

Guy looked down at the water. The ashes like charred snow, were being carried away. Were disappearing into a sunlight that glistened across the water's surface.

He stood with sun and the salt air and summer all around him, and he watched and watched until there was no more to watch. He realized then and understood...Dean's ashes had their appointment with fate, just as he did. But there was also a third fate, the one he and Dean had created together. One that would be there waiting for when they were together again. And there was peace in that, and the beauty of longing.